Praise for *Exploring Islam*

"There are introductory books on Islam that are accurate but rather lifeless. There are others that presume too much knowledge on the part of the reader. This volume is one of those rare texts that is utterly readable for the absolute newcomer and yet also conveys the heart of Islam as only an insider and believer can."

—Michael Birkel, professor of Christian spirituality, Earlham School of Religion, and author of *Qur'an in Conversation*

"Many introductory books on Islam leave students with little understanding of how Islam is lived and what the things they have studied mean to Muslims. *Exploring Islam* overcomes these obstacles through an accessible overview of the central dimensions of Islam that shows how they are integrated with one another and provides examples of how Islam is lived by Muslims from all walks of life. An excellent choice for an introduction to Islam at both college and advanced high school levels."

—Joseph E. B. Lumbard, associate professor of Quranic studies at the College of Islamic Studies, Hamad Bin Khalifa University, Qatar

"Sayilgan transcends the old-fashioned handbook format for introducing readers to Islamic life and faith. He presents a readable blend of historical and theological analysis along with well-chosen descriptions of individual Muslim faith experiences in the contexts of American society. This book will be useful to both the average reader and the religious studies scholar for gaining an understanding of Islam as a major historic religion and an important tradition of individual and communal spirituality."

—John O. Voll, professor emeritus of Islamic history, Georgetown University, and coauthor of *Islam and Democracy after the Arab Spring*

"Salih Sayilgan has written a highly accessible and compelling introduction to Islam, one that does justice to the lived religious experiences of Muslims. Students and readers new to the study of Islam will find Sayilgan's book to be an incredible resource as they seek a better understanding of an often misunderstood and maligned tradition."

—Todd Green, professor of religion, Luther College, and author of *The Fear of Islam: An Introduction to Islamophobia in the West*

"Salih Sayilgan takes readers on a wonderful, guided exploration of foundational themes of faith and practices in Islam. A must-read for those who may serve as a chaplain to Muslim individuals and families in America. So accessible and concise, this is a good primer to understand the sources of theological and spiritual praxis in Islam."

—Bilal W. Ansari, faculty associate in Muslim pastoral theology and
co-director of the Islamic Chaplaincy Program, Hartford Seminary

"Loving our neighbors requires knowing them. Salih Sayilgan's invitation to explore Islam is also an opportunity to get to know Muslims better—through their history, theology, spiritual practices, and daily experiences. This remarkable introductory book reminds us that this knowing—of each other and of God—is God's intention for us as diverse people made in God's image."

—The Rev. Elizabeth A. Eaton, presiding bishop,
Evangelical Lutheran Church in America

Exploring Islam

Exploring **Islam**

Theology and Spiritual Practice in America

Salih Sayilgan

FORTRESS PRESS
MINNEAPOLIS

To Zeyneb

And among His signs is the creation of the heavens and the earth, and the variations in your languages and your colors. Truly in that are signs for those who know.

—QUR'AN 30:22

Contents

Part 5: Contemporary Questions

Acknowledgments

This book builds on the writings of many scholars in Islamic studies, and I am grateful for their work and research. While this is a monograph, in many ways, it feels like a collective work. Numerous people generously offered their time and knowledge for this project.

I am grateful to Heather Lee Miller, Ingrid Berdahl, and Dodd Sims. They read the first draft of the manuscript and made valuable suggestions. Ali Galib Cebeci, Mustafa Tuna, and Amin Gharad provided diligent feedback for some of the chapters. I am indebted to them.

Taalibah Hassan, Merbiye Mollayakup, Tariq and Muslimah 'Ali Najee-ullah, Mohamed Afzal Norat, Fatima Abdulhamid Mangera, Cemal Gumus, Susan Douglass, Osamah Saleh, Jaye Starr, and Mustafa Boz helped me conduct interviews for some of the chapters. I am thankful to all of them. Some of the American Muslims who told their stories for the chapters remain anonymous. I am grateful to them for sharing their experiences of Islam in America.

My students at Wesley Theological Seminary and Georgetown University read the drafts of some of the chapters. Their questions, comments, and critiques helped me improve this work. My heartfelt thanks go to them. I am also thankful for the intellectual exchanges I had with my colleagues at both institutions.

While working on this project, I was awarded with the Louisville Institute's Postdoctoral Fellowship in 2018. I often discussed this work with my cohort during our gatherings. In fact, it was their input that helped me decide on the title of this book. I am thankful to the members of my cohort and the institute's leadership.

A special thanks goes to my acquisition editor, Ryan Hemmer, and his team at Fortress Press. Ryan believed in this project from the beginning. He graciously accommodated my requests and made the entire process smooth. Ryan's editorial skills and theological expertise enriched the manuscript.

Finally, I wish to thank my wife, Zeyneb, who is also specialized in Islamic studies. She was the first reader of this work. Her German critical reading helped me improve the book immensely. While I worked on this project, Zeyneb provided care not only to me but also to our beautiful daughters, Elif and Meryem. This work is dedicated with much love to her.

Introduction

One of the sites that I toured during my first visit to Washington, DC, was the Library of Congress—the oldest federal cultural institution in the United States. Serving as the primary research repository for Congress, the library was the brainchild of James Madison and was originally established under President John Adams in 1800, when the young country's capital moved from Philadelphia to the newly built Washington, DC. After the British destroyed the first congressional library in 1814, Congress purchased the personal collection of Thomas Jefferson, whose dedication to assembling a wide variety of books would serve as the philosophical basis for the Library of Congress as we currently know it. Jefferson believed that to be an inclusive, democratic legislature, lawmakers needed information and ideas from all subject areas.

Jefferson's eclectic and broad-minded approach to civic learning is represented on the ceiling of the library's main reading room—the central and highest point of the building—which opened in 1887 and bears Jefferson's name. Adorning the reading room's dome are twelve murals depicting the civilizations or epochs that contributed most to human progress in general and to US culture in particular.[1] Perhaps surprising to contemporary Americans, one of the twelve murals is dedicated to Islamic civilization and its contributions to physics, the branch of science that studies matter and aims to understand how the universe works. Unfortunately, the image of Islam today in the United States shares little with the depiction that has adorned the walls of the Library of Congress for more than a century.

I have been offering courses on Islam in the United States for over a decade now. I teach not only college students but also seminarians of various faiths and secular communities. And through years of experience, I have come to recognize certain traits and trends among my students concerning their perceptions of Muslims and their understanding of Islam:

---

1. "On These Walls: Inscriptions and Quotations in the Buildings of the Library of Congress," Library of Congress, last updated April 4, 2017, https://www.loc.gov/loc/walls/jeff1.html.

- *widespread religious illiteracy about Islamic faith and practice*
- *preconceptions about Islam that are both numerous and incorrect*
- *dismissal of Islamic theology*
- *ignorance of Islamic spirituality*
- *ignorance of the lived experience of American Muslims*
- *no exposure to Muslim scholars and teachers*

First, given that Islam is a minority religion, there is significant religious illiteracy among my students concerning Islam and its practices. According to a survey conducted in 2017, half of US adults, for example, believe that, unlike Judaism and Christianity, Islam should not be considered a "mainstream" religion.[2] Muslims in the United States are viewed less favorably than any other religious group, including atheists.[3] Many Americans, nevertheless, are inundated with messages about Islam and Muslims on an almost daily basis either through the media or through politics. In the last several presidential elections, Islam and its adherents have been the subject of many conversations. When Barack Obama was running for president in 2008, one of the controversies surrounding his campaign was whether he was a Muslim. The implication was that if Obama were a Muslim, he would be unqualified to be president of the United States. In 2015, one of the presidential candidates was asked whether a US Muslim could be a president. He answered no and claimed that Islam is inconsistent with the Constitution. A US Muslim, therefore, should not be allowed to be a president.[4] And during the 2016 presidential election, major candidates made statements like "Islam hates us," "I would not advocate that we put a Muslim in charge of this nation," and "Patrol and secure Muslim neighborhoods." These assertions went viral on social media.[5]

2. For a study on the reception of Islam in America, see "How the U.S. General Public Views Muslims and Islam," Pew Research Center, July 26, 2017, https://www.pewforum.org/2017/07/26/how-the-u-s-general-public-views-muslims-and-islam/.
3. Travis Mitchell, "Americans Express Increasingly Warm Feelings toward Religious Groups," Pew Research Center, February 15, 2017, https://tinyurl.com/4asr3dbh.
4. See Martin Pengelly, "Ben Carson Says No Muslim Should Ever Become U.S. President," *Guardian*, September 20, 2015, https://www.theguardian.com/us-news/2015/sep/20/ben-carson-no-muslim-us-president-trump-obama.
5. See Trump quoted in Theodore Schleifer, "Donald Trump: I Think Islam Hates Us," CNN, March 10, 2016, https://www.cnn.com/2016/03/09/politics/donald-trump-islam-hates-us/index.html; Carson quoted in Pengelly, "Ben Carson Says"; and Cruz quoted in Sam Sanders and Arnie Seipel, "Cruz: 'Empower Law Enforcement to Patrol and Secure Muslim Neighborhoods,'" NPR, March 22, 2016, https://www.npr.org/2016/03/22/471405546/u-s-officials-and-politicians-react-to-brussels-attacks.

Anti-Muslim attitudes among our recent presidential candidates are reminiscent of the disputes around John F. Kennedy's candidacy sixty years ago. When Kennedy, a Roman Catholic, decided to run in 1960, many Americans raised comparable concerns. To what extent would a Catholic president be able to separate his faith from running the country? Would he take orders from the pope? The root cause of the issue was not Kennedy himself but rather the anti-Catholic prejudice present in mainstream US society. Kennedy addressed the issue head-on, asking, "Are we going to admit to the world that a Jew can be elected Mayor of Dublin, a Protestant can be chosen Foreign Minister of France, a Moslem can be elected to the Israeli parliament—but a Catholic cannot be President of the United States? Are we going to admit to the world—worse still, are we going to admit to ourselves—that one-third of the American people is forever barred from the White House?"[6] It seems that Muslims in the United States are passing through a phase similar to what Catholics went through decades ago.

Second, when I began teaching about Islam, I covered various aspects of the religion—its origins, history, theology, and spiritual practice. I also dealt with contemporary issues such as jihad, sectarian divisions, and gender. But a few classroom experiences persuaded me to be more creative in my instruction. I realized that the focus of my teaching and the questions students were asking were, in the end, unrelated. In one situation, during a lecture about Islamic spirituality, I asked my audience if they had questions. Although I received five questions, not one was related to Islamic spirituality. Instead, my students asked about violence in Islam, sectarian divisions, and Islam in politics. Regardless of what I teach, the questions I receive are usually similar. Why? My audience often seems to already "know" about Islam, but what they've learned has come mainly through the media and political discussions. Although the US media frequently discusses Islam, its coverage is highly negative. Thus I often have an audience that is already informed about various aspects of Islam, if only in a negative fashion. Most of my students come to class having heard some of what they believe are the basics of sharia (Islamic law); however, few know the same about halacha (Jewish law) or dharma (religious and moral law in Hinduism and Buddhism). Many have already heard from the media

---

6. Kennedy's speech is available at "John F. Kennedy and Religion," John F. Kennedy Presidential Library and Museum, accessed July 26, 2019, https://www.jfklibrary.org/learn/about-jfk/jfk-in-history/john-f-kennedy-and-religion.

that Islam is not a religion but a political ideology, that Islam is inherently violent and therefore promotes violence, and that Islam is misogynistic. The challenge of teaching about Islam in the United States is to help my students *unlearn* what they have already learned.

Third, both the media and literature about Islam often dismiss Islamic theology. For the overwhelming majority of Muslims, however, the theological dimension of Islam is what provides answers to life's vital questions: Who is God? Why are we here on Earth? What is the purpose of life? Why did God create the universe? Is there life after death? Why is there so much evil and suffering in this world? Why did God create angels? If God is good, why did he create an evil figure like Satan? How can hell be compatible with God's infinite justice and compassion? Why is there death? Why is there sickness?

Fourth, like Islamic theology, Islamic spirituality and practice rarely enjoy serious coverage. Introductory books on Islam focus on its history, politics, and modern movements but lose the essence of its tradition. For example, it is hard to find in-depth discussions about Islamic prayer, fasting, or pilgrimage, and yet these rituals are the most visible practices of Islam in Muslim societies. Some scholars have taken a more integrated approach to teaching about Islam. Wilfred Cantwell Smith (d. 2000), for example, a prominent comparative religions scholar who taught at Harvard Divinity School for many years, emphasized Islamic practices. He would ask non-Muslim students to observe the fast during the month of Ramadan and to do the five daily prayers. He believed that simply reading books about the practices of Islam was insufficient to understand them and their impact on the spirituality of Muslims.[7]

Fifth, many of my students know very little about how Islam is actually practiced in the United States. Do US Muslims follow sharia? Does Islam bring a different dynamic to public life compared with other religions? Are Muslim and US identities compatible?

Sixth, the majority of students in courses on Islam in the United States are non-Muslims, and in most college classrooms, the religion is taught by a person of another faith or no faith. We need books written by academics specialized in Islam and comparative religions as well as practitioners of Islam in the United States.

---

7. Karen Armstrong, *Twelve Steps to a Compassionate Life* (New York: Anchor, 2011), 157.

As both a scholar and a practicing Muslim living and teaching in America, I have written this book to begin to change these traits and trends.

Exploring Islam is for any reader who wants to be informed about Islam and its practice in the United States. Part 1 begins with a description of the historical context from which Islam emerged and introduces the social, cultural, political, and religious landscape in the Near East on the eve of the birth of Islam. This section also includes chapters on the pre-Islamic narrative and the life of Muhammad and some of the controversies surrounding him. Part 2 focuses on the foundations of Islam: the Qur'an and its interpretation, the legacy of the Prophet Muhammad and his role in the lives of Muslims, and sharia and its practice in the United States. The third part of the book deals with Islamic theology, discussing the fundamentals of faith and major beliefs concerning God, the prophets, the scriptures, angels, predestination and resurrection, and the hereafter. Part 4 is about the spiritual practices of Islam, such as the profession of faith, prayers, fasting, pilgrimage, and paying alms. The last part deals with selected topics and contemporary issues—including jihad, mysticism, and diversity within Islam—and provides a description of various groups of Muslims, including Shiites and Sunnis, Sufis, and women. In all sections, I take the practice of Islam in the United States into consideration and engage with various case studies and living examples from the lives of US Muslims.

Part I

Historical Background

1 The Near East before the Birth of Islam

The story of Islam begins with the first revelation of the Qur'an from the archangel Gabriel to the Prophet Muhammad in Arabia in the early sixth century CE. But before exploring the events of the Prophet's life and their significance in the development of Islam, I will briefly introduce the social, cultural, political, and religious landscape of the time in the Near East.

On the eve of the birth of Islam, two empires dominated the Near East: the Byzantine and the Sasanian (Persian). The Byzantine Empire controlled the western part of Arabia, a geographic area encompassing modern-day Turkey, Syria, and Egypt; the Sasanian Empire controlled the eastern part. These two imperial powers were in constant competition for political, economic, and religious influence in the region.[1] For the last several decades before the collapse of the Sasanian state in the 630s, for example, the Byzantines and Sasanians were at war, vying for control of key areas such as northern Mesopotamia, Armenia, and the Caucasus.[2]

In both civilizations, male elites enjoyed enormous influence. In the Byzantine or eastern Roman Empire, this privileged class mainly consisted of landowners, clergy, and state officials. Their authority over slaves, women, children, and many members of the common class was unquestionable.[3] In the Sasanian Empire, society was divided into hierarchical classes, with slaves solidly at the bottom of the hierarchy.[4]

The Religious Landscape

Religion was an important force in almost all major societies in late antiquity. While Buddhism and Neo-Taoism were gaining significant influence in China,

1. Fred Donner, *Muhammad and the Believers: At the Origins of Islam* (Cambridge, MA: Harvard University Press, 2012), 3.
2. Donner, 24.
3. Donner, 16.
4. Donner, 22.

Hinduism was being promoted by royal powers in Indic lands.[5] By the time of the birth of Islam, the Byzantine Empire had adopted Christianity as its official state religion, hoping to unite all imperial subjects within its vast territory. However, even Christians were divided into various groups over fundamental theological disagreements about the nature of Jesus.

The official church of the Byzantine Empire, which is today commonly known as the Eastern Orthodox Church (a communion of over fourteen autocephalous churches), taught that Jesus was both divine and human—that he had two distinct natures united in one divine person. With this theological position, the official church (based in what was then Constantinople) was able to explain the crucifixion of Jesus: although his human body died on the cross, his divine nature rendered him immortal.[6] This teaching became prevalent in the Balkans, Greece, and Palestine, as the imperial authority was strong in these places. By contrast, the Nestorian churches (today called the Church of the East), located in the Sasanian Empire and central Asia, diverged from orthodoxy by affirming that Jesus had two persons, one human and one divine. As a consequence, Nestorians rejected the idea that Mary was the God-bearer (theotókos), asserting instead that she was the Christ-bearer (Christotokos). This theology was condemned at the Council of Ephesus in 431 CE.

Out of opposition to Nestorianism, Eutyches, a monk and presbyter from Constantinople, taught that not only did Jesus have only one person; he had only one nature. This theology became popular among Christians living in Egypt, Syria, and Armenia, who at the time were called Monophysites (because they believed Jesus had a single nature). Monophysite theology was affirmed at the "Robber Council" held in Ephesus in 449 CE, which concluded without considering Pope Leo I's tome defending two-nature Christology. Amid these theological divisions and at Pope Leo's urging, Byzantine emperor Marcian (d. 457) called for the Council of Chalcedon in 451 CE. Through the council, Marcian attempted to unite the Christian subjects of the empire around one unifying theology.

The Sasanian Empire provided space for a religiously diverse environment but officially endorsed Zoroastrianism (Mazdaism), which emphasizes the cosmic struggle between the forces of good and evil. According to Zoroastrian theology,

---

5. Marshall G. S. Hodgson, *The Venture of Islam: Conscience and History in a World Civilization*, vol. 1, *The Classical Age of Islam* (Chicago: University of Chicago Press, 1977), 125.
6. Donner, *Muhammad and the Believers*, 11.

these forces are represented by light (fire and the sun) and dark. Based on this belief, followers offer special prayers during sunset and sunrise. Rituals centered on temple flames are also key in Zoroastrian worship practices.[7] Zoroastrianism continues to be practiced today among the Parsi and Irani communities of India.

Judaism was also a significant part of the religious landscape of the Near East in the early seventh century. After centuries of Babylonian, Persian, Greek, and Roman rule resulting in major population displacements from Palestine, Jews were spread around the region and in Yemen and North Africa.

Arabia before Islam

The religious landscape in Arabia was rather different from that of the empires. While both the Byzantines and Sasanians were competing for political, economic, and religious influence in the area, no one enjoyed absolute dominance. This state of flux was notable in the Hejaz region, where Mecca and Yathrib (later called Medina) were located (the two cities in which the Prophet Muhammad had lived), perhaps because Hejaz was mountainous and of marginal value for farming.[8] Unlike in the Byzantine and Sasanian Empires, tribal rules and kinship ties dictated social and political order in Arabia.[9] Violating tribal rules could mean death for an individual member of the tribe, and retaliatory feuds were common. When a member of one tribe suffered harm or injury at the hands of another, all members of the perpetrator's tribe were blamed for the crime. Retaliation usually amounted to "an eye for an eye, a life for a life." If the injured group saw itself as stronger than the other group, then the cost of retaliation would be even greater and might lead to war.[10]

Hejaz was a center of commerce, and Mecca in particular drew traders from around western and central Arabia.[11] People from the surrounding areas flocked to the annual market fair in Mecca known as Ukaz. Mecca also attracted visitors wishing to view the Kaaba—a cubic structure regarded as sacred to this day. Islamic tradition relates that Abraham and his family built the Kaaba as the house of God. Since its inception, the Kaaba has represented monotheism. At some point, however,

7. Donner, 19.
8. Hodgson, *Venture of Islam*, 157.
9. Donner, *Muhammad and the Believers*, 28.
10. Hodgson, *Venture of Islam*, 149.
11. Hodgson, 154.

likely as a result of the wide variety of people coming to the town from across the region, it also became a center of polytheism. It started with a Meccan merchant who brought an idol to Mecca. Not long after, many tribes started to have their own idols. Owning an idol would later become a unifying element for each tribe. These idols were believed to be divine protectors, and they were venerated at local shrines.[12] Three of these idols received special veneration, not only by the tribes in Mecca, but also by Arabs from neighboring areas. These divinities were al-Lat, al-Uzza, and Manat.[13] The offerings to these deities were mainly in the form of "I give you, lord, you will give me that favor in return."[14]

While polytheism was more common in Hejaz, Arabs of the region were familiar with monotheistic religious traditions like Judaism, Christianity, and Zoroastrianism. Arabs traded often with people hailing from cities in Yemen, Syria, and Iraq, which were religiously diverse areas with considerable Christian populations.[15] In Mecca, where Islam was born, a number of people followed a form of monotheism described in the Qur'an as *hanif*. Islamic tradition reports that some followers of the *hanif* tradition later converted to Christianity.

As in the Byzantine and Sasanian Empires, a sizable Jewish community lived in Arabia, including in the Hejaz region. Scholars believe that the presence of Jews in Arabia dates from the destruction of the Second Temple in 70 CE. Arabic-speaking Jews could be found in the major oasis towns of northwestern Arabia, including Tabuk, Tayma, Khaybar, and Yathrib (Medina).[16]

Jahiliyya: The Time of Ignorance

Islamic tradition refers to the pre-Islamic period of Arabia as the time of ignorance (*jahiliyya*). The term refers to the polytheistic practices and social injustices of the time, including the worship of idols and the practice of female infanticide. The Qur'an alludes to the latter practice: "When news is brought to one of them, of (the birth of) a female (child), his face darkens, and he is filled with inward grief! With shame does he hide himself from his people, because of the bad news he has

---

12. Donner, *Muhammad and the Believers*, 30.
13. Hodgson, *Venture of Islam*, 156.
14. Hodgson, 159.
15. Donner, *Muhammad and the Believers*, 30.
16. Donner, 30.

had! Shall he keep it in humiliation, or bury it in the ground? Verily, evil is their judgement."[17]

Jafar bin Abi Talib, a cousin to and companion of the Prophet, described this period in detail during his conversation with the Christian king of Abyssinia. When the king asked about Muhammad's message and teaching, Jafar bin Abi Talib replied,

> O King, we were an uncivilized people worshiping idols, eating corpses, committing abominations, breaking natural ties, treating guests badly, and our strong devoured our weak. Thus we were until God sent us an apostle whose lineage, truth, trustworthiness, and clemency we know. He summoned us to acknowledge God's unity and to worship Him and to renounce the stones and images which we and our fathers formerly worshiped. He commanded us to speak the truth, be faithful to our engagements, mindful of the ties of kinship and kind hospitality, and to refrain from crimes and bloodshed. He forbade us to commit abominations and to speak lies, and to devour the property of orphans, to vilify chaste women. He commanded us to worship God alone and not to associate anything with Him, and he gave us orders about prayer, alms and fasting [enumerating the commands of Islam]. So we confessed his truth and believed in him and we followed him in what he brought to us from God; and we worshipped God alone without associating anything with Him. We treated as forbidden what he forbade and as lawful as what he declared lawful.[18]

During *jahiliyya*, residents of Hejaz did not believe in one of the Prophet's key messages, that there is accountability for injustices committed against the poor, vulnerable, and unprotected.

---

17. Qur'an 16:58–59. Unless noted otherwise, I have taken direct citations of the qur'anic verses from Abdullah Yusuf Ali, *The Meaning of the Holy Qur'an* (Beltsville, MD: Amana, 2003), with modifications to make the language more accessible. I also consulted the following translations of the Qur'an: M. A. S. Abdel Haleem, *The Qur'an: English Translation and Parallel Arabic Text* (Oxford: Oxford University Press, 2010); Majid Fakhry, *An Interpretation of the Qur'an: English Translation of the Meanings* (Albany: New York University Press, 2004); Seyyed Hossein Nasr et al., eds., *The Study Quran: A New Translation and Commentary* (New York: HarperOne, 2015); Marmaduke Pickthall, *The Meaning of the Glorious Qur'an* (New York: Everyman's Library, 1992).
18. Ibn Ishaq, *The Life of Muhammad*, trans. A. Guillaume (Oxford: Oxford University Press, 1967), 151–52.

Islamic tradition reports that in pre-Islamic Arabia, Arabs were masters of poetry and literature. During the annual gathering of Ukaz, they would select the best poems and hang them on the walls of the Kaaba. The divine words Muhammad received and memorialized in the Qur'an would bring a new dynamic to Arabic literature. The following chapter outlines the Prophet's life.

2 Muhammad's Life in Outline

In December 2019, US news media outlets reported that *Muhammad* was one of the ten most popular names for baby boys that year in the United States.[1] Around the world, Muslims name children after the Prophet Muhammad because of their love and admiration for him. In this chapter, we will discuss Muhammad's life.

The Early Years

Muhammad was born into the Banu Hashim clan of the Quraysh tribe in early 570 CE in Mecca, a city in the western part of what is now Saudi Arabia. His father, Abdullah, had died before he was born. After his mother, Amina, died when he was six years old, his grandfather Abd al-Muttalib took care of him. Not long after, however, Abd al-Muttalib also died, and responsibility for the boy fell to Muhammad's uncle Abu Talib, a merchant who frequently traveled to Damascus. Young Muhammad worked for his uncle, minding sheep and often traveling with Abu Talib to neighboring cities.

Islamic tradition recounts that unlike many people in Meccan society, Muhammad was among a small number who did not follow the polytheistic beliefs and practices of the *jahiliyya*, observing instead the monotheistic *hanif* tradition. Muhammad was known among his people as a righteous and trustworthy person (*al-amin*). When the leaders of the major tribes wanted to renovate the Kaaba, a dispute occurred concerning the placement of the sacred stone (*hajar al-aswad*), which tradition dates from the time of Abraham. The leaders disagreed on who should have the honor of placing the stone back in its place in the eastern corner of the Kaaba after the completion of the renovation. Each wished for their own tribe to have the honor. As the story goes, Muhammad offered a solution: the stone would be carried on a sheet that all of the leaders could carry equally. In this manner, the dispute was resolved.[2]

1. Harmeet Kaur, "Muhammad Makes List of Top 10 Baby Names," CNN, December 6, 2019, https://www.cnn.com/2019/12/06/us/muhammad-top-10-baby-names-trnd/index.html.
2. Ibn Ishaq, *Life of Muhammad*, 86.

Impressed by Muhammad's good character and success, a widowed business-woman, Khadija, offered Muhammad employment. Khadija fell in love with Muhammad and proposed marriage through her relatives. When they married, Muhammad was twenty-five years old, and Khadija was fifteen years his senior. Muhammad remained faithful to his wife until her death when he was fifty years old. They had five children: a boy who died in infancy and four girls. Of his five children, only his daughter Fatima survived him. Muhammad had many other marriages after Khadija's death, mostly with divorced women in need of assistance and protection. He also entered into political marriages in order to establish peace among the tribes of Arabia. Muhammad reportedly had thirteen marriages, of which eleven were consummated. At one time, he had nine wives. Muhammad also had two concubines. One of them was a Coptic slave with whom he had a son named Ibrahim, who died in infancy.[3]

Two of Muhammad's marriages have become particularly controversial to modern sensibilities. Immediately following Khadija's death, he married Aisha, who was the daughter of the Prophet's close companion, Abu Bakr. (Abu Bakr would become the first leader of the community after the death of Muhammad.) Most Islamic sources report that Aisha was a child of seven or eight when she was engaged to the Prophet; the marriage was consummated after she reached puberty around age ten or eleven.[4] Also controversial is his marriage to Zaynab bint Jahsh, the divorced wife of his adopted son, Zayd bin Haritha. (I discuss Muhammad's marriages in the next chapter.)

Muhammad was involved in what we would today call social justice activism. For example, he participated in the Alliance of the Virtuous (Hilf al-Fudul), an initiative to defend people against injustice in Meccan society, especially visitors to Mecca who sometimes faced having their property confiscated by wealthy residents. The founders and members of the association had pledged to end wrongdoings against the weak, poor, and vulnerable. Young Muhammad was one supporter of this initiative.[5]

3. Jonathan A. C. Brown, *Muhammad: A Very Short Introduction* (Oxford: Oxford University Press, 2011), 49–50.
4. Brown, 24.
5. Ibn Ishaq, *Life of Muhammad*, 57.

Revelation and Transformation

Muhammad frequented the cave of Hira located on Nur Mountain (mountain of light) near Mecca for contemplation, invocation, and worship in the month of Ramadan. During a retreat in 610 CE, when he was forty years old, Muhammad had an experience that would have a substantial impact on the course of world history. In a visitation that was both remarkable and troubling, the archangel Gabriel appeared to Muhammad and commanded him to read (*iqra*). As this was the first revelation Muhammad had ever received, he did not initially understand what was happening. Some sources indicate that he was concerned, even terrified, by the experience. His tentative response to the angelic call was, "I do not know how to read." When Gabriel repeated his command, Muhammad again answered, "I do not know how to read." The archangel then recited the first verses of the revelation to Muhammad.[6] This exchange marks the birth of Islam.

After the incident, Muhammad rushed to Khadija and told her what had happened. She offered the following words of comfort: "Don't worry and don't be sad. God will not put a beloved servant of his to shame. I know that you always speak the truth. You take care of what is entrusted to you. You are good to your relatives and neighbors. You treat them with compassion. You help the poor and needy. You open your door to them. Be patient! You will be the prophet of the community."[7] Khadija's full confidence in her husband would mark her as Islam's first Muslim. Along with Khadija, the Prophet's daughters—Zaynab, Ruqayya, Umm Kulthum, and Fatima—also supported him.

After the revelation, Khadija took Muhammad to her Christian cousin, Waraqa bin Nawfal, a learned scholar of both the Gospel and the Torah. After hearing Muhammad's story, Waraqa affirmed that Muhammad had received a revelation from God. He warned that people would resist Muhammad's message and predicted that his followers would be persecuted and expelled from Mecca. Muhammad did not immediately receive another revelation, which distressed him. But they eventually resumed and continued until his death in 632 CE. In the second revelation,

---

6. Qur'an 96:1–5.
7. Muslim ibn al-Hajjaj al-Naysaburi, *Sahih Muslim*, Sunnah.com, accessed February 8, 2021, https://sunnah.com/muslim, book 1, hadith 2. Unless indicated otherwise, hadith numbers and translations are based on the Arabic references of https://sunnah.com. In some cases, I made slight modifications to make the language more accessible.

God instructed the Prophet to stand up, to teach the message of the new revelation to the community, and to "be steadfast" in God's cause.[8] The revelations in Mecca concerned faith in one God, life after death, resurrection, accountability, worship, and justice.

The second person to accept the new message after Khadija was Ali bin Abi Talib, a cousin of the Prophet who was living with him. Following Ali's conversion, Zayd bin Haritha, the Prophet's adopted son, and Abu Bakr, the Prophet's close friend and businessperson, also converted, along with several slaves, including Bilal bin Rabah.

The growing list of converts became a major concern for elites in Mecca. Many people, including some close members of the Prophet's extended family, opposed his message, fearing that the new religion threatened their tribal practices, economy, and social order. Among the naysayers was Muhammad's uncle Abu Lahab, who, along with his wife, became the symbol of resistance to the new message.[9]

With the conversion of Umar bin al-Khattab, an influential figure among the Meccan elite, the Prophet's message went public. He openly invited his relatives and the larger Meccan community to hear all that had been revealed to him. Members of Muhammad's own Quraysh tribe (who were known to be masters of poetry and literature), including many of his relatives, wanted to undermine the words of the new revelation. Meccan aristocrats (some of these too were his relatives) launched attacks against Muhammad and the new message he proclaimed. One such attack asserted that Muhammad was lying and that he had learned his new teaching not from an angel but from a local Christian.[10] They variously accused him of being insane, a mere poet (not a prophet), and a magician.[11] Some denounced the new revelation as just a tale from the past.[12] Despite his detractors, Muhammad's message continued to attract new followers. The Qur'an invited Muhammad's opponents to produce something similar to the new divine words but asserted that they could not and would not do it.[13]

---

8. Qur'an 74:1–7.
9. Qur'an 111:1–5.
10. Qur'an 16:103.
11. Qur'an 44:14; 52:29; 68:2; 21:5; 6:7.
12. Qur'an 25:5.
13. Qur'an 2:23–24.

Meccan Persecutions

Unable to effectively challenge the new revelation with words, Meccan elites began insulting, boycotting, persecuting, and torturing Muhammad's followers. Soon the situation for these new converts became unbearable, and the Prophet instructed them to find safety in Abyssinia (modern-day Ethiopia/Eritrea), which a Christian king then ruled. Around eighty followers of the Prophet—both men and women—immigrated to Abyssinia as refugees. Among them were the Prophet's son-in-law Uthman bin Affan and his wife, Ruqayya, along with the Prophet's cousin Jafar bin Abi Talib. Concerned that the Prophet's exiled followers might become a threat, the Meccan elite sent a delegation laden with gifts to the king of Abyssinia in an attempt to persuade him to send Muslim refugees back to Mecca. The delegation did everything in its power, including arguing theology, to convince the Christian king to do this. They even told the king that Muhammad and his followers rejected major theological positions of Christianity, including the doctrine of the Trinity. The king, however, chose to listen to Muhammad's followers and their views of Jesus and Mary and told them they could stay in his land as long as they wanted.[14]

Opponents of the Prophet and his followers tried other means to isolate them and put an end to the influence of the new message. One such attempt was a boycott that would last three years, which prohibited anyone from selling to or buying from members of the Prophet's community and left many to starve. Additionally, the embargo disallowed marriage with anyone from the Prophet's clan, Banu Hashim. This prohibition affected two of Muhammad's daughters, Ruqayya and Umm Kulthum, both of whom were engaged to sons of Abu Lahab, one of the Prophet's fiercest enemies. Abu Lahab and his wife forced their children to terminate their engagements to the Prophet's daughters.[15]

Although some good-hearted people in Mecca who had close relations with some of the Prophet's followers eventually broke the boycott, Muhammad's struggle continued. First, his uncle and protector Abu Talib died. Not long after, his beloved first wife, Khadija, passed away. Not only was the year marked as one of great sadness in the Prophet's life, but his opponents also took this opportunity to intensify

---

14. Ibn Ishaq, *Life of Muhammad*, 146–53.
15. Martin Lings, *Muhammad: His Life Based on the Earliest Sources* (Rochester, VT: Inner Traditions, 2006), 72.

their persecution of Muhammad and his followers. Immediately after the death of Abu Talib, Meccans redoubled their offensive actions against the Prophet. On one occasion, an opponent of Muhammad threw dust on him in public as an insult. Upon entering his house with dust in his hair, one of his daughters rushed to him and washed away the dirt. When she burst into tears, the Prophet comforted her: "Don't weep my little girl, for God will protect your father."[16] Amid increasing hostility toward him and his followers, Muhammad then traveled to Taif, a neighboring city, seeking the protection of the tribe of Thaqif. But instead of offering him refuge, the tribe violently expelled him from the town—tradition holds that tribe's youth stoned and chased him away—and he returned to Mecca.[17]

Heavenly Ascent and Life in Medina

In this desperate situation, Muhammad's famous ascension to heaven, known as *mi'raj*, occurred. The aptly named seventeenth chapter of the Qur'an, "The Night Journey," relates how the archangel Gabriel miraculously took the Prophet from Mecca to Jerusalem to heaven and back to Mecca in one night. The Qur'an recounts this occasion, saying, "Glory to Him who did take His servant for a journey by night from the Sacred Mosque to the farthest Mosque, whose precincts We did bless, in order that We might show him some of Our signs, for He is indeed the All Hearing, the All Seeing."[18] Muslims believe that during this journey, Muhammad not only met other prophets, including Moses and Jesus, but also directly encountered God.[19] This event reinforced the Prophet's resolve to pursue his cause.

After the night journey, the Prophet continued to invite people to accept the new message from God that he was conveying. During the annual Ukaz gatherings, which often went on for a couple of weeks, he would meet tribal leaders and invite them to become Muslims. After some from Yathrib brought his message home and the number of his followers began to grow, Muhammad sent Musab bin Umayr, one of his companions, to teach Islam to the people there in a more formal manner. As it turned out, Yathrib was more welcoming to believers than Mecca, and over

16. Ibn Ishaq, *Life of Muhammad*, 191.
17. Ibn Ishaq, 192–93.
18. Qur'an 17:1.
19. Ibn Ishaq, *Life of Muhammad*, 183–84.

time, increasing numbers of the Prophet's followers immigrated there, including Umar bin al-Khattab. The Prophet and his companion Abu Bakr planned to migrate as well. However, aware that most Muslims had departed Mecca for Yathrib, the Quraysh elite wanted to stop those left behind from adding to the strength of the community forming in Yathrib. The elite even attempted to kill Muhammad prior to his departure. Miraculously, the Prophet escaped and made his way to Yathrib in 622 CE.[20] Soon after his arrival, Yathrib came to be known as Medina al-Nabi, or "City of the Prophet." Muhammad's emigration from Mecca to Yathrib/ Medina is known as the *hijra* and marks the beginning of the Islamic calendar.

Muhammad and his followers became a growing force in Medina. The revelation of qur'anic verses continued there—many addressed the practical aspects of the faith, including worship, marriage, dietary restrictions, and relations with other faiths. Companions of Muhammad from Mecca (*muhajir*) who had left everything behind when they journeyed to Medina were warmly welcomed and supported by his followers (*ansar*) there. In order to foster compassion and a sense of kinship between the *ansar* and *muhajir*, Muhammad matched pairs of "brothers" from both communities.[21] The Qur'an echoes the exemplary brotherhoods that formed between the *muhajirs* and the *ansars* in various verses—for example, "And the first to lead the way, of the Emigrants and the Helpers, and those who followed them in goodness, God is well pleased with them and they are well pleased with Him."[22] Another verse refers to the sacrifices the believers made for one another: "Those who entered the city and the faith before them show their love to those who emigrated to them and entertain no desire in their hearts for things given to them. They give them [emigrants] preference over themselves even if they too are poor. Those who are saved from their own souls' greed are truly successful."[23]

Aiming to secure peace in Medina among Jews, non-Muslims, and Muslims, Muhammad entered into an agreement known as the Constitution of Medina with tribes from among these other religious groups. As part of the accord, each group would have the freedom to practice its own traditions. In addition, all tribes would support one another in case of an outside threat. Comprising three major

20. Ibn Ishaq, 222.
21. Brown, *Muhammad*, 29.
22. Qur'an 9:100.
23. Qur'an 59:9.

tribes—Banu Nadir, Banu Qurayza, and Banu Qaynuqa—Jews made up almost half of the Medina population at this time. However, relations between the Muslim community and the Jewish tribes eventually soured. Although some of the Jews of Medina converted to Islam, the overwhelming majority opposed Muhammad and his teachings.[24] Suspecting that some of the Jews who opposed Muhammad were cooperating with the Meccans, the Muslims ultimately expelled the Jewish tribes from Medina.[25]

Muhammad and his companions had mostly avoided armed conflict in Mecca. They had left their city, property, and family members behind to avoid persecution and torture. In a new revelation in Medina, however, God allowed them to defend their rights: "To those against whom war is made, permission is given to fight, because they are wronged; and verily, God is most powerful for their aid. Those who have been driven from their homes unjustly only because they said: Our Lord is God. Did not God check one set of people by means of another, there would surely have been pulled down monasteries, churches, synagogues, and mosques, in which the name of God is commemorated in abundant measure. God will certainly aid those who aid his cause; for verily God is full of strength, exalted in might."[26]

Although Muhammad and his followers were now living in Medina, the Meccan elite still regarded them as an economic threat (and for legitimate reasons). Muhammad had received news that the Quraysh's trade caravan was traveling from Damascus to Mecca and plotted to raid the caravan and seize the property. Although the traders were able to escape the Muslims' raid, the foiled attempt was alarming news to Meccans, who responded by organizing a retaliatory expedition to eliminate the nascent Muslim community. What ensued was the first major battle between the followers of Muhammad and the Meccans in 624 CE. The Quraysh received a devastating defeat at the hands of Muslims.[27]

The following year, the Meccans again waged war against the Muslim community in Medina. But this time, they were victorious. During the battle, the Prophet was injured, and some of his companions, including his uncle Hamza bin Abd al-Muttalib, died. The wars between Meccans and Muslims in Medina continued

---

24. Brown, *Muhammad*, 30.
25. Donner, *Muhammad and the Believers*, 47.
26. Qur'an 22:39–40.
27. Brown, *Muhammad*, 32.

until the Treaty of Hudaybiyya in 628 CE. That year, the Prophet and his companions wanted to visit the Kaaba and make the *umrah*, or "minor pilgrimage." The Quraysh, however, did not let them enter Mecca. Both sides eventually agreed on a truce that required the warring factions to maintain peace for ten years. If a member of Meccan society went to Medina to be a follower of Muhammad, they would be sent back to Mecca. However, if a Muslim from Medina went to Mecca, he would not be sent back. Additionally, the Prophet and his followers would be allowed to visit the Kaaba the next year. Many of the Prophet's companions felt that the agreement was unfair and against the best interests of the Muslim community. Nevertheless, as a result of the settlement, the Quraysh, for the first time, recognized the Muslim community as a political force.

Return to Mecca

In the wake of the peace agreement, an increasing number of people converted to Islam. The Prophet sent letters to major leaders in the Near East, including the Sasanian and Byzantine emperors and the rulers of Egypt and Abyssinia, inviting them to accept his message. When the Quraysh eventually violated the peace agreement, the Prophet organized and led ten thousand of his followers on a major expedition to Mecca. Catching the Meccans unprepared, Muhammad conquered the city with no bloodshed, and many of his prior rivals even accepted Islam.[28]

Not long before he died in 632 CE, Muhammad made his major pilgrimage, the hajj, and delivered his famous farewell sermon. By the time of his death, Muhammad had not only brought peace to Arabia, but almost all of Arabia had also embraced Islam. By the turn of the century, his followers would conquer Armenia, Persia, Syria, Palestine, Iraq, North Africa, and Spain and cross the Pyrenees into France.

---

28. Donner, *Muhammad and the Believers*, 49.

3   Muhammad's Life in Context

The death of Muhammad was a devastating event in the nascent Muslim community. Some of his companions could not believe that the Prophet had died. Abu Bakr, however, reminded Muhammad's followers of the Qur'an's message that "Muhammad is only a messenger, before whom many messengers have come and gone."[1] In this verse, the Qur'an emphasizes that Muhammad is as mortal as any other human prophet. But Muhammad's death was a painful occasion for believers when they realized that with his departure, the channel of revelation had closed.

Muhammad, the Man of Faith

For Muslims, however, the Prophet remained the best model of not only good character but also ways to relate to God and to people. Ali bin Abi Talib, his cousin and son-in-law, described him as follows:

> The Prophet was neither excessively tall nor extremely short. He was of medium height in relation to people. His hair was neither curly nor straight, but it was in between. His face was not swollen or meaty. It was fairly round. He had black eyes that were large with long lashes. His joints were rather large. He had little hairs that stood up, extending from his chest down to his navel, but the rest of his body was almost hairless. He had thick palms and thick fingers and toes. When walking, he lifted his feet off the ground as if he were walking in muddy water. When he turned, he turned completely. Between his two shoulders was the seal of Prophethood. That was the sign that he was the last Prophet. He was known as the most generous, the most truthful of people in speech, and the friendliest of all people, and the most noble of them in his relations. Those who saw him were taken aback by his grandeur and those who knew his high virtues would love him more than anything else while conversing with him. The

---

1. Qur'an 3:144. See also Ibn Ishaq, *Life of Muhammad*, 682–83.

one who tried to describe him would have to say: "I have not seen before him or after him anyone who resembles him."[2]

Islamic literature refers to the Prophet as the exemplar of worship and prayer to God. He was keen on fulfilling the practices of Islam, including the five daily prayers, fasting, pilgrimage, and almsgiving. Muhammad fasted every Monday and Thursday. He often performed ablution for each prayer. He got up for prayer from his sleep and spent a third of his night in devotion; he sometimes prayed so long that his feet would go numb.[3] When asked why he prayed so much, given that paradise had been granted to him, he responded, "Should I not be a grateful servant of God?"[4] Muhammad spent the last ten days of the month of Ramadan in the mosque dedicating his time to worship and contemplation. He was mindful of God in every aspect of his life. He performed daily supplications (dua) and invocations (dhikr) for almost every good act. Seventy times a day, he said words of repentance (tawba) and sought refuge in God (istighfar). Muhammad made supplications to God when he ate and drank, when he went to sleep and arose, when he entered and exited his house, and when he got dressed. After eating, he would pray, "Praise be to God who feeds us and gives us drink and has made us among those who submit to Him."[5] When he rode his camel, he would pray, "In the name of God. Praise is to God. Glory to Him Who has provided this for us though we could never have had it by our efforts. Surely, unto our Lord we are returning. Praise is to God. Praise be to God. Praise be to God. God is the Most Great. God is the Most Great. God is the Most Great."[6] Before going to bed, he would pray, "With Your Name my Lord, I lay myself down; and with Your Name, I rise. And if You take my soul, have mercy on it, and if You send it back, then protect it as You protect Your righteous servants."[7] In times of distress, he often prayed, "O Ever Living and Self Sustaining Sustainer, in your mercy do I seek relief."[8]

2. Muhammad bin Isa al-Tirmidhi, Jami' al-Tirmidhi, Sunnah.com, accessed February 8, 2021, https://sunnah.com/tirmidhi, book 49, hadith 399. While this hadith is considered weak (da'if), it is widely known among Muslims. In fact, many Muslims have the Arabic calligraphy of this depiction of the Prophet in their houses.
3. M. Yaşar Kandemir, "Muhammed," in İslam Ansiklopedisi (Istanbul: TDV, 2005), 30:427.
4. Muhammad bin Isa al-Tirmidhi, Shama'il Muhammadiyya, Sunnah.com, accessed February 10, 2021, https://sunnah.com/shamail, book 40, hadith 262.
5. Brown, Muhammad, 39.
6. Al-Naysaburi, Sahih Muslim, book 15, hadith 425.
7. Al-Naysaburi, book 48, hadith 85.
8. Al-Tirmidhi, Jami' al-Tirmidhi, book 48, hadith 155.

Muhammad regarded his time praying before God as the best moments of his life. One tradition narrates that after completing two cycles of the dawn prayer, he would say, "The pleasure of the entire world is nothing compared to the pleasure I get from these two cycles of prayer."[9] He never doubted God's compassion and the forgiveness he gives to his servants. In another narrative, one day the Prophet saw a woman who had been separated from her child. The woman was hugging and feeding any child she saw on the street. The Prophet asked his companions, "Would this woman ever throw her child into fire?" They replied that she would never do so. The Prophet then said, "You should know that the mercy and compassion of God toward his servants is much higher than this woman's compassion toward her child."[10]

The Prophet also instructed his companions to be moderate in worship and prayer. Not wanting them to shirk their familial responsibilities, Muhammad discouraged them from spending all of their time in worship and prayer; instead, he told them to be mindful of their family and other fellow humans. On one occasion, for example, the Prophet learned that Abdullah bin Amr, one of his companions, had decided to dedicate the remainder of his life to praying all night and fasting all day. Muhammad discouraged Abdullah from such excessive displays of spirituality. The Prophet then told him that his body, wife, and children had rights over him too, implying that such extreme worship would compromise their well-being.[11]

Muhammad, the Man of Compassion

For Muslims, Muhammad possessed an exemplary character. He was gentle not only with his fellow humans but also with animals and the environment. Muhammad lived in a humble clay house until his death. As the Prophet and leader of his society, everyone in the community had access to Muhammad. But still no leader was obeyed the way the followers of the Prophet obeyed him. At home, he did housework, including sewing his own clothes. He was good to his neighbors

---

9. Al-Tirmidhi, book 2, hadith 269.
10. Muhammad bin Ismail al-Bukhari, *Sahih al-Bukhari*, Sunnah.com, accessed February 8, 2021, https://sunnah.com/bukhari, book 78, hadith 30.
11. Al-Bukhari, book 30, hadith 84.

and generous to others. In a tradition reported by his wife Aisha, after the family slaughtered a goat, Aisha distributed most of it to the poor. She told Muhammad that only a small piece from the shoulder was left for them. The Prophet replied that "everything remains except the shoulder piece," a metaphor for the idea that what is given to charity will eventually return as a spiritual reward.[12] The Prophet was echoing the qur'anic message, "What is with you will vanish, but what is with God will endure. And We will certainly bestow on those who patiently persevere, their reward according to the best of their actions."[13] In another tradition, the Prophet said, "If you are merciful, God is merciful to you too. Have mercy on the creatures on the earth, so those in the heaven have mercy on you too."[14] Another reported that the Prophet remarked, "He who sleeps on a full stomach while his neighbor is hungry is not from us."[15]

When Byzantine emperor Heraclius asked one of the Prophet's initially most fierce enemies, Abu Sufyan, about Muhammad's character, Abu Sufyan answered, "Muhammad never breaks his promises, he never lies and always speaks of the truth."[16] Abu Sufyan also said, "I have never seen anyone who was as loved as Muhammad was by his companions."[17] Muhammad's companions loved him even more than their own children and parents.[18] His wife Aisha related that Muhammad would never respond to evil with evil. He was forgiving and did not focus on people's shortcomings.[19]

Embodying the qur'anic teaching that piety formed the base for "being superior in the eyes of God," Muhammad discouraged his followers from discriminating against anyone because of race and rank. Although during his time slavery was an entrenched institution, he encouraged his followers "to dress them [slaves] from what they [his followers] dress, to offer them from what they eat."[20] They should also treat slaves as equals when standing before God, shoulder to shoulder in the same prayer line. When one of his prominent companions discriminated against a

---

12. Al-Tirmidhi, Jami' al-Tirmidhi, book 37, hadith 2658.
13. Qur'an 16:96.
14. Al-Tirmidhi, Jami' al-Tirmidhi, book 27, hadith 30.
15. Al-Bukhari, Sahih al-Bukhari, book 6, hadith 12.
16. Al-Naysaburi, Sahih Muslim, book 32, hadith 89.
17. Brown, Muhammad, 38.
18. Brown, 37.
19. Al-Tirmidhi, Jami' al-Tirmidhi, book 27, hadith 122.
20. Al-Bukhari, Sahih al-Bukhari, book 2, hadith 1.

Black Ethiopian follower, Muhammad chastised the companion for displaying the sentiments of *jahiliyya*, or ignorance from the pre-Islamic period.[21]

Within a short time, Muhammad was able to reform Arabian society in many ways. Until that time, Arabs had followed tribal norms. Muhammad brought law and justice for all. Even if an injustice were to go unnoticed, he warned that accountability exists and that God always knows what is in one's heart.[22]

Muhammad and Controversy

While Muslims hold up Muhammad as the model of piety and excellent character, others in the West, especially after the rise of what historians consider to be modernity (around the seventeenth century CE), have criticized aspects of his life. From early on, critics of Muhammad offered different narratives about him. Scottish historian W. Montgomery Watt noted that "of all the worlds' great men none has been so much maligned as Muhammad."[23]

Many Western people expressed concern about Muhammad's multiple marriages. As mentioned, Muhammad had a monogamous relationship with his first wife, Khadija, until her death, and he was in his fifties when she died. Only after Khadija's death did he enter into polygamous relationships. According to Islamic sources, he had eleven consummated marriages and was married to nine women at one time.[24] Most of his wives were divorced and in need of protection. Some of these marriages were also politically expedient means of solidifying more positive relationships among the tribes. Polygamous relations and marriages for political purposes were common in the Near East: "Prior to Christianity, . . . the Near East from Pharaonic Egypt to ancient Mesopotamia was a world in which polygamy was not foreign at all. For most men, it would have been too expensive, but for rulers or men of great import it was an expectable tool of politics and propagation. Perhaps the most famous exemplar for such 'harem politics' was King Solomon, whom the Bible says had 700 wives and 300 concubines

---

21. Al-Bukhari, book 2, hadith 23.
22. Qur'an 3:29.
23. W. Montgomery Watt, *Muhammad: Prophet and Statesman* (Oxford: Oxford University Press, 1978), 231.
24. Brown, *Muhammad*, 49.

(1 King 11). Among them was the daughter of the Pharaoh of Egypt, whom he had married to cement an alliance."[25]

Two of the Prophet's marriages have been particularly controversial in the West. One was his marriage to Zaynab bint Jahsh, who was initially married to Zayd bin Haritha, the Prophet's adopted son and the only companion the Qur'an mentions by name. The marriage was not working, and Zayd told the Prophet he was considering divorce. Although Muhammad asked them to stay married, they divorced. The Qur'an explains, "When you [Prophet] said to the man who had received the grace of God and your favor, 'Keep your wife and fear God,' you concealed in your heart what God would later disclose. You were afraid of people, but it is more fitting that you fear God. When Zayd dissolved his marriage with her, We gave her to you in marriage so that there might be no fault in believers marrying the wives of their adopted sons after they no longer wanted them. God's command must be fulfilled."[26]

With this qur'anic instruction, Muhammad married Zaynab. His opponents were shocked and claimed that Muhammad was motivated by lust. How could he marry his adopted son's divorced wife? Yet with this marriage, Islam was reforming another practice in Arabia: an adopted son is not like a biological son. The Prophet's marriage to Zaynab confirmed that a Muslim could marry a divorced wife of his adopted son.[27]

The other marriage that has caused a lot of controversy in the West was Muhammad's marriage to Aisha, the daughter of his close companion Abu Bakr. Most Islamic resources relate that the marriage was consummated when Aisha reached puberty around age ten or eleven. It is noteworthy that this marriage did not become an issue until modern times. In the context of Muhammad's own time, marriage at an early age was quite routine; it was not unusual for both men and women to marry once they reached puberty. According to one of Muhammad's biographers,

> The reason that no pre-modern critics paid attention to the Prophet's marriage to a ten-year-old was because marrying girls considered under-age today was commonplace in the pre-modern world. Under Roman law, the earliest permitted age for marriage was twelve. In the heyday

25. Brown, 76.
26. Qur'an 33:37.
27. Qur'an 33:37.

of the Roman Empire (2nd century CE), by fourteen a girl was considered an adult whose primary purpose was marriage. In many pre-modern day law codes, such as Hebrew biblical law and Salic Frankish law, marriage age was not a question at all. It was assumed that when a girl reached puberty and was able to bear children, she was ready for marriage. As a result, we find that average marriage ages in the pre-modern world were remarkably young. Surviving evidence from several centuries of imperial Roman history suggests that as many as 8 percent of women married at ten or eleven. In Italy in the 1300s and 1400s, the average age for women was between sixteen and seventeen. Even in an 1861 census in England, over 350 women married under the age of fifteen in just two counties that year. According to both Christian and Muslim teachings, the Virgin Mary was not the mature maternal figure seen in the artwork about the Bible. She was at most in her mid-teens, having only just begun menstruating, and is reported to have been as young as ten years old.[28]

As we will see in chapter 5, Muhammad's private life became as important as his public life for Muslims in practicing their religion. We probably do not know about any other historical figure on such an intimate and detailed level—information that his wives played a key role in revealing. The Prophet educated his wives about the most intimate issues, and the community—especially Muslim women—learned from them. Aisha, for example, narrated many hadiths, or reports attributed to the Prophet; she is among the top four contributors of Muhammad's narrations. This is partly because of her youth and partly because of her good memory. Many companions as well as successors sought Aisha's advice concerning matters of jurisprudence as well as hadiths from the Prophet. Aisha transmitted more than two thousand of the three thousand hadiths attributed to his wives.[29]

The Prophet's life has also been controversial in the West because of his involvement in wars. (According to Islamic sources, Muhammad fought actively in nine wars.[30]) Some have even argued that he spread Islam through force and that con-

---

28. Brown, *Muhammad*, 78.
29. Muhammad Zubayr Siddiqi, *Hadith Literature: Its Origin, Development, and Special Features* (Cambridge: Islamic Text Society, 1993), 18.
30. Brown, *Muhammad*, 38.

temporary Muslims have taken the Prophet's involvement in wars as their example of and justification for jihad. Here, Muhammad is usually seen in stark contrast to Jesus. As shown in the first chapter, in the Near East of late antiquity, religion was one of the most important aspects of a person's identity. Wars were as common as peace. And it's important to remember that unlike Jesus, Muhammad was not only the Prophet of God but also the leader of the entire Muslim community in an often hostile environment. In dealing with issues of peace, violence, and war, he conformed at times to the rules of his environment. Also, unlike Jesus, who practiced his ministry for three years, Muhammad was a political leader for more than two decades.[31]

In the last several decades, the Prophet has also been at the center of debates about freedom of expression. These controversies have arisen with the publication of some images that depicted Muhammad in a degrading way. Such ridiculing is not new. According to the Qur'an, Muhammad's opponents continuously looked for opportunities to criticize him and to delegitimize his message. He was called a liar, a magician, and a deceiver. Naturally, such derogatory remarks have pained his followers, as the Prophet is dearer to them than their parents and children. Muslims of the past as well as today continue to look up to Muhammad as someone who positively informs their identity and is a model of personal growth in many aspects of human life.

In part 2, I turn to the sacred foundations of Islam: the Qur'an, the legacy of Muhammad (the Sunna), and Islamic law (sharia). I begin with the scripture.

---

31. David Chidester, *Christianity: A Global History* (New York: HarperOne, 2000), 12.

Part 2

Foundations

4 Scripture

The Qur'an

In January 2020, I attended a formal gathering at a mosque in Virginia. The event was held in the mosque's community hall, which was decorated as if for a wedding. Around 250 members of the community were present, including a diverse array of men, women, and children. During the event, teachers of the Qur'an gave talks about Islamic scripture and the significance of knowing it by heart. On a special stage, two teenage girls sat in fancy chairs. They recited short chapters of the Qur'an. The event concluded with the late evening prayer followed by a dinner.

As it turned out, the community had come together to celebrate the accomplishment of Janan and Asena, two sisters who had memorized the entire Qur'an. The girls had been born in the United States to a Uyghur Muslim family after their mother moved to the United States to pursue an education. Enjoying the religious freedom the Constitution guarantees, their mother wanted her children to have an Islamic education and dreamed that her children would memorize the Qur'an. The sisters were well motivated to carry the divine words in their hearts, and they embarked on the journey of memorizing the scripture. However, doing so was not a straightforward process. In addition to attending school, they studied with teachers at various qur'anic schools. After three years, they had committed the Qur'an to memory and thus became *hafiza*, or a Muslim woman who knows the entire Qur'an by heart. Janan and Asena are not the only US Muslims who have achieved this feat. Hundreds of Muslim children have memorized the sacred words in the United States. In this chapter, I explore the Qur'an and its significance and role in Muslim life.

The Qur'an and the Birth of Islam

The history of Islam begins with the Qur'an. While many communities of religious believers have created their own texts, Muslims assert that the Qur'an itself formed their community. For Muslims, the Qur'an has served as a book of wisdom, prayer, supplication, invocation, law, worship, contemplation, and science as well as a source of happiness and morals. It is a sacred guide to navigating the hereafter. The book reveals the meaning of life and serves as an introduction to divine attributes and their manifestations in the universe.[1]

The Qur'an describes itself as the "Word of God" (*kalamullah*), and Muslims consider it as such. As explained in chapter 2, the first verses of the Qur'an were revealed in 610 CE, when Muhammad was on a spiritual retreat in the outskirts of Mecca. The first revelation began with the word *read* or *recite* and then pointed to the embryonic development of humans as a sign of God's power in their creation.[2]

God revealed the Qur'an gradually, over many years, until Muhammad's death in 632 CE. The Prophet mostly received these revelations through the archangel Gabriel. Sometimes Gabriel arrived as himself, in his own form; at other times, he appeared to the Prophet in the form of one of his companions (known as Dihya); and on still other occasions, he manifested in the form of an unknown human. Whenever the Prophet received a revelation, his companions could see that the Prophet's attitude had changed. The divine words would be brought to him in many ways. When they were delivered on cold days, for example, he often broke into an unusual sweat. According to some hadith narratives, the Prophet's companions asked him how the revelations would come to him. He answered that it was "like the ringing of a bell." He continued, "When it departs, I remember what Gabriel said, and this is the hardest on me. And sometimes the angel comes to me in the form of a man and reveals it to me."[3]

Some revelations addressed a specific case or issue within the nascent Muslim community. On one occasion, for example, Abdullah bin Umm Maktum, a blind man, came to the Prophet Muhammad seeking his guidance. At the time, the Prophet was in conversation with a number of elites of the Meccan society conveying the message of Islam. When Abdullah kept asking for guidance, the Prophet then frowned at him and continued his conversation with the unbelievers. Upon this occasion, the first ten verses in chapter 80 of the Qur'an were revealed, in which

---

1. Bediuzzaman Said Nursi, *Signs of Miraculousness*, trans. Şükran Vahide (Istanbul: Sözler, 2004), 16.
2. Qur'an 96:1–5.
3. Al-Tirmidhi, *Jami' al-Tirmidhi*, book 49, hadith 3994.

God admonished Muhammad for frowning at the blind man.[4] The same chapter of the Qur'an also takes its name from the occasion: "He Frowned" ("Abasa").

Muhammad was eager to preserve the revelations and transmit them to his companions. He would recite every revealed verse, and his scribes would take dictation. The Prophet and the archangel Gabriel would recite the revealed verses to each other and review them once a year during the month of Ramadan. They did this traditional recitation and review of the revelation twice in the last year of Muhammad's life.[5] In addition, the revealed portions of the Qur'an would be recited communally during the Prophet's time, especially during the month of Ramadan. Muslims continued this tradition after Muhammad's death. From early times, recitation was one of the most common ways of engaging with the Qur'an. This form of engagement with the words of God made them accessible to the entire community, as men, women, and children were able to hear and recite scripture from the beginning of the revelations.

Compilation and Canonization

While the Prophet was alive, scribes engraved the verses of the Qur'an on leather and bones, but the preservation of the revealed words was mainly done orally through memorization and recitation. A sizable number of Muhammad's companions, for instance, were known as memorizers (huffaz) of the Qur'an. During the reign of Abu Bakr (r. 632–34), some of these people died in a battle. These deaths raised concern within the Muslim community over possibly losing some of Muhammad's precious revelations. In order to preserve the Qur'an in a formal and durable way, Abu Bakr formed a committee and appointed Zayd bin Thabit, one of the Prophet's scribes, as chair. The committee brought together both the written versions of the revealed verses and the huffaz. The committee members were able to come to a consensus on the text of the Qur'an as a book (mushaf), which they entrusted first to Abu Bakr and then to his successor, Umar (r. 634–44). Tradition recounts that the copy was then passed to Umar's daughter Hafsa, who was married to Muhammad.

4. Joseph E. B. Lumbard, Commentary on Surat 'Abasa, in Nasr et al, Study Qur'an, 1475.
5. Al-Bukhari, Sahih al-Bukhari, book 1, hadith 6.

During the reign of the third caliph, Uthman (r. 644–56), Islam expanded into non-Arabic-speaking regions. This raised the issue of access to the Qur'an as well as its proper recitation. Some oral versions included minor differences, which all had been considered valid readings since the time of Muhammad. To address these differing readings, more copies of the Qur'an were needed. A committee of a dozen Muslims came together and copied the Qur'an. They then sent an exact copy of the same version of this Qur'an along with reciters to each of the seven major areas of the Muslim world, including Yemen, Kufa, Basra, Damascus, and Mecca. These books are known as the Uthmanic copies. While having copies in various regions of Islam settled many issues concerning the text as well as the recitation, some textual matters remained unresolved. The Uthmanic copies, for example, did not have diacritical marks or vowel symbols, which made reading the Qur'an a challenge. To make the Qur'an more accessible, a dotting and diacritical system was introduced in the late seventh century CE during the Umayyad dynasty. Khalil bin Ahmad, an Arab philologist, approved the system in use today in the eighth century CE.[6]

Form and Structure

The Qur'an neither follows a chronology nor concerns itself with genealogy. Although it contains 114 chapters and more than six thousand verses, the Qur'an is a relatively short text compared to the Bible or the Hindu Vedas. The chapters are divided into two groups: those that Muhammad received in Mecca and those that he received in Medina. The Meccan chapters confronted unbelievers who opposed the new message. They are centered on the belief in one God (*tawhid*), issues of moral accountability, and the resurrection. Because Meccans already believed themselves to be advanced in literature and poetry, the Qur'an challenged them with "the highest styles of eloquence [*i'jaz*]" in words.[7] Many of the Meccan chapters are short and poetic. Unlike the Meccan chapters, the Medinan chapters focus more on issues related to faith and practice. They provide guidelines for how believers should conduct both their personal and public lives. Given that a sizable number of Jews and Christians lived in Medina, these chapters also engage some theological and practical aspects of Judaism and Christianity.

6. Abdulhamit Birışık, "Kur'an," in İslam Ansiklopedisi (Istanbul: TDV, 2002), 26:386.
7. Bediuzzaman Said Nursi, *The Words* (Istanbul: Sözler, 2008), 469.

Major Themes

Some major themes recur throughout the Qur'an. The first is *tawhid*, or the unity of God, which almost all chapters of the Qur'an directly or indirectly discuss. The qur'anic verses repeatedly point to God's creations around us, continually referring to such things as the stars, mountains, seas, trees, birds, humans, fruits, and milk as signs of God (*ayat*). Many of the chapters of the Qur'an are named after things God created. For example, chapter 2, which is the longest, is titled "The Cow." Others are named "The Cattle," "The Thunder," "The Bee," "The Light," "The Spider," "The Mount," "The Star," "The Moon," "The Human Being," and so on. The Qur'an uses different names for God and presents creation as the manifestation of his names. In one of the verses, for example, God is described as light: "God is the Light of the heavens and the earth. The Parable of His Light is as if there were a niche and within it a lamp. The lamp enclosed in glass. The glass is a shining star kindled from a blessed olive tree, neither of the east nor of the west. Its oil would almost glow even if untouched by fire. Light upon light! God guides to His light whomever He pleases and gives examples for people. God has knowledge of everything."[8]

The second major theme of the Qur'an is prophecy (*nubuwwa*). For the journey of knowing God (*marifah*), there are three major sources: scriptures, the universe, and the prophets. The Qur'an repeatedly invokes the stories of the prophets—Abraham, Jesus, Moses, Noah, Ishmael, and Joseph—and points out that there are messages in these stories for believers: "There is, in their stories, a lesson for those who understand. It is not a tale invented, but a confirmation of what came before it, a clear exposition of all things, and a guide and a mercy for people who believe."[9]

The third theme is the hereafter and resurrection. The Qur'an alludes to the signs (*ayat*) in the universe when it points to the resurrection. It emphasizes that everything done in life is recorded and that there will eventually be a bodily resurrection to a realm of accountability. When Meccan unbelievers questioned the rationality of a bodily resurrection, the Qur'an pointed to the creation of humans, stating that the One who created humans in the first place could give them life again.[10] The Qur'an mentions spring—the resurrection of creation after winter—as

8. Qur'an 24:35.
9. Qur'an 12:111.
10. Qur'an 36:77–83.

more evidence of life after death: "Look, therefore, at the prints of God's mercy, how He gives life to the earth after its death. Indeed, this is the same God who will give life to the dead for He has power over all things."[11]

The fourth major theme of the Qur'an is worship. The Qur'an frequently refers to believers as those who worship and glorify God and remarks that God created humans so that they could worship him in response to his manifestations throughout creation.[12]

The fifth central theme is justice: "You who believe," the Qur'an tells us, "Stand out firmly for justice, as witnesses to God, even if it is against yourselves, or your parents, or your close relatives, and whether it be (against) rich or poor for God can best protect both. Do not follow your desire to avoid justice. If you distort (justice) or decline to do justice, verily God is fully aware of what you do."[13] In another verse, believers are asked to be just in their affairs, even in difficult situations: "You who believe! Stand out firmly for God, as witnesses to fair dealing, and let not the hatred of others to you make you swerve to wrong and depart from justice. Be just, that is nearer to piety and be mindful of God. God is fully aware of what you do."[14] Although the Qur'an repeatedly encourages the believer to be a just person who longs to restore justice on earth, it also ties the concept of justice to the idea of resurrection and life after death. The reasoning is that God's justice is partly revealed in this world and will have its complete manifestation in the hereafter. It is also important to point out that while the Qur'an is often presented as a book of law, only around three hundred of its over six thousand verses address legal issues.

The Qur'an in Muslim Living

I spent the summer of 2011 in Egypt. I heard recitations of the Qur'an not only in mosques but also in markets, cafés, and even a cab. The country's soundscape is suffused with the language of the Qur'an. Perhaps the most unique experience I had was in an elevator in a building in Cairo. When I pushed the button to go up or down, a voice came over a speaker and recited the following verse from the

11. Qur'an 30:50.
12. Qur'an 51:56.
13. Qur'an 4:135.
14. Qur'an 5:8.

Qur'an: "Glory be to God who has given us control over this, for we could never have accomplished this by ourselves."[15] This message applies to more than elevators. When Muslims ride on a ship or an animal, they remember God's blessings and contemplate his grace. To embody this qur'anic message in modern life, some Muslim airlines make sure that passengers listen to this prayer before the airplane takes off. Muslims even install this prayer in their cars. When they start the engine, it recites the same verse.

The most common way Muslims have engaged with the Qur'an since its inception is through recitation, whether from memory or readings of the Qur'an. This approach makes the words of God more accessible to believers. Many Muslims memorize the divine words just by listening to daily recitations in Muslim societies. In addition to recounting verses during worship and prayers, observant Muslims engage with the Qur'an during their daily affairs. At funerals, for example, attendees recite particular sections of scripture, usually from "Surat al-Yasin" (chapter 36). Upon hearing that a fellow Muslim has died, Muslims recite the following passage: "We belong to God and to Him we shall return."[16] At weddings, they say, "People, be mindful of your Lord, who created you from one soul and created from it its mate and dispersed from both of them many men and women. And be mindful of God, through whom you appeal one another and invoke family relationships. Indeed, God is always watching over you."[17] People in Muslim societies gather often and at various venues simply to enjoy the recitation of the Qur'an.

Muslims, whether they are native Arabic speakers or not, usually memorize some portions of the Qur'an in Arabic, especially the first chapter, "Al-Fatiha." Committing the Qur'an to memory has long been a tradition among Muslims, and today, thousands of qur'anic schools around the world teach children to memorize the entire book. A chain of qur'anic schools in Pakistan, for example, has been giving the certificate of memorization to around 60,000 students annually.[18] In Turkey, more than 150,000 Muslims were certified as *huffaz* between 1970 and 2019.[19]

---

15. Qur'an 43:13.
16. Qur'an 2:156.
17. Qur'an 4:1.
18. "Pakistan Tops World with Qur'an Huffaz," Darul Ihsan Humanitarian Centre, July 17, 2014, https://darulihsan.com/index.php/news/item/5840-pakistan-tops-world-with-qur'an-huffaz.
19. Ayhan İşcen, "'Türkiye'deki hafız sayısı 150 bini geçti,'" AA.com, May 10, 2019, https://www.aa.com.tr/tr/turkiye/turkiyedeki-hafiz-sayisi-150-bini-gecti/1603171.

Those who carry the divine words in their hearts enjoy a special respect within the Muslim community. Many are internationally recognized.

The Qur'an has also had a significant effect on Islamic art, especially calligraphy. qur'anic calligraphies adorn not only mosques but also offices, houses, and stores. Major monuments of the Muslim world such as the Taj Mahal in India, the Alhambra in Spain, and the Dome of the Rock in Jerusalem are also decorated with qur'anic verses. Upon building the Taj Mahal in memory of his beloved deceased wife, Mughal emperor Shah Jahan (d. 1666) inscribed on its walls verses from the Qur'an concerning judgment day, rewards, and heaven. On the southern part of the main gate, the following verses are inscribed: "O you soul at peace, return to your Lord, well pleased and well pleasing unto Him. Join My devotees and enter my Paradise."[20]

The Qur'an has also shaped Muslims' daily language. Arabic terms and phrases such as "In the name of God" (bismillah), "God willing" (inshaallah), "Praise be to God" (alhamdulillah), and "God's peace be upon you" (assalaamu alaikum) come from the Qur'an and have become part of a shared Muslim language. Many Muslim names such as Ayaat (signs), Akbar (greatest), Bushra (good news), Huda (guidance), Ibrahim (Abraham), Ihsan (kindness), Iman (faith), Isa (Jesus), Jamil (beautiful), Jannah (paradise), Maryam (Mary), Musa (Moses), Naeem (bliss), Nasr (victory), Qamar (moon), Salam (peace), Saleh (pious), Shakir (thankful), Tayyib (virtuous), and Yunus (Joseph) are all based on the Qur'an.

Quite literally, Muslims elevate the Qur'an whenever there is a chance—for example, by placing their copy on a high shelf. In addition, before reciting from the Qur'an, Muslims usually perform minor ablutions, physically purifying themselves with water.[21]

Interpretations

Muhammad's death left Muslims with the challenge of determining how to accurately interpret the Qur'an. Before the Prophet died, believers would come to him seeking clarification on the sacred words. In their eyes, Muhammad was the living Qur'an. His

---

20. Qur'an 89:27–30.
21. For the etiquette of approaching the Qur'an, see Abu Hamid al-Ghazali, *Ihyā' 'Ulūm al-Dīn* (Cairo: al-Quds, 2012), 1:450–77.

departure from this world left his followers with many questions. How would they understand the scripture without the Prophet's earthly presence? How should they conduct their lives according to the will of God? Naturally, Muslims turned first to the Qur'an for answers. But not everything in the Qur'an was clear. So how should they interpret the ambiguous parts? What did God intend with each verse?

Attempting to answer these questions became the most important mission of Muslim exegetes (*mufassirun*). Scholars of the Qur'an already knew that the ultimate meaning of the divine words was hidden in the mind of God. They believed, therefore, that the interpretations of the qur'anic verses could never be exhausted, since the Qur'an was itself the eternal word of God. This approach generated a great diversity of interpretations, and *mufassirun* often concluded their commentaries with the phrase "God knows best," humbly acknowledging that their understanding of the Qur'an was just one of many.

Two major exegetical categories have emerged: tradition-based commentary (*tafsir bi al-ma'thur*) and independent reasoning–based commentary (*tafsir bi al-ra'y*). Tradition-based commentary is heavily focused on the text. According to this approach, the exegete begins to interpret a verse through other verses in the Qur'an, then looks at the hadith texts, and finally consults the works of the first and second generations of Muslims.[22] Independent reasoning–based commentary broadens the resources available to exegetes' interpretations. In addition to the sources used for the tradition-based commentaries, they also look at the perspectives of later scholars, principles of jurisprudence, and the writings of Muslim theologians. Within these two broad categories, diverse traditions developed: commentaries based on Sunni or Shiite interpretative approaches, theology, law, mysticism, and philosophy. In modern times, in response to the need for qur'anic commentaries that are compatible with and speak to the spirit of the age, modernist, scientific, sociopolitical, feminist, as well as contextualist commentaries have emerged.

Translations

Whether Muslims should accept as sacred text the translation of the Qur'an in any language other than Arabic has been a pressing question since Islam began being

22. Abdullah Saeed, *The Qur'an: An Introduction* (New York: Routledge, 2008), 179.

practiced among non-Arab speakers. When it comes to the translation of the holy text, many compare it to the ways Christians judge different versions of the Bible. However, while Christians regard translations as legitimate and authoritative, Muslims believe that engaging with the Qu'ran in Arabic is always preferable.

Translating the Qur'an into other languages has been a contentious issue among Muslim scholars from the early years of Islam. On the one hand, some claimed that the scripture could not be translated. They based their argument on the orthodox approach—namely, that the Qur'an is miraculous in not only content but also form and that both aspects would be lost in translation. On the other hand, the Qur'an states that it is a divine message for all humanity. Considering that only a small percentage of people could access the Qur'an in Arabic, others argued that it should be more broadly available. Muslim scholars generally agree that the Qur'an is not translatable but has been translated anyway. Thus most scholars regard any translation as an interpretation. This is why one finds so many different versions of the English translation, each with a distinct approach, including orthodox, progressive, Sufi, and feminist translations.

Any discussion of translations of Islamic scripture needs to highlight two important characteristics of the Qur'an. First, Muslim scholars have emphasized that in addition to its content, God also revealed its inimitable (*i'jaz al-Qur'an*) form and structure. The Qur'an itself teaches this lesson. Addressing those who doubt that it is a revelation, for example, the Qur'an points out that "if you are in doubt about what We have revealed to Our servant, then produce a Sura like it; and call upon your supporters other than God if you are truthful."[23] The verse concludes by stating that anyone who tries to do so will fail. Another verse emphasizes the inimitability of the Qur'an: "If the whole of mankind and jinns came together to produce the like of this Qur'an, they could not produce the like of it, even if they backed up each other with help and support."[24] Many major qur'anic exegetes, therefore, dedicated volumes of their commentaries to this feature. Among them are al-Jahiz (d. 868), al-Baqillani (d. 1013), al-Jurjani (d. 1078), al-Razi (d. 1210), and al-Zamakhshari (d. 1144).

Second, reciting the Qur'an *in Arabic* is a key component of Islamic spirituality. To do so is a form of contemplation (*tafakkur*), an act of remembrance (*dhikr*),

23. Qur'an 2:23.
24. Qur'an 17:88.

and a supplication to God (*dua*). Since any translation would lack these aspects of qur'anic spirituality, any translation of the Qur'an technically cannot be received as the "Qur'an."

The Qur'an in the United States

The journey of the Qur'an to the United States dates from early colonial times. Documents from the 1500s mention Muslim names, and scholars believe around 15 percent of West Africans brought to the United States as slaves were Muslims. Many of these slaves were educated and well versed in both the Arabic language and the Qur'an.[25] These slaves' engagement with Muslim scripture often impressed their masters. Because of the slaves' knowledge about Christianity—its theology and its scriptures—they were able to engage in conversations about theological issues in their encounters with Christians.

Ayuba Suleiman Diallo, also known as Job Ben Solomon, was enslaved around 1730 in the eastern part of today's Senegal and brought to Annapolis, Maryland. His knowledge of the Qur'an and Arabic impressed James Oglethorpe, the founder of Georgia and a member of the British parliament. He bought Job and took him to England. According to his biographer, Thomas Bluett, Job made three copies of the Qur'an from memory.[26] Based on his knowledge of Jesus that he learned from the Qur'an, Job was able to discuss the concept of the Trinity and belief in the virgin birth of Jesus with his sponsors.[27]

The Qur'an is also vividly present in dialogues between Abd al-Rahman Ibrahima and Christians. A Muslim noble and military leader, Abd al-Rahman was brought to the Americas as a slave from today's Guinea. When he was asked to write the Lord's Prayer in Arabic, he wrote the first chapter of the Qur'an, "Al-Fatiha." Like Job Ben Solomon, because of his knowledge of the Qur'an, he was able to engage with Christian scripture and its theology.[28]

---

25. Carl W. Ernst, *Following Muhammad: Rethinking Islam in the Contemporary* (Chapel Hill: University of North Carolina Press, 2003), 18.
26. Edward E. Curtis, *Muslims in America: A Short History* (Oxford: Oxford University Press, 2009), 2.
27. Curtis, 3.
28. Curtis, 9.

The Qur'an played a significant part in the life of Omar bin Sayyid. Omar was brought from West Africa to Charleston, South Carolina, around 1807.[29] In his 1831 autobiography, Omar engages with qur'anic verses and extensively quotes from chapter 67, "Surah al-Mulk."[30] Muslims often memorize this section of the Qur'an, and it is therefore not surprising that Omar knew it by heart. The chapter emphasizes that dominion or power belongs to God, not to humans: "Blessed be He in whose hands is sovereignty; and He has power over everything. He who created death and life, that He may test which of you is best in deed; and He is the Mighty, the Forgiving. He who created the seven heavens one above another."[31] As a slave, believing this qur'anic message helped Omar find comfort and hope.

Lamen Kebe, who was a teacher in West Africa before his enslavement in 1795, told a man named Theodore Dwight about methods of teaching the Qur'an and the meaning of the Arabic words.[32] Thus one of his owners bought him a copy of the Qur'an and an Arabic Bible.[33]

Some qur'anic verses even found their way into antislavery debates. A few decades before the Civil War began, some abolitionists engaged with Islam in order to challenge slavery. An edition of the *New Hampshire Patriot* from 1810, for example, relates a story from Islam:

> A singular instance of forbearance, arising from the powerful influence of religious principles, is recorded in the history of Caliphs. A slave one day during a repast, was so unfortunate as to let fall a dish which he was handing to the Caliph Hassan, who was severely scalded by the accident. The trembling wretch instantly fell on his knees, and quoting the Qur'an, exclaimed: "Paradise is promised to those who restrain their anger." "I am not angry with thee," replied the Caliph, with a meekness as exemplary as it was rare. "And for those who forgive offences," continued the slave. "I forgive thee thine," answered the Caliph. "But above all, for those who

29. Ala Alryyes, *A Muslim American Slave: The Life of Omar Ibn Said* (Madison: University of Wisconsin Press, 2011), 61–63.
30. Curtis, *Muslims in America*, 13.
31. Qur'an 67:1–3.
32. Allan D. Austin, *African Muslims in Antebellum America: Transatlantic Stories and Spiritual Struggles* (New York: Routledge, 1997), 121.
33. Alryyes, *Muslim American Slave*, 73.

return good for evil," adds the slave, "I set thee at liberty," rejoins the Caliph, and "give thee ten dinars."[34]

Verse 134 in chapter 3 of the Qur'an is at the center of this story. It teaches that God loves those who give to charity in ease and in hardship, restrain their anger, and forgive people.[35]

When Thomas Jefferson's library was moved to the Library of Congress in the early 1800s, among his more than six thousand books was a copy of the Qur'an, which currently occupies a shelf in the reading room. Keith Ellison, the first US Muslim elected to Congress from Minnesota, took his oath on Jefferson's copy of the Qur'an.[36]

Today, the Qur'an is still a major influence in the lives of Muslims in the United States. One can find qur'anic schools as well as study circles around the country in which Muslims learn not only to understand and recite the Qur'an but also to memorize it and learn its language. They try to live up to its message in their daily lives as much as they can. However, since not everything is clearly laid out in the Qur'an, Muslims rely on another sacred source, the Sunna of the Prophet Muhammad, which is the subject of the following chapter.

34. Cited in Peter Manseau, *One Nation, under Gods: A New American History* (New York: Little, Brown, 2015), 236.
35. Qur'an 3:134.
36. "Thomas Jefferson's Copy of the Koran to Be Used in Congressional Swearing-In Ceremony," Library of Congress press release, January 3, 2007, https://www.loc.gov/item/prn-07-001/.

5 The Legacy of Muhammad

The Sunna

Tariq and Muslimah 'Ali Najee-ullah are a second-generation Muslim African American couple. Muslimah is a trained anatomist with a PhD from Howard University, and Tariq currently serves as the imam and Muslim chaplain at Johns Hopkins University. In January 2020, they invited their colleagues and family friends to an event celebrating the birth of their fourth child, Zuhayrah Manar, at the Johns Hopkins Interfaith Center in Baltimore. Zuhayrah's parents and siblings educated the audience on the religious significance and meaning of the occasion, and a local imam offered reflections. In addition, the speakers recited chapters from the Qur'an. The event concluded with food and festivities.

With these birth rituals, parents fulfill one of the Sunna of the Prophet Muhammad known as *aqiqa*.[1] *Aqiqa* usually refers to the sacrifice of an animal as a form of gratitude toward God following the birth of a child. The infant's family cooks and eats the meat of the animal, shares it with family and friends in the form of a banquet, and also distributes some to the needy. The *aqiqa* ritual also involves naming the child, shaving the infant's head, and giving the weight of its hair in silver or gold to the poor.[2] The Qur'an does not mention *aqiqa*, but the Prophet Muhammad strongly recommended it. Therefore, Muslims around the world as well as in the United States often have an *aqiqa* for their newborns as part of the Prophet Muhammad's legacy, which is referred to as Sunna. In this chapter, we examine the role of Muhammad's Sunna, or his example in the lives of Muslims.

The death of the Prophet Muhammad is, for Muslims, one of the saddest events in the history of Islam. He was the transmitter of divine words, and early Muslims had direct access to new revelations through him. His death marked the end of this unique revelatory period. The story of Umm Ayman, a woman the Prophet referred to as "my mother after the death of my mother," reflects this loss. Umm Ayman took

---

1. Imam Tariq Najee-Ullah, telephone interview with the author, January 31, 2020.
2. Matthew B. Ingalls, "Aqiqah," Oxford Islamic Studies Online, accessed January 20, 2020, http://oxfordislamicstudies.com/article/opr/t349/e0002#.

care of Muhammad during his childhood and numbered among his first followers. The Prophet had profound respect for Umm Ayman and visited her often up until his death. After the passing of the Prophet, his companions spent time with Umm Ayman out of respect for Muhammad's special relationship with her. One day, as they arrived for a visit, the Prophet's companions found Umm Ayman distressed and crying about his death. The companions tried to console her, saying, "Don't you know that being with God is better for the Prophet?" Umm Ayman affirmed she did not have any doubt that the Prophet was in a better place, yet she said, "I am sad that with the Prophet's death we are disconnected from divine revelation."[3]

The Prophet's death meant the end of the revelation and also created challenges for understanding the Qur'an, which contains ambiguous verses. During the Prophet's lifetime, people turned to him directly when questions arose. But now that Muhammad was gone, they wondered how they could understand the Qur'an, practice their religion, and conduct their lives in a way that was pleasing to God. They turned to the way or example of the Prophet, which is known as the Sunna (literally, "path" or "custom"). *Sunna* usually refers to what Muhammad said, what he did, and what he approved of.[4]

Many Muslim scholars regard the Sunna of Muhammad as the most valuable resource for understanding the Qur'an. The Qur'an itself repeatedly instructs Muslim believers to follow and obey the Prophet. In one case, the scripture says that if one loves God, then they should follow the Prophet.[5] The Qur'an implies that the love of God requires following the Sunna. It also characterizes the Prophet as the best model for believers.[6] Based on interpretations of these qur'anic references, Muslim scholars consider the Prophet's words and actions as "the archetype of a life lived in full submission to God."[7] Many Muslims regard living in accordance with the prophetic example, both in conducting one's life and in practicing the rituals, as a way of remembering and loving God.[8] As a result, Muslims take every aspect of the Prophet's life seriously. After the Qur'an itself, the Sunna has served as the

3. Muhammad bin Yazid Ibn Majah, *Sunan Ibn Majah*, Sunnah.com, accessed February 2021, https://sunnah.com/ibnmajah, book 6, hadith 1704.
4. Hamza Yusuf Hanson, "The Sunna: The Way of the Prophet Muhammad," in *Voices of Islam*, vol. 1, ed. Vincent J. Cornell (Westport, CT: Praeger, 2007), 129.
5. Qur'an 3:31.
6. Qur'an 33:21.
7. Joseph E.B. Lumbard, Commentary on *Surat al-Ahzab*, in Nasr et al., Study Qur'an, 1025.
8. Qur'an 3:31.

most important source for Islamic spirituality and moral conduct. The Prophet himself emphasized the Sunna. One of the hadiths reports that he admonished the community: "I have left two things by which, as long as you hold to them, you will not go the wrong way: the Book of God and my Sunna."[9]

The Sunna as Guidance for Manners and Moral Conduct

The Sunna also serves as a guide for moral conduct in the Islamic tradition. As mentioned before, Muslims regard the Prophet Muhammad as the embodiment of the Qur'an and as the pinnacle of moral character. Even his opponents called him "the Trustworthy" (al-Amin). The Qur'an establishes the moral excellence of the Prophet and the authority of the Sunna. Muslim scholars agree that the verse "Truly you have an exalted character" refers to the beautiful and noble conduct of the Prophet Muhammad.[10] When one of the companions asked Muhammad's wife Aisha about his personality, she answered that the Prophet's character was the Qur'an (khuluquhu al-Qur'an).[11]

One of many proofs that the Prophet was indeed the qur'anic embodiment of perfect morality and reflected the highest ideal of ethical behavior was his radical transformation of a society that was, morally speaking, deficient. If he had not embodied strong moral qualities himself, he would have failed to bring about such a large-scale social revolution as the religion of Islam. Muhammad's transformation of pre-Islamic tribal society was a permanent one because he conquered the hearts of people before they turned to Islam.[12]

By following the Sunna, every habit and human act becomes a prayer, sacred and meaningful for a Muslim believer. Following the Sunna is not just a matter of simple imitation; every detail of the Sunna contains wisdom, light, and a moral lesson.[13] Moreover, the Sunna defies the dichotomy between sacred and profane by demonstrating that all human acts—even smiling, dressing, or studying, for example—can be acts of

9. Malik bin Anas, *Muwatta*, Sunnah.com, accessed April 28, 2021, https://sunnah.com/malik, book 46, hadith 1623.
10. Qur'an 68:4.
11. Abu Dawud al-Sijistani, *Sunan Abu Dawud*, Sunnah.com, accessed February 8, 2021, https://sunnah .com/abudawud, book 5, hadith 93.
12. Bediuzzaman Said Nursi, *İşaratül İ'caz* (Istanbul: Söz Basim, 2009), 227–28.
13. Bediuzzaman Said Nursi, *The Flashes* (Istanbul: Sözler, 2004), 85.

worship. Therefore, life in all its aspects becomes full of worship and meaning. God values all human deeds, and by following the Sunna, humans add sanctity and meaning to their lives. Emulating the Prophet leads to the remembrance of God, who is the most compassionate and sovereign of the world. He is the one who sends messengers as moral ideals and human models to be followed. Practicing a simple Sunna, like entering a house with the right foot, connects the observant believer to the heavenly realm. One then lives in a state of constant awareness of God and is conscious that God is at the center of human life. Knowing that God concerns himself with his creation in every act creates a deep sense of connection to the divine. One then feels valued and honored, and a sense of meaning and sacredness infuses human life.

The Sunna as Guidance for Islamic Ritual Practices

The Sunna is not only a source of instruction on manners and moral conduct; it also guides Islamic ritual practices. The Qur'an does not provide the details about how to conduct a specific ritual and points to the Prophet as the one who can clarify and explain its meanings.[14] The Qur'an contains references to ablution (wudu), the five daily prayers, and fasting. However, it is the Sunna that details how Muslims are to perform these rituals.[15]

From the beginning, therefore, Muslims followed the prophetic example for conducting Islamic practices. For example, the Qur'an calls on believers to pray five times daily but provides no details about how they should do so.[16] Thus following the Sunna becomes essential to performing Muslim rituals. Prominent jurist Imam al-Shafi'i (d. 820) explained,

> The Prophet specified that daily prayers shall number five, that the number of cycles in the noon, afternoon, and evening prayers shall number four, repeated twice in the towns, and that the cycles for the sunset prayer are three and for the dawn prayer two. He decreed that in all the prayers there should be recitation from the Qur'an, audible in the sunset, evening, and

14. Qur'an 16:44.
15. Hanson, "Sunna," 127.
16. Ingrid Mattson, *The Story of the Qur'an: Its History and Place in Muslim Life* (Oxford: Wiley-Blackwell, 2013), 211.

dawn prayers, and silent in the noon and afternoon prayers. He specified that at the beginning of each prayer, the *takbir* should be said and at the end, the *taslim*, and that each prayer consists of *takbir*, recitation, bowing and two prostrations after each inclination but beyond that, nothing is obligatory [only recommended]. He decreed that the prayer made on a journey can be shorter, if the traveler so desires, in the three prayers that have four cycles, but he made no change in the sunset and dawn prayers.[17]

Al-Shafi'i demonstrates the Prophet's crucial role in modeling how to conduct the rituals laid out in the Qur'an. Following the example of the Prophet in rituals is the cornerstone of Islamic spirituality.

Hadith in Relation to the Sunna

Hadith is regarded as the most important source of the Sunna after the Qur'an. While the term *hadith* is often used synonymously with the Sunna, it more properly refers to reports concerning the Prophet's sayings and actions rather than the sayings and actions themselves. In order to reveal and preserve the example of Muhammad, Muslim scholars tried to record almost every detail about the Prophet. Those details later found their way into the hadith collections. Muslim scholars distinguish three stages of development of hadiths. One is the prophetic stage, which refers to the time when companions in the Prophet's circle learned from him and absorbed his teachings. After this period came the compilation stage, during which many hadiths were collected after Muhammad's death. Last is the codification stage, when scholars approached hadith literature critically and classified the reports.[18] Muslim scholars regard this stage as the golden age of hadith scholarship.

Following the first civil war after the death of Muhammad, many hadiths were forged in order to justify political beliefs. Within this context, Muslim scholars developed the field of hadith scholarship in order to assess the authenticity of the reports concerning the Prophet's sayings and actions. According to this science,

17. Muhammad bin Idris al-Shafi'i, *Islamic Jurisprudence: Shafi'i's Risala*, trans. Majid Khadduri (Baltimore, MD: Johns Hopkins University Press, 1961), 158–60, cited in Mattson, *Story of the Qur'an*, 211.
18. Muslim jurist Ahmad Zarruq's (d. 1493) made this classification. See Hanson, "Sunna," 131.

one of the most important principles for determining authenticity was whether the chain of transmission (*sanad* or *isnad*) was reliable.[19] Scholars sorted hadith narratives into three broad groups: sound (*sahih*), good (*hasan*), and weak (*da'if*). They then grouped the sound hadiths into subcategories: (1) *mutawatir*, a hadith many narrators reported throughout the first three generations of Muslims and considered to be authentic; (2) *mashur*, a tradition narrated by multiple chains of transmission at most stages; and (3) *ahad*, a hadith that only a few narrators reported.[20] Around five hundred *mutawatir* hadiths exist.

Scholars also evaluated hadiths based on their type (*qudsi* and *nabawi*), their number of narrators, their soundness, and the existence of possible disconnections in their chain of transmission (*sanad*). In addition, hadith scholars evaluated the character of the narrators based on their state of memory, moral conduct, and piety.

In the Sunni tradition, six hadith collections became prominent. First is *Sahih al-Bukhari*, which Imam al-Bukhari (d. 870) compiled. For his work, he traveled to major Islamic areas—including Syria, Egypt, Basra, Balkh, Kufa, and the Hejaz—in order to both study with well-known scholars and gather hadith narratives.[21] His anthology includes around seven thousand hadiths. Scholars believe he studied around six hundred thousand hadith narratives to select the most reliable ones. *Sahih al-Bukhari* consists of ninety-seven chapters on such broad topics as revelation, belief, knowledge, peacemaking, marriage, fasting, jihad, prayers, pilgrimage, medicine, and food. The second collection is the *Sahih Muslim*, which Imam Muslim (d. 875) compiled and includes over seven thousand hadiths. Scholars report that he studied more than three hundred thousand hadiths during the process of compilation.[22] The other four books are *Jami' al-Tirmidhi* of Imam al-Tirmidhi (d. 883), *Sunan* of Muhammad bin Yazid b. Majah (d. 886), *Sunan* of Abu Dawud al-Sijistani (d. 888), and *Sahih al-Nasai* of Ahmad bin Shu'ayb al-Nasa'i (d. 915). The collections of al-Bukhari and Imam Muslim are considered more authentic compared to other hadith works.

Hadith collections are also important in the Shiite tradition, which also holds that following the Prophet's example is essential to Muslim life. Shiites, however, attribute unique authority to Muhammad's descendants through his daughter Fatima

---

19. Hanson, 132.
20. Siddiqi, *Hadith Literature*, 110.
21. Diyanet İşleri Başkanlığı, *Hadislerle Islam* (Istanbul: Diyanet Yayınları, 2011), 1:74.
22. Diyanet İşleri Başkanlığı, 1:75.

and his cousin and son-in-law, Ali bin Abi Talib. Shiites usually refer to hadiths as *akhbar*, meaning "news" or "reports." While in the Shiite tradition, hadith collections remain a key source of jurisprudence after the Qur'an, Shiites reject some of the narratives that the Prophet's prominent companions relayed. From a Shiite perspective, the political position of these companions regarding Ali's leadership after the Prophet's death is problematic. Also, unlike Sunnis, Shiites believe the twelve imams played a key role in transmitting the hadiths. Nevertheless, many of the traditions that made their way into the Shiite collections are similar to those that are part of the Sunni sources.[23]

Women played a key role in the transmission of hadiths. Just four of Muhammad's companions related more than two thousand hadiths. One was the Prophet's wife Aisha. Those who study hadiths will recognize the names Hafsa, Umm Habiba, Umm Salama, and Maymuna, all of whom reported hadiths directly from the Prophet. Women even played key roles in the field of hadith in later centuries. Ibn Hajar al-Asqalani (d. 1449), a major hadith expert, lists over 170 women scholars in his biographical work. Umm Hani Maryam of Cairo (d. 1466), for example, was known for her knowledge of Islamic sciences and traveled widely in the Muslim world to study hadith. Umm Hani was also a prominent lecturer in Cairo schools. According to her biographer,

> She taught hadith for a long time, and many eminent scholars heard them from her; everything I have learned from her teachers, I learned through her. However, I believe that she knew much more than I was able to learn. Her grandfather presumably taught her the rest of the Six Books and taught her Nashawiri's (d. 1388) version of *Sahih al-Bukhari*. She was a good woman who used to weep profusely when the names of God and the Prophet were mentioned; she was consistent in her fasting and night prayers and firm in her religion. . . . She performed the pilgrimage thirteen times, often staying for months to study and teach in Mecca and Medina.[24]

Unlike their male counterparts, one could barely find any woman hadith scholar who forged reports about the Prophet.

23. Hanson, "Sunna," 137–38.
24. Hanson, 139.

Hadith collections contain descriptions of every aspect of the Prophet's life, including his spirituality, outward appearance, manners, morals, social relations, and family life. Significant portions of the hadiths are concerned with what the Prophet said about certain rituals and how he performed them. For example, see the following excerpts:

On the implications of being part of good Islam: A man asked the Prophet (pbuh),[25] "What sort of deeds or (what qualities of) Islam are good?" The Prophet (pbuh) replied, "To feed (the poor) and greet those whom you know and those whom you do not know."[26]

None of you will have faith till he wishes for his brother what he likes for himself.[27]

If a man spends on his family (with the intention of having a reward from God) sincerely for God's sake then it is a (kind of) charity in reward for him.[28]

You will be rewarded for whatever you spend for God's sake even if it were a morsel which you put in your wife's mouth.[29]

Gabriel kept recommending treating neighbors with kindness until I thought he would assign a share of inheritance to one's neighbor.[30]

A man came to the Prophet (pbuh) asking his permission to take part in jihad. The Prophet (pbuh) asked him, "Are your parents alive?" He replied in the affirmative. The Prophet (pbuh) then said to him, "Then exert yourself in their service."[31]

25. Whenever Muslims mention the Prophet Muhammad's name, they say, "Peace be upon him," often abbreviated as "pbuh." They use the same phrase for other prophets too.
26. Al-Bukhari, Sahih al-Bukhari, book 2, hadith 5.
27. Al-Bukhari, book 2, hadith 6.
28. Al-Bukhari, book 2, hadith 48.
29. Al-Bukhari, book 2, hadith 49.
30. See a translation at Imam al-Nawawi, "Forty Hadith of an-Nawawi," Sunnah.com, accessed February 8, 2021. https://sunnah.com/nawawi40.
31. Al-Bukhari, Sahih al-Bukhari, book 56, hadith 213.

These examples show that the hadiths of the Prophet Muhammad address many aspects of Muslim life, guiding followers to conduct themselves in accordance with the teachings of the Qur'an and the Sunna of the Prophet.

Criticism of Hadith Literature

With the rise of modernity, both Muslim and non-Muslim scholars posed challenges to traditional hadith scholarship. Hungarian scholar Ignaz Goldziher (d. 1921), for example, specialized in Jewish law and used the historical-critical method in his study of both the Jewish legal tradition and hadiths. Given that hadiths were mainly transmitted orally, Goldziher believed they are subject to fabrication and manipulation and thus cannot be relied on as historical truth.[32] In addition, the later hadith collections have disproportionately larger numbers of reports than earlier compilations, and many of them contradict each other. Goldziher argued that scholars should approach later hadith additions with skeptical caution. Those who forged hadiths had political, sectarian, and legal motivations.[33] Joseph Schacht (d. 1969) echoed Goldziher's arguments, claiming that legal hadiths emerged during the Umayyad dynasty (661–750) in order to justify state policies.[34] He argued that the early followers of Muhammad did not consider him to be a law maker and pointed out that early scholarly writings do not use arguments from hadiths.[35]

Several Muslim hadith scholars have refuted the claims of Goldziher and Schacht in their works. Muhammad Azami (d. 2017) pointed out that both Goldziher and Schacht drew major conclusions concerning hadith literature without providing substantial evidence. Schacht not only relied on a few sources in his broad generalizations but also misunderstood the nature of early Islamic legal studies.[36] Yasin Dutton, a scholar specializing in early Islamic law, also challenged the views of Goldziher and Schacht. He contended that Imam Malik's (d. 795) *Muwatta* disproves their approach to hadith scholarship because *Muwatta* included hadiths based on the teachings and practices ('*amal*) of Muslim scholars in Medina. In this regard,

---

32. Jonathan A. C. Brown, *Hadith: Muhammad's Legacy in the Medieval and Modern World* (London: Oneworld, 2009), 205.
33. Brown, 206.
34. Hanson, "Sunna," 141.
35. Brown, *Hadith*, 211.
36. Brown, 219–20.

the hadith accounts were not only transmitted in oral and written forms but also based on the actions of Muslims in Medina. Goldziher and Schacht have dismissed this aspect of the hadiths.[37]

Muslim scholars have also critiqued hadith scholarship. Rashad Khalifah rejected hadiths and proposed that Muslims should rely only on the Qur'an for guidance. Similarly, Muhammad Shahrur noted that there was no need to rely on the example of Muhammad, as his Sunna served only in his time and environment for understanding the Qur'an. He argued that Muslims should not interpret the Sunna too literally and should instead apply the Prophet's guidance within the specifics of their own time and context.[38]

US Muslim scholars like Fazlur Rahman and Amina Wadud have questioned the reliability of hadiths and emphasized the overall principles of the Qur'an as sufficient guidance for Muslims. Rahman, like some Western historians, believed that many hadiths were fabricated and unreliable. He argued that the Sunna should not be understood as a set of fixed rules; the teachings should evolve according to the conditions of human life and society.[39] Wadud has stated that many hadiths are not only misogynistic but also interpreted by male scholars who do not provide gender-inclusive readings.[40]

The Legacy of Muhammad in the United States

In his 1978 book *The 100: A Ranking of the Most Influential Persons in History*, Michael H. Hart ranks Muhammad as number one. Hart explains, "[Muhammad] was the only man in history who was supremely successful on both the religious and secular levels."[41] He concludes, "It is this unparalleled combination of secular and religious influence which I feel entitles Muhammad to be considered the most influential single figure in human history."[42]

---

37. For more details, see Yasin Dutton, *The Origins of Islamic Law: The Qur'an, the Muwatta' and Madinan 'Amal* (New York: Routledge, 2002).
38. Hanson, "Sunna," 141.
39. Jonathan A. C. Brown, *Misquoting Muhammad: The Challenge and Choices of Interpreting the Prophet's Legacy* (London: Oneworld, 2014), 202.
40. Amina Wadud, *Inside the Gender Jihad* (London: Oneworld, 2007), 7.
41. Michael H. Hart, *The 100: A Ranking of the Most Influential Persons in History* (New York: Citadel, 1978), 2.
42. Hart, 6.

Muhammad's legacy and his Sunna continue to be major sources of inspiration for Muslims in the United States. In matters concerning charity, good citizenship, love, or coexistence, Muslims often refer to the hadiths of the Prophet alongside qur'anic verses. Today, many of the rituals in which US Muslims engage—for example, at weddings, births, and funerals—are still based on the Sunna.

Major American figures like Muhammad Ali, Malcolm X, and Elijah Muhammad either renamed themselves after the Prophet or were inspired by his legacy. Muslim leaders addressing questions of race have often turned to Muhammad's teachings on equality, as exemplified by his relationship with Bilal bin Rabah. A native of what is today Ethiopia, a young Bilal was abducted by a tribal leader of Mecca and enslaved. With the coming of Islam, he was drawn to the Prophet's message of the equality of all people in the eyes of God, and he became Muslim. His conversion led his master to persecute him. Abu Bakr, another companion of the Prophet, eventually purchased Bilal's freedom. Bilal then became not only a major companion of the Prophet but also the one who offered the call to prayer (*muezzin*) for the Prophet's community in Medina. On one occasion, a companion of the Prophet referred to Bilal as the "son of a black woman." Perturbed, the Prophet retorted, "You are the man who still has the traits of *jahiliyya* or ignorance in him."[43]

During the Prophet's farewell speech, he stressed the importance of dismantling injustices of the *jahiliyya* in Arabia, including racism: "An Arab has no superiority over a non-Arab, nor does a non-Arab have any superiority over an Arab; a white has no superiority over a black, nor does a black have any superiority over a white; [none have superiority over another] except by piety and good action."[44] Islamic practices rely significantly on the Sunna of the Prophet. In prayer, for example, believers should stand shoulder to shoulder during worship regardless of their color, rank, or ethnicity.

Muhammad's legacy in the realm of law is so vast that the US Supreme Court building contains a marble frieze of the Prophet. When the building was completed in 1935, the architect hired a sculptor to create friezes of the "great lawgivers of history" that would adorn the courtroom. The sculpture depicts eighteen figures,

---

43. Al-Bukhari, *Sahih al-Bukhari*, book 2, hadith 23. It is important to note that this hadith does not mention Bilal's name. However, hadith commentaries widely point out that the discriminated person mentioned here is Bilal bin Rabah.
44. Bünyamin Erul, "Veda Hutbesi," in *İslam Ansiklopedisi* (Ankara: TDV, 2012), 42:592.

including Hammurabi, Moses, Solomon, and Confucius. According to the Office of the Curator of the Supreme Court, the Prophet of Islam "is depicted holding the Qur'an. The Qur'an provides the primary source of Islamic Law. Prophet Muhammad's teachings explain and implement Qur'anic principles. The figure above is a well-intentioned attempt by the sculptor, Adolph Weinman, to honor Muhammad and it bears no resemblance to Muhammad. Muslims generally have a strong aversion to sculptured or pictured representations of their Prophet."[45]

In relation to their US neighbors, Muslims often remember this hadith of the Prophet: "He is not a true believer whose neighbor is not safe from his annoyance. Give to the one whose door is nearer to you. He is not a believer whose stomach is filled while the neighbor to his side goes hungry."[46] In conducting their lives according to God's will, Muslims turn to Muhammad's Sunna. Following the prophetic example shows one's love for God and his messenger in Islam. In times of spiritual and moral turmoil, the Sunna serves as a compass for Muslims and provides a meaningful perspective for the followers of Islam everywhere, including in the United States. In many ways, from birth to death, the Sunna of the Prophet Muhammad shapes Muslims' lives. And yet, throughout the centuries, Muslims have faced many issues that neither the Qur'an nor the Sunna explicitly addresses. In those cases, they have turned to sharia, the subject of the next chapter.

45. "Courtroom Friezes: South and North Walls," information sheet, US Supreme Court, accessed April 18, 2020, https://www.supremecourt.gov/about/northandsouthwalls.pdf.
46. For the Prophet Muhammad's hadiths on the rights of the neighbor, see Diyanet İşleri Başkanlığı, *Hadislerle İslam* (Istanbul: Diyanet Yayınları, 2014), 4:335–43.

6 Islamic Law

Sharia

In 2011, a Muslim inmate on death row sued the Ohio Department of Rehabilitation and Correction. While the department was providing kosher meals prepared according to halacha (Jewish law) for its Jewish prisoners, it provided no halal meals prepared according to sharia (Islamic law). The Muslim inmate argued that this inequity compromised his constitutional freedom to practice his religion.[1] Immediately after the case was filed, prisons in Ohio removed pork products from their menus, and the case was eventually settled. According to a study from 2019, Muslim inmates comprise around 9 percent of the prisoner population in the United States (as high as 20 percent in some states). The study also identified 163 federal lawsuits brought by Muslim prisoners between October 2017 and January 2019. Forty percent of these cases involved food, with Muslim inmates alleging that they were not provided meals prepared according to sharia.[2] What is sharia? How is it understood and practiced by Muslims? This chapter aims to answer these questions.

Sharia outlines the ideal way to conduct one's life according to God's will. In this regard, sharia has similarities to Christian canon law, Jewish halacha, or dharma in Eastern religions such as Buddhism or Hinduism. Islamic literature refers to the sharia of the Muslim community as well as the sharia of other Prophets such as Abraham, Moses, and Jesus. Each prophet outlined laws that were relevant to their specific cultural environments but were not necessarily universal. In addition, the law of the prophets was subject to change and alterations by their successors.[3] With the increased intermingling of humans, these once separate cultural zones became increasingly connected, and the law of common sense became more tangible.[4]

---

1. "Death Row Inmate Wants Muslim Meals," *Columbus Dispatch*, October 3, 2011, https://www.dispatch.com/article/20111003/NEWS/310039810.
2. Muslim Advocates, *Fulfilling the Promise of Free Exercise for All: Muslim Prisoner Accommodation in State Prisons*, Free Exercise Report, July 2019, https://tinyurl.com/vazukx3v.
3. Bediuzzaman Said Nursi, *Sözler* (Istanbul: Söz, 2009), 553.
4. Nursi, 553.

Sharia is attuned to the dynamic nature of humans, who unlike other living creatures have countless desires, wishes, and necessities. In seeking to fulfill these needs, every individual inevitably interacts with other individuals and must learn how to cooperate with them. God, however, placed no specific limits on human desire, anger, or intellect, which, when used improperly or in an unbalanced way, lead to tyranny, aggression, or injustice. In addition, not every member of a society can grasp what is right or wrong, what is just and unjust. Sharia serves to balance the emotions, desires, and powers of humans in order to nurture justice in society and help humans discern right from wrong. A collective intellect is needed to establish principles of law that speak to every member of the society. In Islam, this general law is called sharia, and the Prophet Muhammad was the one who embodied and taught it.[5]

The term *sharia* literally means "the way or path that leads to the source of water." Water was a powerful symbol for the Arabs of the Prophet's time, as finding it in the barren desert often meant the difference between life and death. Taken in a spiritual dimension, then, sharia is the path that leads to peace in this world and salvation in the world to come. That is why sharia regulates all human activity—spiritual, moral, and legal. As shown in two previous chapters, in conducting their lives in accordance with God's will, Muslims turn to the Qur'an and Sunna of the Prophet Muhammad. However, not everything is clear in these sources. The Qur'an is not a book of law, and only a few qur'anic verses deal with legal issues. How, then, should Muslims deal with matters that are not clearly addressed in either the Qur'an or the Sunna, especially when living in new cultural or social contexts? The answer can be found in the sophisticated science of legal thought that has developed around the concept of sharia.

Fiqh: Understanding Sharia

One hadith reports that Prophet Muhammad asked Muadh bin Jabal, one of his closest companions, to go to Yemen to teach and mentor newly converted Muslims there. The Prophet then asked Muadh how he might judge if a dispute arose between two persons. Muadh answered that he would judge according to God's

---

5. Nursi, *Signs of Miraculousness*, 161.

book, the Qur'an. The Prophet then asked what he would do if the Qur'an did not address the issue. Muadh answered that he would turn to the Sunna. The Prophet then asked what he would do if he also found no answer in the Sunna. Muadh answered that he would judge according to his own judgment. The Prophet was pleased with Muadh's answer.[6]

Muadh's story provides indications about the roots of sharia. When dealing with important questions, Muslims turn to the revealed sources. But what if the revealed texts are either ambiguous or silent on the issue? Answering this question became Muslim scholars' goal, an effort that has come to be known as *fiqh*, or Islamic jurisprudence, a key field in the Islamic sciences. *Fiqh* literally means "understanding," but as a term, it is specified to mean "understanding of sharia." *Fiqh* experts study the revealed texts and use their judgment to ascertain what God would want humans to do in various situations. Jurists usually categorize human actions into five types.

The first type of action is obligatory (*fard*) for believers. This category generally involves worship of or duties due to God (*huquq Allah*). Reciting the profession of faith (*shahada*), praying five times daily, fasting during the month of Ramadan, performing the pilgrimage, and giving alms all fall under this category. Fulfilling what is obligatory results in rewards. Unless followed by repentance (*tawba*), noncompliance incurs punishment, especially in the hereafter.

The second type of human action is forbidden (*haram*)—the opposite of obligatory action. Among the forbidden acts in sharia are holding other deities or humans equal to God; committing murder, theft, or adultery; backbiting; dying by suicide; gambling; consuming intoxicants or pork; disrespecting one's parents; lying, and being wasteful. Committing something *haram* requires punishment, while avoiding *haram* is rewarded.

The third type of human action is recommended (*mustahab*). This type is also known as Sunna (matters that follow the Prophet's example) and includes being good to one's neighbor, greeting people with the phrase "Peace be upon you," helping the needy, giving extra charity in addition to the obligatory alms, performing the minor pilgrimage (*umrah*), dressing cleanly and well, reciting supplications while making an ablution for the prayers, doing extra prayers, and fasting more

---

6. Al-Sijistani, *Sunan Abu Dawud*, book 25, hadith 22.

than required. Fulfilling this category is considered rewardable in the hereafter, but unlike the obligatory acts, one is not punished if they do not complete them.

Neutral (*mubah*, which also translates as "indifferent" or simply "permitted") is the fourth type of human action. Doing what is neutral—for example, sleeping, sitting, eating, or walking—does not have an effect on one's relationship with God. However, performing these actions in a particular manner can make them meritorious for believers. For example, one can sleep on one's right side, eat with one's right hand, step into a mosque with one's right foot, and enter a restroom with one's left foot—all acts the Prophet himself performed.

The fifth type of human act is a disliked act (*makruh*). Unlike the *haram*, one is not punished for committing these acts, but one is rewarded for avoiding them. The most common example of a disliked act is divorce. While the process of divorce is remarkably simple in Islamic tradition, Muslims also know that it is one of the acts most disliked by God. The fact that it is disliked encourages couples to try hard to find solutions before resorting to divorce. Other examples of disliked acts include wasting water during ablution prior to prayer, eating garlic before going to the mosque or a social gathering, eating while walking, and talking while in the restroom.

Sources of Sharia

In order to derive laws concerning human acts from the sacred sources, Muslim jurists formulated a theory of jurisprudence. To reach a legal ruling, they first turn to the Qur'an and the Sunna of the Prophet. If these sources do not have a definite or explicit ruling on the specific issue at hand, the jurists resort to consensus (*ijma*) as the third source of Islamic law. Muslims understand consensus as "the agreement of the community as represented by its highly learned jurists living in a particular age or generation, an agreement that bestows on those rulings or opinions subject to it a conclusive, certain knowledge."[7] While consensus is part of legal reasoning, it must be grounded in revealed texts.

Cases in which a consensus was reached are rare—less than 1 percent of Islamic law may be attributed to consensus.[8] Some examples are the form of various rituals,

7. Wael Hallaq, *An Introduction to Islamic Law* (Cambridge: Cambridge University Press, 2009), 21.
8. Hallaq, 22.

such as the five daily prayers, fasting, and pilgrimage. Other instances of consensus pertain to the requirement of taking major ablution after sexual intercourse, the impermissibility of adultery, and the consumption of intoxicating beverages. Further agreement outlined the collective duty of Muslims to attend funerals, allowed Muslim women to be absent from the Friday communal prayers, and ruled that the text of the Qur'an is unaltered. Moreover, jurists agreed that the verses of the Qur'an recited in daily prayers can only be recited in Arabic and that it is spiritually rewarding to pray them in a congregation. Because all of these matters had a basis in the Qur'an and its living embodiment, the prophetic Sunna, Muslim jurists were able to reach a consensus concerning their legal authority.

If jurists were not able to derive a legal ruling through the Qur'an, the Sunna, or consensus, they then turned to analogical reasoning (qiyas). In this process, jurists used previously legislated cases that are similar in nature to the case at hand to derive applicable judgments. For example, when tobacco was introduced into Muslim societies in the late sixteenth century, jurists could find no guidance in the Qur'an or the Sunna and were unable to come to a consensus on whether it should be allowed. While the first three sources were unanimous that harmful and intoxicating substances are impermissible, smoking remained an ambiguous issue. So the jurists turned to the instrument of analogical reasoning to draw a ruling about smoking. However, smoking generated many diverse opinions among Muslim scholars of jurisprudence. The resulting positions fall into three categories. While some scholars argued that smoking is permissible, others disputed that it is disliked (makruh). Another group of scholars maintained that smoking is forbidden (haram). Those who argued that it is permissible pointed out that there is no evidence in the three sources—the Qur'an, Sunna, and consensus—to say that smoking is forbidden. According to this view, tobacco does not have the same attributes as intoxicants and harmful things. Some scholars even listed the benefits of smoking with regard to the people's overall well-being.[9]

Those who opposed tobacco argued that the usual sources gave sufficient evidence to conclude that smoking should be forbidden. Smoking, they argued, has harmful attributes, and as the Qur'an and the Sunna state, what is harmful must be avoided. These jurists gave many reasons for why smoking is harmful: it

---

9. One is Abdülganî b. İsmâil en-Nablusî. For information concerning the debate about tobacco in Islamic jurisprudence, see Sükrü Özer, "Tütün," in İslam Ansiklopedisi (Istanbul: TDV, 2012), 42:5–9.

is filthy, its smell disturbs people, it poses a threat to one's health, it is a form of extravagance and waste, and it has the attributes of an intoxicant that lead to addiction. To support their positions, these jurists alluded to certain verses from the Qur'an: "Spend in the way of God, and make not your own hands contribute to your destruction; but do good; for God loves those who do good" and "Eat and drink, but do not be extravagant. Truly, God does not like those who are extravagant."[10] Ömer Müfti Kilisi, a renowned Ottoman jurist of the nineteenth century, wrote a treatise on smoking in which he argued by analogy that both smoking and selling tobacco products should be forbidden.[11] Even some contemporary scholars in the Muslim world consider smoking impermissible, pointing to studies that conclude that smoking is harmful to human health. Egyptian scholar Yusuf al-Qaradawi, for example, took the following approach concerning tobacco: "If it is proved that the use of tobacco is injurious to health, it is *haram*, especially for a person whose physician has advised him to stop smoking." Al-Qaradawi further pointed out that even if tobacco "is not injurious to health, it is still a waste of money, spent neither for religious nor for secular benefit, and the Prophet (pbuh) forbade wasting of property. This becomes even more serious when the money is otherwise needed for the sustenance of oneself or one's family."[12] Despite these scholarly arguments and conclusions, a large percentage of Muslims smoke tobacco.[13]

Drug use is another issue adjudicated by applying *qiyas*. Muslim jurists are unanimous that intoxicants are impermissible, particularly wine. Using the qur'anic prohibition on wine as their point of reference, Muslim jurists extend the prohibition to include marijuana, cocaine, opium, and other drugs.

In addition to the four major sources of sharia outlined above, Muslim jurists subsequently developed two others: juristic preference (*istihsan*) and public interest (*maslaha*). Istihsan allows jurists to exercise personal opinions (*ra'y*) in order to prevent rigidity or injustice resulting from the literal interpretation of the law. *Maslaha* allows them to choose a weaker precedent over a strong precedent if it is in the interest of justice.[14] In addition, local customs (*'urf*) are also considered

10. Qur'an 2:195; 7:31.
11. Hüseyin Baysa, "Ömer Müftü Kilisinin sigaranın hükmü hakkındaki görüşünün değerlendirilmesi," *Kilis 7 Aralik Universitesi Dergisi* 1 (2015): 37–57.
12. Yusuf al-Qaradawi, *The Lawful and Prohibited in Islam* (Plainfield, IN: American Trust, 1999), 79.
13. See "The Tobacco Atlas," accessed April 18, 2020, https://tobaccoatlas.org.
14. See "Istihsan," Oxford Islamic Studies Online, accessed April 18, 2020, http://www.oxfordislamicstudies.com/article/opr/t125/e1136.

as valid sources of law as long as they do not contradict the objectives of sharia. The sum of this intellectual exercise of deriving rules by following the principles of Islamic jurisprudence is known as *ijtihad*.

Five Objectives of Sharia

Muslim jurists agree that Islamic law has five major universal objectives (*maqasid al-sharia*): the protection of life, mind, religion, offspring, and property.[15] Islamic law aims to guarantee individual and social prosperity not only in this life but also in the hereafter. Sharia lays the groundwork for establishing these necessities and provides rulings for their preservation. To preserve life, sharia not only forbids killing, including suicide, but also prohibits harmful acts to fellow humans, animals, and even plants. It aims to create a space for people to live with dignity and in harmony. For violators of this principle, sharia ensures punishment in this world as well as in the hereafter. To protect the mind, sharia promotes knowledge and asserts that education is an individual right. It forbids intoxicants such as alcohol and drugs that can corrupt one's morals or weaken one's intellect. To ensure the establishment and continuity of faith, Islam requires worship. Therefore, sharia regulates the rituals based on the Qur'an and the Sunna of the Prophet Muhammad. To protect lineage and continue human life, sharia encourages marriage and prohibits adultery. It also regulates issues that may arise in marriage. Concerning the protection of wealth and property, sharia promotes the right to earn, own, and invest. It regulates transactions to ensure fair dealing and economic justice and also forbids usury (*riba*), theft, deception, and misappropriation of another person's wealth.

Schools of Jurisprudence

Because Islamic law develops organically and leaves room for diverse interpretations depending on the scholars' sociopolitical context, the early centuries of Islamic jurisprudence witnessed the creation of a wide variety of legal approaches. However, the opinions of a few prominent jurists and their schools of thought

---

15. Hallaq, *Introduction to Islamic Law*, 26.

(*madhhab*) eventually came to dominate Islamic law. In order to understand how the opinions of certain jurists came to dominate, we must briefly discuss Islamic education during the formative period of these schools—in particular, *halaqas*.

Halaqas were informal open circles of study that anyone could attend regardless of economic or ethnic background.[16] *Halaqas* almost always revolved around a pious and knowledgeable person in the religious sciences.[17] Often these circles were set up in the form of intimate sittings (*jalasa*), which helped form close bonds between the teacher and student, with the student carrying on the legacy of the teacher even after their instruction had ended. The teacher was not only the source of knowledge for the student but also a companion and mentor.[18] *Halaqas* did not have a set curriculum. Each *halaqa* could be different from the next one in style, structure, and context.[19] Neither did they grant degrees like European universities. A participant of the *halaqa* would receive a certification (*ijāza*) signifying that the individual had studied with a particular teacher.[20] Often translated as "permission," *ijāza* meant that a student could transmit a particular text acquired from the teacher.[21]

The dissemination of jurists' opinions was tied to the number and range of *halaqas*, their students, and the students of their students in various parts of the Muslim world. Gradually, these *halaqas* crystallized into distinct legal schools, with four gaining the most prominence among Sunni Muslims (Hanafi, Maliki, Shafi'i, and Hanbali) and one becoming the most prominent in Twelver Shiism (Jafari).

The Hanafi school was named after jurist Abu Hanifa (d. 767), a student of Imam Jafar al-Sadiq, the sixth imam in Twelver Shiism and founder of the Jafari school. The Hanafi school first became influential in today's Iraq, the birthplace of Abu Hanifa. Students of the Hanafi school then spread Abu Hanifa's teachings around the Muslim world. Compared to other schools, Hanafi jurisprudence is more flexible and liberal on certain issues, especially in matters of criminal law, the status of non-Muslims in Muslim lands, individual freedoms, and marital and family

16. Wael Hallaq, *Shari'a: Theory, Practice, Transformations* (Cambridge: Cambridge University Press, 2009), 138.
17. Jonathan P. Berkey, *The Formation of Islam: Religion and Society in the Near East, 600–1800* (Cambridge: Cambridge University Press, 2003), 225.
18. Hallaq, *Shari'a*, 137.
19. Hallaq, 139.
20. Berkey, *Formation of Islam*, 225.
21. Hallaq, *Shari'a*, 139.

issues. This was partly because Abu Hanifa, in addition to the major sources of Islamic law, relied on personal opinion (ra'y) and juristic preference (istihsan) as sources of law.[22] More readily than other Islamic schools, Hanafi jurisprudence integrates local customs.[23] Today, it has the largest number of followers among the five schools and is especially influential in Turkey, Central Asia, and Europe and on the Indian subcontinent.

The Maliki school was named after Malik bin Anas (d. 795). Imam Malik was born and lived his entire life in Medina, and his school first became influential in the city and the surrounding Hejaz area. Today, Maliki jurisprudence is the dominant school on the African continent, especially in Sudan, Morocco, Mauritania, and Nigeria. The school is known for its reliance on the practice ('amal) of Medina, and jurists emphasize the practices of the Prophet and his major companions.[24]

The Shafi'i school was founded by Imam al-Shafi'i (d. 820), who was born in Damascus. Though jurists of his own school especially venerated him, Imam Shafi'i also had a significant impact on the development of the entire system of Islamic jurisprudence (usul al-fiqh). The Shafi'i school has been influential in Syria, Egypt, Palestine, and the Kurdish areas in Turkey and Iraq as well as among most of the Malays in Southeast Asia, especially in Indonesia, Malaysia, Singapore, and Thailand.[25]

Named after its founder Ahmad bin Hanbal (d. 855), the Hanbali school has relied mainly on the Qur'an and hadiths when interpreting and developing Islamic law. Hanbali jurists are also known for their emphasis on literal interpretations of the sacred texts. While this school was historically influential in various parts of Muslim societies, today most of its followers live in Saudi Arabia.

The Jafari school, which was named after the sixth imam, Jafar al-Sadiq (d. 765), has held and continues to hold prominence among Shiites. The Iranian constitution draws significantly from Jafari legal texts, and the school has the largest number of followers in today's Iran, Bahrain, southern Iraq, southern Lebanon,

---

22. Christie S. Warren, "The Hanafi School," Oxford Bibliographies, last modified May 28, 2013, http://www.oxfordbibliographies.com/view/document/obo-9780195390155/obo-9780195390155 -0082.xml.
23. Seyyed Hossein Nasr, The Heart of Islam (New York: HarperOne, 2002), 68.
24. Delfina Serrano, "Mālikīs," Oxford Bibliographies, last modified July 30, 2014, https://tinyurl.com/ pzaafb6b.
25. Nasr, Heart of Islam, 69.

and Azerbaijan.[26] Although Jafari jurisprudence is the most influential among Shi-ites, other schools, such as the Zaydi and Ismaili, also exist. Today, Zaydi Shiite jurists are influential in Yemen, and followers of the Ismaili school can be found in Pakistan, Afghanistan, India, the United Kingdom, Canada, the United States, and East African countries such as Tanzania, Kenya, and Uganda. Unlike Sunnis, Shiite scholars rely on the teachings of the imams—descendants of the Prophet's cousin Ali—as a major source of Islamic law (in addition to the Qur'an and hadiths).[27]

Despite their differences, what unites the various Islamic schools of law has been the goal of understanding what God wants from humanity in every choice of life. Even minor questions about Islamic practices, like the ablution (*wudu*) before prayer, have generated extensive literature among the scholars of these schools. For example, because the Qur'an lists "wiping over heads" (*wamsahu bi ruusikum*) as a step in making an ablution, all of the schools agreed that wiping the head with wet palms is necessary. However, they disagreed about how to understand this qur'anic phrase in practice, with each school basing their unique interpretation of the different hadiths on the practices of the Prophet and his companions. While Hanafi and Jafari jurists agreed that wiping one-fourth of the head is sufficient to meet that requirement, Maliki jurists held the view that the entire head from the upper part of the forehead to the neck needs to be wiped. Shafi'i scholars insisted that the requirement is met if even a small part of the head is wiped, while adherents to the Hanbali school claimed that the entire head should be wiped, including the ears.

Divisions of Legal Acts: *'Ibadat* and *Mu'amalat*

Islamic law deals with all aspects of life—spiritual, moral, and legal. Its goal is to form and maintain a just society. In Islamic law, legal matters are usually divided into two categories: acts of worship (*'ibadat*) and social transactions (*mu'amalat*). In a typical Islamic law book, a jurist examines these two categories under four major fields: rituals, marriage, sales, and injuries.[28]

Rituals revolve around purity and include minor and major ablutions, the five daily prayers, funerals, alms, fasting, retreat in a mosque (*i'tikaf*), and pilgrimage.

26. Hallaq, *Introduction to Islamic Law*, 37.
27. Nasr, *Heart of Islam*, 123.
28. Hallaq, *Introduction to Islamic Law*, 28.

Each chapter of typical legal treatises also contains subchapters. In the case of rituals, for example, subchapters could include the requirements of the prayer, the call to prayer, conditions that invalidate prayer, how to dress while praying, information about the direction of prayer (qibla) and how to locate it, the elements of prayer (such as postures and what portions of the Qur'an to recite), nonobligatory prayers, congregational prayers, Friday prayers, prayers during the holidays, prayers made by a sick person, and prayers while traveling.

Sales concern partnerships, usury, bartering, oral and written agreements, unlawful transactions, gifts and bequests, nonrefundable deposits, personal loans, bankruptcy, debt, renting, job wages, endowments, and so on. Chapters concerning marriage deal with such things as the elements of the marriage agreement, deciding on a suitable partner, the wedding ceremony, spousal marital responsibilities, childcare, custody, and divorce. Injuries cover crimes, such as theft and homicide; qur'anic punishments; war; and peace.

Crimes and Punishments in Sharia

While a significant portion of Islamic legal books is dedicated to matters of worship, a small percentage relates to crimes and punishments. Muslim jurists divided crimes into two categories: those that violate the rights of God (huquq Allah) and those that violate the rights of his servants (huquq al-'ibad). Some offenses that require punishments are outlined in the Qur'an and hadiths of the Prophet. Among these crimes are adultery/fornication (or wrongfully accusing someone of it), consuming intoxicants, some types of theft, armed robbery, and banditry.[29] Known as hudud crimes, the Qur'an provides guidance on punishment—for example, cutting off the hands of a thief or doling out one hundred lashes to someone who commits fornication.[30] Such hudud punishments, however, were rarely if ever implemented in premodern Islam because of the strict evidentiary standards required to prove someone had actually committed the crime.[31] Sharia dictated that people could

29. The section on prayer, for instance, would almost always enjoy the longest share compared to other books. According to Jonathan A. C. Brown, the general percentage for a multivolume book on law is usually around 2 percent. See Brown, "Stoning and Hand Cutting: Understanding the Hudud and the Shariah in Islam," Yaqeen Institute, January 12, 2017, https://tinyurl.com/fmkcdj8.
30. See Qur'an 5:38; 24:2.
31. Hallaq, Introduction to Islamic Law, 173.

only be punished if there was absolute certainty the crime had been committed.[32] Moreover, expressing mercy before carrying out *hudud* punishments was a core principle of sharia based on one of the Prophet's hadiths, which says, "Avert the legal punishments from Muslims as much as possible, if you find a way out for the person, then let them go, for it is better for the authority to make a mistake in forgiving than to make a mistake in punishment."[33]

Muslim jurists interpreted this hadith as guidance to avoid handing out *hudud* punishments if legal ambiguities (*shubuhat*) existed. Whenever judging a case, they would try to exhaust all reasonable doubts before handing down a decree (fatwa) requiring actual punishment for a *hudud* offense. This way, they could avoid dubious punishments.[34] Muslim scholars created a lengthy list of ambiguities. For instance, Taqi al-Din al-Subki (d. 1356), a major Shafi'i jurist and chief judge of Damascus, issued a fatwa concerning someone who had committed theft. Al-Subki listed eighty-two conditions that must be met before the punishment can be applied. Among them were that the theft should not be from the public treasury, that the thief was of sound mind and a reasonable age, that he was free, that he was not drunk, that he was not forced by hunger, that he stole from a secured location and stole by his own hand, and that at least two witnesses saw the theft take place and their testimony was consistent. Additionally, a month should not have passed since the theft occurred.[35] In adultery/fornication cases, four witnesses have to testify independently in order to justify a *hudud* punishment. Their testimonies have to be consistent with each other; otherwise, the accusers would be charged with slander and whipped eighty lashes each.[36]

Because sharia requires that all ambiguities be resolved before carrying out any *hudud* punishment, it is "nearly impossible for a thief or fornicator to be sentenced, unless he wishes to do so and confesses."[37] In the same vein, when the British East India Company became influential in India and was in charge of implementing sharia among Muslims in the late 1700s, British officials were disappointed with

---

32. Brown, "Stoning and Hand Cutting."
33. Al-Tirmidhi, *Jami' al-Tirmidhi*, book 17, hadith 2.
34. Intisar A. Rabb, "'Reasonable Doubt' in Islamic Law," *Yale Journal of International Law* 40, no. 1 (2015): 41–45, 93.
35. Brown, "Stoning and Hand Cutting."
36. Hallaq, *Introduction to Islamic Law*, 173.
37. Rudolph Peters, *Crime and Punishment in Islamic Law* (Cambridge: Cambridge University Press, 2016), 54.

sharia, as they found it almost impossible to execute people for criminal offenses under Islamic law.[38]

Today, a considerable number of Muslims believe in the idea of sharia, but there are major disagreements concerning the degree to which it should be part of a country's official law.[39] The overwhelming majority of Muslim countries do not include *hudud* punishments in their constitution—exceptions are Iran, Saudi Arabia, Sudan, and Nigeria. But even in these countries, the number of *hudud* cases is low. In Saudi Arabia, a country known for its *hudud* punishments, there were four executions by stoning and forty-five amputations for theft between 1981 and 1992. From 1982 to 1983, there were two amputations out of 4,925 convictions for theft. As scholar Jonathan Brown notes, "Fornication and *hudud*-level theft are offenses almost by definition done in private, as intoxication could be as well. They are done out of the sight of all but God. Perhaps these stringent laws, which God's mercy has made almost impossible to apply, exist primarily to remind people of the enormity of the sins that they usually get away with."[40]

Sharia in the United States

Sharia has been one of the most controversial aspects of Islam in the United States over the last two decades. The term appears often in media and politics. References to sharia appear in the remarks of presidential candidates. For example, in 2010, presidential candidate and former Speaker of the House Newt Gingrich remarked, "I believe sharia is a mortal threat to the survival of freedom in the United States and in the world as we know it."[41] In 2016, he said, "Western civilization is in a war. We should frankly test every person here who is of a Muslim background, and if they believe in sharia, they should be deported. Sharia is incompatible with Western civilization. Modern Muslims who have given up sharia—glad to have them as citizens. Perfectly happy to have them next door."[42] Many states—including Alabama,

38. Brown, "Stoning and Hand Cutting."
39. For a study on Muslims' view of sharia, see "Chapter 1: Beliefs about Sharia," Pew Research Center, April 30, 2013, https://tinyurl.com/j2mts9vs.
40. Brown, "Stoning and Hand Cutting."
41. For Gingrich's remarks, see Conor Friedersdorf, "Singling Out Islam: Newt Gingrich's Pandering Attacks," *Atlantic*, January 31, 2012, https://tinyurl.com/yjdjrbe5.
42. For the related remarks, see "Newt Gingrich: Deport Every Muslim Who Believes in Sharia," Fox News, July 15, 2016, https://video.foxnews.com/v/5036444136001/#sp=show-clips.

Arizona, Arkansas, Kansas, Louisiana, Mississippi, North Carolina, Oklahoma, South Dakota, Tennessee, Texas, and Washington—enacted bills negatively referencing sharia. One such bill from Tennessee reads, "The threat from sharia-based jihad and terrorism presents a real and present danger to the lawful governance of this state and to the peaceful enjoyment of citizenship by the residents of this state." The bill also authorizes the attorney general to designate sharia organizations, which it defines as "two (2) or more persons conspiring to support, or acting in concert in support of, sharia or in furtherance of the imposition of sharia within any state or territory of the United States." Furthermore, anyone who "knowingly provides material support or resources to a designated sharia organization, or attempts or conspires to do so" in Tennessee could be charged with a felony and face a minimum of fifteen years in jail.[43]

Despite this toxic antisharia environment in the United States, the growth of the Muslim population has led to increased requests for arbitration based on Islamic law. Before taking cases to the civil courts, some members of the Muslim community seek Muslim sharia experts who can provide resources and spaces in which members of the Muslim community can resolve disputes. While Jewish halacha and Christian canon law play similar roles to sharia in relation to the civil law in the United States, Muslim practices face more scrutiny than those of Christians and Jews for a number of reasons. First, unlike Jewish and Christian communities, Muslims in the United States do not have enough experts among them who are specialized in both civil and Islamic law. As a result, when Muslims go to a so-called religious expert, the person may make a poor case if not a major mistake in terms of civil law. Second, due to misconceptions about Islam, many people in the United States have negative connotations of both Muslims and sharia, especially after 9/11.[44] A Muslim's ability to practice Islam in the United States according to sharia is as connected to their freedom of religion as a Christian's or a Jew's ability to adhere to canon law or embrace halacha.

43. "Material Support to Designated Entities," Tennessee Senate Bill 1028, quotations on 5, 13, n.d. [ca. 2011], http://www.capitol.tn.gov/Bills/107/Bill/SB1028.pdf.
44. Michael Broyde, "Sharia in America," Washington Post, June 30, 2017, https://www.washingtonpost.com/news/volokh-conspiracy/wp/2017/06/30/sharia-in-america/.

Conclusion

A few features of sharia need emphasizing. First, and most important, sharia has a dichotomous nature. On the one hand, it is a stable law based on a fixed set of sources. Its rituals are mostly nonnegotiable—prayer, fasting, the pilgrimage, and the alms tax are all pillars of Islam that have endured throughout centuries without change. On the other hand, it is an ever-evolving, flexible, and adaptable system. On many emerging issues, from bioethics to financial ethics, modern Muslim jurists are constantly developing new rulings depending on the context of time and location. Based on principles found in the Qur'an and hadiths of the Prophet, Muslim jurists continue to derive rulings in order to create a just and peaceful society.

Second, contrary to popular perception, guidelines on how to worship and perform certain rituals and not *hudud* punishments comprise the most significant portion of Islamic law. In this sense, one cannot imagine a Muslim without sharia. In performing their duties for God, Muslims turn to the books of sharia. Sharia also provides guidelines on how to live in peace with oneself as well as with society.

Third, plurality is a key feature of Islamic law. Because of the linguistic ambiguities in the sacred text as well as new cultural contexts, Muslim jurists in every century have disagreed about certain issues.

Fourth, unlike modern law, access to sharia has been and continues to be free; everybody can seek justice at a public court.

Finally, the rulings were made not by the state but rather by jurists who were known to be pious and knowledgeable in their communities.

In the following part, I discuss the major themes of Islamic theology in light of the six articles of faith (*iman*).

Part 3

Theology

Articles of Faith

7 Who Is God?

Overview of Islamic Theology

Belief in God is the first article of faith in Islam. But before I examine the Islamic concept of God, I will briefly introduce Islamic theology as a whole. *Iman* ("faith" or "belief") is among the most important domains of Islamic theology. The word *iman* originates from the Arabic root *amana*, which connotes freedom from fear, calmness, conviction, confidence in truth, and trust. In Islam, *iman* means "to believe in the message from God that was revealed through the Prophet Muhammad." A person who accepts the Prophet Muhammad's message becomes a believer (*mu'min*) or Muslim (a person who submits to the message). The opposite of faith is *kufr*, which literally means "covering the truth." *Kufr* is also described as being contrary to *shukr*, which is often translated as "thankfulness" or "gratitude." The person who carries the trait of *kufr* is an unbeliever (*kafir*).

The Qur'an frequently engages with theological issues concerning faith and characterizes believers as those who have faith in God, angels, scriptures, messengers, and the hereafter.[1] It also addresses the idea of predestination and of what is evil and what is good.[2]

The hadith collections also discuss theological issues related to faith. A number of hadiths attributed to Muhammad discuss the fundamentals of faith in Islam. In one of these reports, a man in white garb visited the Prophet while he was sitting with his companions. To his companions' surprise, the man sat knee to knee with the Prophet and began asking him questions. When the man queried the Prophet on the meaning of *iman*, the Prophet answered, "Faith means to believe in God, His angels, His scriptures, His messengers, the resurrection and the hereafter, and predestination, both its good and its evil."

"You have spoken the truth," the man responded. He then asked the Prophet, "What is Islam?"

1. Qur'an 2:185; 2:177; 4:136.
2. Qur'an 57:22–23; 64:11; 15:21; 36:12.

The Prophet replied, "Islam means to bear witness that there is no god but God and that Muhammad is God's messenger, to perform the five daily prayers, to pay the zakat or alms tax, to fast during the month of Ramadan, and to make the hajj or pilgrimage to the Kaaba."

Affirming the Prophet's answer, the man then asked, "What is ihsan?"

The Prophet replied, "Ihsan means that you should worship God as if you see Him, for even if you do not see Him, He sees you." The conversation continued with a few other questions. The companions of the Prophet were astonished to see a man they did not know questioning the Prophet and affirming his answers. Once the man left, the Prophet told his companions that the visitor was the archangel Gabriel, who had come to teach them about religion.[3]

On another occasion, the Prophet said that Muslims who embody the following qualities would enjoy the sweetness of faith: holding God and his messenger dearer than anything else, loving a person for God's sake alone, and after finding faith, avoiding unbelief so they would escape being cast into the fire.[4] He also said that faith has over seventy branches. The highest branch of faith is to say, "There is no god but God." Its lowest branch is to remove injuries from the paths of people. Modesty is another branch of faith.[5] Looking at the hadiths, Muslim scholars listed reciting the Qur'an, maintaining cleanliness, believing in the six articles of faith, practicing the five pillars of Islam, being thankful to God, avoiding waste, being truthful, avoiding hatred toward people, being just and pious, helping those in need, being humble, managing anger, taking care of one's family, responding to the greeting of a person, visiting the sick, attending funeral prayers, being generous, being respectful to the elderly, not gossiping, not killing, and not eating impermissible food, among other activities, as being among the branches of faith.[6]

In one of the hadiths, the Prophet said, "Faith is knowledge in the heart, words on the tongue, and action with the physical faculties (limbs of the body)."[7] Based on this statement, Muslim scholars emphasize faith's three dimensions.

---

3. This report is narrated in major hadith collections, including Sahih al-Bukhari, Sahih Muslim, and Sunan Abu Dawud.
4. Al-Naysaburi, Sahih Muslim, book 1, hadith 67.
5. Al-Naysaburi, book 1, hadith 60.
6. Diyanet İşleri Başkanlığı, Hadislerle Islam, 1:512.
7. Ibn Majah, Sunan Ibn Majah, book 1, hadith 68.

According to the first dimension, faith begins in the heart. The Prophet said that God would save whomever sincerely believed in their heart that there was no god but God and that Muhammad was his messenger.[8] This hadith also echoes a verse in the Qur'an that says that those who say they have faith in fact do not have faith, as "faith has not yet entered their hearts."[9] On one occasion, the Prophet's companions were at war with a hostile tribe. One of his companions, Usama bin Zayd, captured a fighter from that tribe. When Zayd was upon his enemy, all of a sudden, the man said, "There is no god but God." Zayd killed him despite his having said that. When the Prophet heard about the incident, he asked Zayd why he had killed the person when he had declared his faith in God. Zayd answered that the enemy had invoked the statement of faith in order to save his life. The Prophet then rebuked Zayd by saying, "Did you check his heart?"[10]

The second dimension of faith involves utterances of the tongue. The Prophet repeatedly encouraged his followers to voice their faith in God by saying, "There is no god but God." Muhammad himself repeated words of repentance (tawba) and sought refuge in God (istighfar) seventy times every day. The third dimension of faith is acting with one's body. Faith in God can only become rooted and meaningful once it is put into action. For the salvation of Muslims, the Prophet often invoked practices as well as faith. That is why Muslim theologians listed works ('amal), including especially the five pillars of Islam, as being part of faith. In this sense, faith requires practice.

While he was alive, the Prophet could clarify ambiguous matters of faith on which his followers sought clarification. As the messenger of God, Muhammad's explanations satisfied those seeking his guidance. However, after he died, Muslims became preoccupied with theological inquiries for two prominent reasons. First, the Prophet's death created a void in authority that led to disagreements among Muslims concerning various aspects of faith. Second, as Muslim territories expanded, followers of Islam increasingly engaged with people of other faiths, including Jews, Christians, Zoroastrians, and those who were learned in Greek philosophy. These dynamics led to the rise of Islamic theology known as kalam ("speech" or "discourse"), a science that aimed "to give precise formulation to the

8. Al-Bukhari, *Sahih al-Bukhari*, book 3, hadith 70.
9. Qur'an 49:14.
10. Al-Naysaburi, *Sahih Muslim*, book 1, hadith 183.

articles of faith."[11] According to one scholar of Islam, *kalam* "represents one of the most original and distinctive of the Islamic sciences of religion, as comprehensive as it is intricate."[12]

While *kalam* has remained an important discipline in Islam, it has not played the leading role that theology has played in the Christian tradition. Instead, sharia has enjoyed that place of prominence: "The vast majority of practicing Muslims have known nothing about *Kalam*, although they all have had some degree of familiarity with the Shariah. One can be a good Muslim without *Kalam*, but it is impossible to be any sort of Muslim without the Shariah. Many of the great Muslim authorities, such as al-Ghazali, warned people against studying *Kalam*, since it focuses on intellectual issues that are of no practical use for most people."[13]

Another important characteristic of Islamic theology is that it is open to diversity. Because of the lack of sacraments and a true hierarchy, "Islam possessed no mechanisms for imposing dogmatic conformity."[14] History documents two major exceptions, however. First, from 833 to 848 CE, Mutazilite theology was backed by the Abbasid Caliphate and enforced on the people. Second, Shiite doctrine was imposed on Iranian Sunnis under the Safavids in the sixteenth century.[15] Apart from these examples, one generally finds great diversity in theological opinion because "in Islam, there exists no special category of individuals, no special profession, whose task it is to dispense salvation; all Muslims are laypersons."[16] This made space not only for the emergence of diverse theological schools—such as Mutazilism, Asharism, Maturidism, and Hanbalism—but also for major differences of opinion about law and mysticism.[17] When there were disagreements about theological issues, Muslim theologians often turned to the Prophet's famous hadith: "In my community, disagreement is a sign of divine mercy."[18]

Among the questions that Muslim theologians have addressed are the following:

---

11. Eric Ormsby, "Islamic Theology," in *The Oxford Handbook of World Philosophy*, ed. William Edelglass and Jay L. Garfield (Oxford: Oxford University Press, 2011), 432–46, https://tinyurl.com/2h7jzxhr.
12. Ormsby, 433.
13. Murata Sachiko and William C. Chittick, *The Vision of Islam* (Saint Paul, MN: Paragon House, 1994), 239.
14. Tim Winter, ed., *Classical Islamic Theology* (Cambridge: Cambridge University Press, 2008), 7.
15. Winter, 7.
16. Josef van Ess, *The Flowering of Muslim Theology*, trans. Jane Marie Todd (Cambridge, MA: Harvard University Press, 2006), 13.
17. Winter, *Classical Islamic Theology*, 7.
18. Van Ess, *Flowering of Muslim Theology*, 18.

- *What is God's nature in relation to his attributes?*
- *Do humans have free will or are they predestined to act in a certain way?*
- *If God is all knowing and all powerful, why is there still accountability in the hereafter, given that he already knows what humans will do?*
- *What is the status of a mortal sinner?*
- *Who is eligible to lead the Muslim community and what is legitimate governance?*
- *Do mortal sinners remain as believers or do they become unbelievers?*
- *Is there a middle way for a mortal sinner?*
- *Is the capacity for reason sufficient to guide humans?*
- *Is the Qur'an eternal or created?*
- *What is the relationship between faith and works?*

Mainstream Muslim theologians eventually came to a consensus that the fundamentals of faith concern belief in the following:

- *God*
- *angels*
- *the prophets*
- *scriptures*
- *the resurrection*
- *the hereafter*
- *predestination*

This section treats each of these fundamentals, beginning with the Islamic belief in God.

The One God

A professor at a private evangelical Christian college in a Chicago suburb was at the center of a major controversy in late 2015. Concerned about negative political rhetoric involving Muslims at the time, she donned a hijab in solidarity and made the following statement on social media: "I stand in religious solidarity with Muslims because they, like me, a Christian, are people of the book. And as Pope Francis stated last week, we worship the same God."[19] College administrators initially placed the professor on administrative leave and issued a statement indicating that their decision was not about the hijab but rather about her statement that Muslims and Christians worship the same God. The college and the professor eventually parted ways. On this issue, camps continue to be divided: many non-Muslims argue that Muslims believe in a different divinity, while others claim that they all believe in the same God even though conceptions about this common God might differ. So who is the God of Muslims? How do Muslims relate to their divinity?

While Muslims refer to God by many different names, the most common name used to invoke or address and praise God is Allah. Arabic-speaking Jews and Christians also use this word, which derives from the combination of the Arabic article *al* and the word *ilah*. In this regard, *Allah* literally means "the God." Grammatically speaking, the word *Allah* has no plural form or associated gender.

Islamic tradition relates that in Mecca, the birthplace of Islam, people already had a notion of Allah but associated other gods with him. While the Meccans considered Allah to be their supreme creator, they also believed that other deities existed that interceded between them and Allah. Islamic tradition dates the history of Mecca to Abraham, his concubine Hagar, and his son Ishmael, who brought monotheism to Mecca. But it is believed that at some point, through interactions with neighboring cities, Mecca was introduced to polytheism. By the dawn of Islam, the Kaaba—built by Abraham and his family as the house of the one God—was full of deities. With the coming of Islam, Arab society was reintroduced to its monotheistic roots and the belief in one God, or Allah. But who is this God whom Muslims worship?

To understand and know the ways of God, Muslims turn to three sources: the Qur'an, the Prophet Muhammad, and the created universe itself. When trying to comprehend God, Muslims believe that one should first turn to creation. The Qur'an relates the following verse: "I [God] created jinn and humankind only that they might worship me."[20] The purpose of creation is to know, worship, and remember God. This form of worship and remembrance is by choice, not force. Some of the

---

19. Manya Brachear Pashman and Marwa Eltagouri, "Wheaton College Says View of Islam, Not Hijab, Got Christian Teacher Suspended," *Chicago Tribune*, December 16, 2015, https://tinyurl.com/zwyc9ja9.
20. Qur'an 51:56.

Qur'an commentaries interpret the phrase "only to worship Me" as "only to know me."[21] In line with this interpretation, a widely circulated sacred narration (*hadith al-qudsi*) reports that God said, "I was a hidden treasure, and I loved to be known; so I created creation in order to be known."[22] In the center of the story of the creation stands God's desire to reveal and introduce himself.

A few analogies might help us understand the Islamic theology of creation. Perhaps one of the most enjoyable things for artists is to exhibit their work. Through their exhibits, artists not only delight in seeing their pieces displayed but also enjoy visitors' appreciation and admiration. For teachers, one of the most pleasing things is to show their knowledge and share it with an audience. In the same way, people who are beautiful or perfect in some way or possess specific knowledge and skills naturally aim to reveal, display, and manifest these qualities and abilities. They would especially like to express their skills to those capable of both understanding and offering a proper response.[23] From an Islamic point of view, knowledge, love, and worship of the creator is that appropriate response. God exhibits his large treasure of skills and blessings in this universe and invites his creation, particularly humans, to freely and consciously acknowledge him as their only creator. That, in short, is the main purpose of creation in Islam.

God's Names: *Asma al-Husna*

The most important way of knowing God is through his most beautiful names (*asma al-husna*). God reveals himself through these names, which the Qur'an refers to as follows: "The most beautiful names belong to God, so call on Him by them."[24] In another verse, the Qur'an instructs followers to "call upon God, or the Compassionate—whatever names you call Him, the most beautiful names belong to Him."[25] The Qur'an repeatedly mentions God by different names and attributes. In chapter 59, for example, many of God's names are listed together:

21. Joseph E. B. Lumbard, Commentary on *Surat al-Dhariyat*, in Nasr et al., 1280.
22. Nasr et al., 1280. A *hadith al-qudsi* is a report that is attributed to God from the perspective of its meaning, but it is articulated with the words of the Prophet Muhammad.
23. Nursi, *Sözler*, 178.
24. Qur'an 7:180.
25. Qur'an 17:110.

He is God, there is no god other than Him; who knows all things both secret and open. He is the Most Beneficent, the Most Merciful. He is God, there is no god other than Him, the Controller, the Holy One, the Source of Peace, the Guardian of Faith, the Preserver of Safety, the Exalted in Might, the Irresistible, the Supreme. Glory be to God, He is above all that they associate as partners with Him. He is God, the Creator, the Evolver, the Fashioner, to Him belong the most beautiful names. Everything in the heavens and earth glorifies Him. He is the Mighty, the Wise.[26]

While Islamic literature often references the ninety-nine names of God, the Qur'an mentions more than a hundred. Therefore, the number ninety-nine should not be taken literally, since scripture contains more than that. All chapters of the Qur'an except one begin with these names of God. God is al-Rahman and al-Rahim, the most compassionate and the most merciful. God is al-Khaliq, the one who brings everything from nonexistence to existence. God is al-'Adl, the embodiment of justice. God is al-'Alim, the all-knowing one; there is nothing beyond his knowledge. God is al-Razzaq, the provider. God is al-Latif, the most gracious one. God is al-Ghafur, the all-forgiving one. God is al-Wadud, the all-loving one. God is al-Mumit, the one who inflicts death. God is also al-Muhyi, the one who gives life. God is al-Quddus, the most holy one—the one who is pure and without imperfection. The self-cleansing of the universe through alteration, transformation, death, and re-creation is regarded as the manifestation of this name. God is also al-Qayyum, the self-sufficient one, who depends on nothing but on whom everything depends.

The Qur'an refers to this attribute of God with the following verse: "God: there is no god but He, the Living, the Self-Subsisting. Neither slumber nor sleep overtakes Him. His are all things in the heavens and on the earth. Who is there that can intercede with Him except by His permission? He knows what is before them and what is behind them, but they do not comprehend of His knowledge except what He wills. His throne encompasses the heavens and the earth, and their preservation does not tire Him. He is the Exalted, the Magnificent."[27] Muslims often know this verse by heart and usually recite it in their daily supplications.

26. Qur'an 59:22–24.
27. Qur'an 2:255.

God's Essence, Attributes, and Acts

Muslim theologians have classified God's names in numerous ways. One way is to think of God's names as being related to his essence (*dhat*), attributes (*sifat*), and acts (*af'al*). The names concerning God's essence belong only to him—there is nothing created that can share the qualities enumerated by these names. In this regard, the Qur'an affirms, "There is nothing like Him."[28] Among the attributes of his essence is existence (*wujud*). Thus God's existence stems from himself. He is not created, and his existence depends on nothing. Everything will perish except God. God has neither beginning nor end.

Another way to categorize God's names is by his attributes (*sifat*), such as power (*qudra*), knowledge (*'ilm*), will (*irada*), life (*hayat*), speech (*kalam*), hearing (*sam'*), and sight (*basar*). While these attributes are unlimited in God, humans can only partially embody these names. For example, whereas God is all knowing, humans have limited knowledge. Whereas God has life without imperfection, humans and other creatures have life only because of God. Their life depends on God and is subject to imperfections, including illness and death. God also has the attribute of will (*irada*). Human beings share this attribute, but while God's will is unlimited, humans' free will is highly limited.

Other names relate to God's active role (*af'al*) in the creation (*khalq*) of the universe. Everything is created by God. God creates the universe from nothing (*insha*). He gives life (*ihya*) as well as death (*imata*). As part of his active role, God is also the one who provides (al-Razzaq) for his creation. In order for his creatures to continue living, God meets all their needs.

God's Nearness and Distance

To understand God's essence and attributes, Muslim theologians point to his nearness and distance. The Qur'an states that everything is near to God and in his control: "To God belong the East and the West. Wherever you turn, there is the presence of God. No leaf falls without His knowledge."[29] In another verse, God's nearness to humankind is stated: "We are nearer to him than his jugular

28. Qur'an 42:11.
29. Qur'an 2:115; 6:59.

vein."[30] But Islamic theology also emphasizes God's distance from creation. God is everywhere, so no particular thing or place is associated with God. In emphasizing God's distance, the Qur'an states that angels ascend to God "on a day whose measure is fifty thousand years."[31] One hadith reports that God is behind seven thousand veils.[32] God is close to creation through the manifestations of his names and attributes, while creation itself is distant from God's essence.[33]

God's *Jamali* and *Jalali* Names

Islamic theology speaks of the two modes of God, or his dual nature. God's names are also divided into beauty and mercy (*jamali*) and glory and majesty (*jalali*) aspects. *Jamali* names are manifested in the universe as beauty, mercy, compassion, forgiveness, love, and kindness. The beauty of creation, with its distinctive forms, fashions, and colors; generosity; and blessings are also among these names. Others are the Most Beautiful (al-Jamil), the Most Generous (al-Karim), and the Giver of Life (al-Muhyi).

The *jalali* names are revealed in the forms of majesty, awe, and fear. Life, light, and existence are manifestations of the *jalali* names, as are death, separation, fear, punishment, wrath, and major natural disasters. These names include the Majestic/ Exalted (al-Jalil), the Subduer (al-Qahhar), the Almighty (al-Aziz), the Bringer of Death (al-Mumit), the Avenger (al-Muntaqim), and the Compeller (al-Jabbar).

In the universe, one can also observe that the *jamali* names are revealed within the *jalali* names. For example, within God's unity (*wahdaniyya*) is the manifestation of divine oneness (*ahadiyya*). As the light of the sun encompasses the entire earth, so does God's glory and unity. As the sun's light, heat, colors, and shadows are found in transparent objects and drops of water, so is God's *jalal* and oneness. God is present in the universe and is the provider for all of creation. But God is also particular in providing according to the distinctive needs of every being. All the flowers on earth together, for example, manifest God's glory and unity. However, every single flower, with its distinctive beauty and color, manifests God's *jamal* and oneness.

30. Qur'an 50:16.
31. Qur'an 70:4.
32. Nursi, *Sözler*, 277.
33. Nursi, *Words*, 215.

Muslims believe that the *jalali* names will be fully revealed in hell, while the *jamali* names will have their full manifestation in heaven. But in Islam, God's mercy is emphasized over his wrath. In one of the *hadith al-qudsi*, God says, "My mercy overcomes my wrath."[34] The Qur'an also emphasizes God's mercy: "Your Lord has prescribed mercy upon Himself, if any of you did evil in ignorance, and thereafter repented, and amend his conduct, indeed He is Forgiving and Merciful."[35] Referring to the coming of the Prophet Muhammad, the Qur'an notes that he was sent as a mercy to all creatures.[36]

Humankind in Relation to God and His Names

At the center of the theology of God's names is humankind. Unlike in the Christian tradition, the notion of original sin is absent in Islamic theology. Muslims believe that God created Adam and Eve and that they slipped "individually," as the Qur'an puts it. Both repented, and God eventually forgave them. The Qur'an points out that Adam and Eve were abiding in heaven. God gave them permission for everything except for approaching a particular tree. Satan tempted them with the idea of becoming eternal if they ate fruit from the forbidden tree.[37]

Muslims believe that humans are the mirror of God's names in the most comprehensive way. That is why they are—along with the Qur'an and universe—also considered a book to be read in relation to God. According to a hadith that often appears in Sufi literature, "God created humankind in his image."[38] Humankind was not only created in the image of God, but humans are the ones who read and contemplate God's names better than any being in the universe.

In the story of the creation in Islam, one learns that "Adam was taught the names" by which humans are made superior even to the angels. The ability to recognize the manifestation of God's names in creation is one of the most important ways to know God. To believe that there is one God is different from knowing God. Once humans know God and have knowledge of him, they will be led to have admiration as well as love for him. Love for God is followed by strong faith and worship. In this regard, contemplating the universe in relation to God (*tafakkur*) is an act of worship.

34. Al-Naysaburi, *Sahih Muslim*, book 50, hadith 18.
35. Qur'an 6:54.
36. Qur'an 21:107.
37. Qur'an 7:19–25.
38. Al-Naysaburi, *Sahih Muslim*, book 45, hadith 1.

Being the Mirror of God's Names

Humans not only reflect on the names of God and have the ability to contemplate their manifestations in the universe; they also have the responsibility to embody God's names in their acts. In line with the qur'anic principle "Do good to others as God has done good to you," believers are asked to exemplify God's names in their lives. God is the most compassionate one, and humans are encouraged to have compassion for each other and for God's creation. God is the most generous one, and humans are encouraged to be generous. God is just, and humans are encouraged to stand for justice. God creates with wisdom and does not waste, and likewise, humans are encouraged to do the same in their affairs.

In embodying God's name, the Most Merciful One (al-Rahim), al-Ghazali (d. 1111) wrote that believers should show mercy for the poor and provide them with whatever they need. In order to embody God's name the Peace and Source of Peace (al-Salaam), believers should not be prisoners of their anger and greed. Al-Salaam is the one whose essence is free from imperfection. To be the mirror of this name of God, believers should overcome such deficiencies. A Muslim is the one from whose tongue and hand believers are safe.[39]

Humankind remains at the center of Islamic theology because humans embody God's names (asma al-husna) in the most comprehensive way. They are also the ones who can read and contemplate the manifestation of these names in the universe better than any other creature. Humankind, therefore, carries a unique responsibility, which is to believe in God, to know and contemplate him, and to worship him. Departing from this responsibility is regarded as veiling God's signs (kufr); in other words, not reading the creation as it relates to God. A further step in kufr is shirk, which means to put other deities or humans on an equivalent footing with God.

Islamic ontology is not limited to human beings; it includes supernatural beings such as angels, which are the subject of the next chapter.

---

39. Abu Hamid al-Ghazali, *Ninety-Nine Names of God in Islam*, trans. Robert Charles Stade (Ibadan: Daystar, 1970), 14, 23.

8 Angels and Their Nature

When it comes time during the academic year to discuss the subject of angels, I always stop first to ask my students whether they believe in angels. A few inevitably affirm their belief, others will say they are agnostic, but the majority of the students respond in the negative. With modernity and progress in science, belief in supernatural beings like angels is waning. While the number of those who believe in the existence of angels is declining, the majority of Americans still believe angels are present. According to a 2016 study, 72 percent of Americans believe in the existence of angels; in 2001, 79 percent believed in angels.[1]

Belief in the existence of angels has been part of the teachings of many religious traditions, including Zoroastrianism, Judaism, and Christianity. Zoroastrianism, for example, recognizes several types of angels, each with a distinctive function. Followers of this tradition choose an angel for protection or an angel who serves as a guide to them. They dedicate prayers to that angel throughout their lives. In the Hebrew Bible, angels appeared to major figures like Abraham, Moses, and Jacob. When Abraham was about to sacrifice his son Isaac, an angel appeared and stopped him. Abraham sacrificed a ram instead. In the Jewish sacred texts, angels are depicted in a variety of roles—healers, messengers, guardians or protectors, teachers, and warriors. Jewish scholars, including the medieval philosopher Maimonides (d. 1204), wrote of angelic hierarchies. Angels in each category have distinct features and functions.

Angels also appear frequently in the New Testament. One of the first mentions is in the Gospel of Luke when an angel appears to Zachariah in Jerusalem's temple. The angel brings the good news of the birth of John the Baptist.[2] In the same gospel, the archangel Gabriel appears to the Virgin Mary and tells her she will miraculously conceive and give birth to a son who will be called Jesus.[3] The New Testament

1. "Religion," Gallup, accessed April 18, 2020, https://news.gallup.com/poll/1690/religion.aspx.
2. Luke 1:11–20.
3. Luke 1:26–32.

relates many other occasions of angelic appearances. As in the Jewish tradition, angels often appear as messengers, guardians, and teachers.

Probably no other religion emphasizes its belief in angels as much as Islam. Given that the Qur'an and the hadiths repeatedly refer to angels and that belief in angels is one of the articles of faith, not believing in angels calls into question the sincerity of a Muslim's faith. The Qur'an stresses that those who deny the existence of angels are misguided.[4]

Prominent Muslim scholar Al-Suyuti (d. 1505) compiled around 750 hadiths about angels in his work dedicated to their study in Islam.[5] Despite its importance in sacred texts as well as in the popular literature of Islam, the study of angels is often dismissed as unimportant.

Why Angels?

Since belief in angels is a key component of Islamic theology, Muslim theologians attempt to articulate reasons for their significance. One explanation is God's desire to be known through different manifestations of his creative activity. He revealed himself through creation, of which angels are an important part. God creates beings who can observe his creation, contemplate its significance, and worship him as an expression of praise and gratitude. Following this line of thought, Islamic theologians argue that because God created humankind as beings capable of reflecting on his creation by virtue of their intellect, God could create other beings that could do so too. Creation as a whole is the manifestation of God's names. One of God's names is the Living One / the One Who Gives Life (al-Hayy). The manifestation of this name—of life itself—is present not only in the material world but also in other parts of the universe, including the spiritual.

If God is life, there is no nonexistence. Life is reflected to different degrees in both visible and invisible ways in every spot of the cosmos. Angels are part of this living system. Since God is the hidden treasure and eternal life himself, he longs to be known and glorified endlessly. Due to many obstacles and distractions, humankind, however, is unable to worship and praise God ceaselessly and perfectly. For

4. Qur'an 4:136.
5. For a study on Al-Suyuti's work on angels, see Stephen Burge, *Angels in Islam* (New York: Routledge, 2012).

this reason, angelic beings respond to divine beauty and perfection in the most comprehensive way and fill the cosmic atmosphere with meaning, illuminating and making it "alive" in line with God's name.[6]

The Nature of Angels

What kinds of creatures are angels? What is their nature? The word for "angel" in Islamic theology is *malak* (pl. *malaik*). Angels are God's messengers. While God is not existentially in need of other beings, his majesty and sovereignty make it fitting that those beings exist. Angels mediate between God and humans. It is believed that angels are created from light (*noor*). Unlike humans, they do not eat or sleep, as these needs are not part of their nature. As in the Bible, the Qur'an recounts occasions when angels appeared to Abraham. On one occasion, he received four people as guests. Known for his generous hospitality, Abraham rushed home and returned with a roasted calf. He placed it in front of his guests. But Abraham noticed that they were not touching the food. Seeing that Abraham was concerned, the guests comforted him and gave him the good news of a son. Abraham came to realize that his visitors were angels.[7] So angels often appear in human form.

Angels constantly glorify and worship God. The Qur'an mentions that angels "never disobey God's commands to them, but do precisely what they are commanded."[8] In another verse, angels are described as those who submit to God and are free of arrogance.[9] In this regard, there is no characterization of angels as either bad or fallen in Islamic theology. Angels' lack of free will differentiates them from humans and places humankind on a higher level in the creational hierarchy: humankind has a self or ego and therefore freedom of choice, while angels simply follow what they are ordained to do. In Islamic theology, angels have no gender. And while they are depicted as physical beings, even with wings, Islamic theology asserts that such descriptions are metaphors for their faculties or skills.[10]

---

6. Nursi, *Words*, 191.
7. Qur'an 51:26–28.
8. Qur'an 66:6.
9. Qur'an 16:49.
10. Diyanet İşleri Başkanlığı, *Hadislerle Islam*, 1:535.

The Role of Angels

Sacred texts of Islam not only refer to the existence of angels and their nature but also describe their roles and attributes. The four chief angels are the archangels Gabriel, Michael or Mikail, Azrael, and Israfil or Raphael. According to a hadith reported by the Prophet's wife Aisha, the Prophet would often recite the following prayer at night: "O Allah, Lord of Jibreel [Gabriel], Mikail and Israfil, Creator of heaven and earth, Knower of the unseen and the seen, You are the Judge of the matters in which Your servants differ; guide me with regard to disputed matters of truth by Your permission, for You guide whomever You will to the straight path."[11]

Gabriel is known as the angel of revelation. Because of the distance of God from humans, revelation to the prophets is received through Gabriel. The Qur'an mentions Gabriel as the one who brought the Qur'an down to Muhammad's heart with God's permission.[12] Gabriel would appear to the Prophet in diverse ways, including in human form. According to various hadiths, the archangel would often come to the Prophet in the form of one of his handsome companions.[13] In the Qur'an, Gabriel also appears to Mary in the form of a man.[14]

While Michael or Mikail is God's messenger in charge of issues related to nature, Azrael is known as the angel of death. The Qur'an asserts, "'The Angel of Death put in charge of you will take your souls, and then you will be returned to your Lord.'"[15] Death is part of God's own creation and design.[16] According to a story widely shared among Muslims, when Azrael was assigned to be the angel of death, he was concerned that people would hate him because of what he does. God answered that he would establish elements for death so people would not criticize Azrael as death's main source. Rather, they would think of the secondary causes as the reason for the loss of a loved one.[17] Finally, Israfil or Raphael is the angel who is in charge of eschatological signs and who will blow the trumpet at the end of the world.[18]

---

11. Al-Naysaburi, *Sahih Muslim*, book 6, hadith 239.
12. Qur'an 2:97.
13. Al-Bukhari, *Sahih al-Bukhari*, book 66, hadith 1.
14. Qur'an 19:17.
15. Qur'an 32:11.
16. Qur'an 67:2.
17. Nursi, *Şualar* (Istanbul: Söz, 2009), 342–43.
18. Diyanet İşleri Başkanlığı, *Hadislerle Islam*, 1:536.

The Qur'an mentions other angels as well. Among them are the *hafaza* angels, who are always present with humans, one on the left shoulder and one on the right. God assigns a *hafaza* to each individual to record all that person's deeds. Nothing a human says or does remains secret.[19] Considering that most crimes and injustices, including domestic violence and abuse, happen behind closed doors, the Qur'an warns the perpetrators of such crimes that eventually, everything will be unveiled. Islamic theology also mentions angels (*munkar* and *nakir*) who have the role of questioning humans immediately after their death.[20]

Between Angels and Human Beings: Jinns

In addition to angels, Muslims believe in the existence of jinns, supernatural beings believed to be created from fire. According to Islamic sources, "Jinn, as psychic beings, unseen to most humans, occupy an intermediate state between the material realm of our physical experiences and the angelic and spiritual realms."[21]

God sent Muhammad as a prophet not only to humans but also to jinns. Human beings and jinns are mentioned together in twenty different verses in Muslim scripture. Not only does the Qur'an repeatedly mention jinns; one of its chapters is even named after them.[22] The chapter relates an occasion when a group of jinns sat with humans listening to the Prophet Muhammad recite the Qur'an. The jinns were awed by the divine words. The Mosque of the Jinn in Mecca takes its name from that event. The Qur'an also points to the Prophet Solomon's relationship with the jinns in his service. Unlike angels, jinns can choose freely to become believers or disbelievers. In this regard, there can be good jinns and bad jinns.

Satan among the Jinns

Muslims believe that Satan is a jinn. The Qur'an refers to Satan as Iblis, the first jinn God created. Because of his piety and surrender to God, Iblis was initially part of a group of angels, though was not an angel himself. According to the Qur'an,

---

19. Qur'an 50:17–18.
20. Diyanet İşleri Başkanlığı, *Hadislerle Islam*, 1:536.
21. Lumbard, Commentary on *Surat al-Jinn*, Nasr et al., Study Qur'an, 1427.
22. Qur'an 22:72.

when God told the angels that he would create a human on earth, their concerned response was, "Will you place someone there who will cause harm and bloodshed, while we glorify you with praises and thanks?"[23] God responded, "I know what you do not know," and proceeded to create Adam, whom God taught his most beautiful names (*asma al-husna*).[24] He then asked the angels, including Satan, to prostrate before Adam. Everyone did so except Satan.[25]

When God asked Satan why he refused to obey, Satan reasoned that Adam was created from clay, while he was created from fire. Satan argued that he was superior to Adam and was therefore unwilling to prostrate before him. (For this reason, some Muslim scholars consider Satan to be the first bigot.) As a consequence, he was cursed and banished from heaven. Satan then made it his mission to tempt people away from the divine path. God granted him the freedom to do so while stressing that pious humans would be able to resist such deception.

Satan represents evil. However, according to Islamic theology, neither jinns nor Satan have power over humans. In the Qur'an, Satan's tactics are described as weak.[26] Yet as noted in one of the hadiths, "Satan circulates inside the human similar to the blood in the veins."[27] He is always nearby and can have an influence on those who turn to him.[28]

According to Islamic theology, Satan is not a power or entity in the universe independent of God's creative agency. Satan is a creature, not a creator. God gave him the freedom to test believers in this world.[29] But humans can spiritually and morally thrive through the temptations and challenges of Satan—and even rise to a higher level than angels.

Human Nature

The nature of angels and jinns can be clarified by contrasting it with Islamic theology's view of human nature. According to Islam, humans were created from clay and came into existence after they were equipped with a divine spirit. The Qur'an

23. Qur'an 2:30.
24. Qur'an 2:31.
25. Qur'an 2:34.
26. Qur'an 4:76.
27. Al-Bukhari, *Sahih al-Bukhari*, book 93, hadith 35.
28. Qur'an 22:4.
29. Qur'an 34:20–21.

says that God first created humans from clay and fashioned their descendants from semen, an extract of humble fluid. He shaped them and breathed into them his Spirit. He then gave them hearing, sight, and minds.[30] According to Islamic theology, the exact nature of the spirit (*ruh*) is ultimately unknowable; humans have only a limited knowledge of it.[31]

The combination of both spirit and clay is known as soul. Once the spirit merges with the body, the human self (*nafs*) comes into existence. The soul tends to forget its nature and the reality that it "does not reside in the body but in the spirit and in God."[32] In this regard, the word *nafs* has a negative connotation in Islamic literature: "It refers to all the darkness within people that keeps them wandering in ignorance and distance from God."[33]

Unlike angels, humans are granted free will; they can choose to obey or disobey God, who is constantly testing them. The Qur'an mentions that humans were created with dignity "in the most beautiful state."[34] But because of their freedom of choice, they can also descend to "the lowest of the low."[35] Compared to angels and jinns, humans have more limitations due to their nature.

Islamic theology emphasizes human weakness. Being aware of one's inherent weakness leads to full reliance on God and is an essential step toward becoming a servant of God—who is beyond all weakness. Recognition of human impotence is thus a fundamental means by which the believer is led to explore God's attributes—to come to know God as the almighty, the most merciful, and the most generous.[36] Without understanding their own powerlessness, God remains unknown to humans.

Humans are mirrors of God's attributes, but they must be aware of their limits in relation to God. Awareness of these polar opposites—the unlimited weakness of humans and the unlimited power of God—provides insight into God's power, richness, and glory.[37] As part of their created nature, humans are dependent.[38] Being

30. Qur'an 32:7–9.
31. Qur'an 17:85.
32. Sachiko and Chittick, *Vision of Islam*, 100–101.
33. Sachiko and Chittick, 101.
34. Qur'an 17:70; 95:4.
35. Qur'an 95:5.
36. Nursi, *Lem'alar* (Istanbul: Söz, 2009), 546.
37. Bediuzzaman Said Nursi, *Mesnev-i Nuriye* (Istanbul: Söz, 2009), 152.
38. Nursi, *Words*, 491.

aware of this disposition brings one closer to God. Without the boundless spiritual poverty of humans, one cannot understand the boundless richness of God.[39]

The Qur'an and hadiths not only refer to humans' weakness and the fact that they are in need but also allude to their longing for eternity and attachment to wealth. The Qur'an points out that humans are often "excessive in their love of wealth" and think their possessions will help them live forever.[40] Therefore, the Qur'an repeatedly emphasizes that everything will perish except that which is turned toward God.[41] What is done according to the will of God can remain permanent. Humans are asked to be grateful for what they have been given. Being superior in the eyes of God is related not to wealth, rank, color, or race but to piety. Thus the superiority of humans to angels is a function of divine wisdom, not power or prestige.

As God created humans to choose freely to worship him, so he created angels and jinns to worship and glorify him by the necessity of their nature. Despite the fact that modernity and science have caused a decline in the belief in angels, this belief remains a key component of Islamic theology. In the following chapter, I discuss the third and fourth articles of faith: belief in the revealed books and the prophets.

39. Nursi, Lem'alar, 39.
40. Qur'an 100:8; 104:3.
41. Qur'an 28:88.

9 Prophets and Scriptures

In 1965, near the end of Vatican II, the council issued its Declaration on the Relation of the Church to Non-Christian Religions, entitled *Nostra Aetate*. The decree includes a short section on the Catholic Church's view of Muslims. While it does not directly reference the Qur'an or the Prophet Muhammad, it does highlight three other major figures of Islamic scripture as inflection points of similarity and appreciation. The first is Abraham. *Nostra Aetate* briefly describes the God in which Muslims believe and concludes that their God is the God of Abraham, the same God whom Christians worship as the God Jesus Christ. The second figure discussed is Jesus. The document mentions that while Muslims do not believe Jesus to be God, they revere him as a prophet of God. The third is Mary, Jesus's mother, whom Muslims honor. Like Christians, they also believe in the virgin birth.[1] These three biblical and qur'anic figures continue to generate conversations between Christians and Muslims in the United States. This chapter explores the Muslim understanding of prophets and scriptures, which are central to those conversations.

The third and fourth articles of faith in Islam are belief in the prophets and belief in the revealed books the prophets received from God. The Qur'an instructs believers not to distinguish among his messengers: "Those who deny God and His messengers, and those who wish to separate God from His messengers, saying, 'We believe in some and disbelieve in others,' and seeking to choose a way in between. They are truly disbelievers. We have prepared for the disbelievers a humiliating punishment."[2] Consequently, being selective among the prophets is considered a form of unbelief according to Muslim scripture.

As mentioned in the chapter on God, one of the divine attributes is speech (*kalam*). Because of this attribute, one of God's names is the One Who Speaks (al-Mutakallim). The manifestation of this name is the creatures' ability to both speak and be spoken to. If God creates beings with life and the ability to express themselves, naturally, he will also communicate with them. If he speaks, he will do

---

1. See Pope Paul VI, "Declaration on the Relation of the Church to Non-Christian Religions: *Nostra Aetate*," October 28, 1965, Vatican archives, accessed March 3, 2020, https://tinyurl.com/44hehnhn.
2. Qur'an 4:150–51.

so to those who are the most deserving. According to Islamic theology, the prophets are those most qualified to be directly addressed by God. God is also known as the All-Knowing One (al-'Alim). Naturally, the one who knows will deliver knowledge.[3]

In this regard, God's divinity requires that he interact with the most qualified ones, the prophets. While we cannot know the nature of God's speech, we know, at least, that it is different from human conversation. The Qur'an explains, for example, that when Moses asked God to reveal himself, it was impossible due to the limitations of human nature in relation to God. Instead, God's majesty was revealed in the burning bush. Even though this divine disclosure was somewhat limited, Moses fainted. Because of human limitation, God speaks to creation through revelation. It is thus that God spoke to the prophets. One hadith reports that God sent 124,000 prophets to Earth. And while the core beliefs contained in their messages were similar, prophets instructed their particular audiences on different laws depending on their context. Given that cultures were not as connected as they are today, the legal aspects of God's message remained flexible.

Characteristics of the Prophets

Based on both the Qur'an and hadiths, Muslim theologians have identified features common to all the prophets. First, with divine aid, prophets were able to perform miracles.[4] In one of the hadiths, Muhammad stated, "There is no prophet who did not perform miracles with God's permission so that their people would believe in their message." He then said, "My miracle is the Qur'an, that is why I will have the largest community on the day of judgment."[5] The Qur'an mentions the miracles of Abraham and recounts that when Abraham had doubts about the resurrection, God asked him to catch four birds, cut them into different pieces, place them on separate hilltops, and then call them back. Abraham did so, and the birds miraculously flew to him.[6] In another instance, because of his message of the unity of God (tawhid), an oppressive king threw Abraham into the fire, which miraculously did not burn him.[7]

---

3. Nursi, Flashes, 288.
4. Yusuf Şevki Yavuz, "Peygamber," in İslam Ansiklopedisi (Ankara: TDK, 2007), 34:259.
5. Al-Bukhari, Sahih al-Bukhari, book 96, hadith 7.
6. Qur'an 2:260.
7. Qur'an 21:51-70.

The Qur'an also describes the miracles of Moses, which began in infancy. Pharaoh was persecuting the Israelites and taking the lives of newborns. God inspired Moses's mother to take action and cast Moses into the river. He was found by Pharaoh's people and eventually adopted and raised by Pharaoh's wife. However, Moses refused to suckle from a foster mother. They eventually found Moses's own mother to feed him. He grew up in Pharaoh's palace.[8] As is well known, during an exchange with Pharaoh, Moses's staff turned into a giant serpent.[9] His greatest miracle, however, was the Exodus. While Moses and his followers crossed the Red Sea, Pharaoh and his followers drowned in it.[10]

The Qur'an discusses the miracles of Jesus as well. Like Moses, his miracles began in infancy. Muslims believe in his virgin birth. When people shamed his mother, Mary, and questioned her, Jesus responded from his cradle: "I am indeed a servant of God: He has given me revelation and made me a prophet; and He has made me blessed wheresoever I be, and has enjoined on me prayer and charity as long as I live; He has made me kind to my mother, and not overbearing or miserable. So peace is on me the day I was born, the day that I die, and the day that I shall be raised up to life again."[11] Among Jesus's miracles, the Qur'an also mentions that upon his disciples' request, Jesus asked God to send a table of food from heaven, and God responded to his prayer. The Qur'an also recounts that Jesus healed the blind and the leper, that clay became a bird in his hands, and that he gave life to the dead with God's permission.[12]

The Qur'an also refers to the miracles of the Prophet Muhammad. Many Muslim scholars stressed that the most important miracle of Muhammad is the Qur'an itself. While the tradition reports hundreds of different miracles he made, the Qur'an mentions only some of them: he ascended to the heavens (the night journey), split the moon with the mere sign of his finger, and was miraculously able to flee Mecca and eventually become victorious over the Meccans.[13]

A second characteristic of prophets is that they receive revelation from God. According to Islamic theology, only prophets can be recipients of formal divine

8. Qur'an 28:7:13.
9. Qur'an 27:10.
10. Qur'an 28:40.
11. Qur'an 19:27–34.
12. Qur'an 5:112–14; 5:110; 3:49; 3:49.
13. Qur'an 17:1; 54:1; 9:40.

messages.[14] An important distinction exists between formal revelation (*wahy*) and inspiration (*ilham*). While only prophets can receive revelation, any pious servant of God can have an inspiration. The Qur'an points out that God revealed his messages both to Moses's mother and to Mary.[15] Muslim scholars have interpreted this type of revelation as inspiration. The Qur'an also mentions that it is through God's inspiration that the bee provides honey.[16]

A third characteristic is that prophets are human and do not have a divine nature.[17] While they are known as special servants of God because of their piety and commitment, they are like any other human in that they are born, live, and then die. Except for Adam and Jesus, all the prophets were born to human parents. Being fully human, they are considered the best role models for morality and spirituality because they are more relatable, and people can emulate them. The majority of Muslim scholars argued that only men could be designated as prophets. However, some Muslim scholars such as Abul Hasan al-Ashari (d. 936), Ibn Hazm (d. 1064), and Qurtubi (d. 1273) argued that some women could also be considered prophets. Given the status of women in the Qur'an, they held out the examples of Jesus's and Moses's mothers.[18]

A fourth characteristic of prophets is that God has selected them. Just because a person is pious and highly moral does not mean they are qualified to become a prophet. Being a prophet is a blessing bestowed by God alone.[19]

Fifth, Muslim theologians include sinlessness (*ismah*) among the characteristics of the prophets. While they are human and subject to temptations, God protects prophets from committing major sins. They are fallible and can make mistakes, but prophets are committed to obeying God.[20]

A sixth characteristic of prophets is that they possess the traits of truthfulness (*sidq*) and trustworthiness (*amanah*). In other words, they do not lie, and they are reliable. Prophets not only are just in their own affairs and relations but also promote justice.[21]

14. Yavuz, "Peygamber," 259.
15. Qur'an 28:7; 19:17.
16. Qur'an 16:68.
17. Yavuz, "Peygamber," 259.
18. Yavuz, 260.
19. Yavuz, 260.
20. Yavuz, 260.
21. Yavuz, 261.

One of the most important missions of the prophets is to convey the message of the unity of God (*tawhid*) as expressed in the Qur'an: "We have sent no messenger before you [Muhammad] without revealing to him: 'There is no god but Me, so worship Me.'"[22] In another verse, the Qur'an reads, "We indeed sent a messenger to every community, saying, 'Worship God and shun false deities.'"[23] Based on this qur'anic content, the prophets teach their followers to look at every creature in the universe with the creator in mind. Thus when people look at a beautiful creature, instead of saying, "How beautiful they are," they should say, "How beautifully they are made."[24]

Prophets guide people according to the will of God. Life after death, as well as human accountability, are the hallmarks of their common message. Muslim theologians also referred to some of the prophets as the arch-prophets (*ulul 'azm*). These people committed themselves to God, even at the expense of their lives and families. The tradition usually lists Abraham, Noah, Moses, Jesus, and Muhammad among the arch-prophets.[25] Still, Muhammad is considered to be the seal of the prophets, which means God will not send any other prophet after him. Muslim theologians believe that the gate of revelation closed with Muhammad's death. God sent many prophets throughout history to different nations and tribes. But the Prophet Muhammad came with a universal message that could speak to distinct cultural contexts, which is why the Qur'an refers to him as "the last of the prophets."[26] The Qur'an also asserts that God approved and perfected the religion, Islam, revealed in the Qur'an, through the Prophet Muhammad.[27] In line with these qur'anic verses, some of the hadiths also mention Muhammad as the last prophet sent to humanity. In one of the hadiths, the Prophet said, "No prophethood shall remain after me, save for true visions."[28] In another one, Muhammad described his place among other prophets as the following: "My place among the prophets before me is that of a man who has built a house, completed it, and beautified it, yet left empty a place for a brick. Then people came to the house, were amazed

---

22. Qur'an 21:25.
23. Qur'an 16:36.
24. Nursi, *Sözler*, 873.
25. Muhammad Aruçi, "Ülü'l-'Azm," in *İslam Ansiklopedisi* (Istanbul: TDV, 2012), 42:294–95.
26. Qur'an 33:40.
27. Qur'an 5:3. While the majority of Muslim scholars have interpreted the word *Islam* in this verse as the religion revealed in the Qur'an, some also believe that it refers to the universal understanding of submission to God. See Maria Massi Dakake, Commentary on *Surat al-Ma'idah*, Nasr et al, Study Qur'an, 276.
28. Quoted in Nasr et al., *Study Quran*, 1031.

by it, and said, 'If only you were to put in place this brick, your house would be complete!' I am this brick."[29]

Belief in Scriptures

Belief in all of the revealed books that were brought by divine messengers and by the Prophet Muhammad is also part of the Islamic creed. God sent these books to guide people, and the prophets were those who explained and lived up to their message, modeling what it means to be a true servant of God. In one of the hadiths, the Prophet was asked about the number of revealed books. He answered that 104 books were revealed, among them the Torah, the Gospel, the Psalms, the Qur'an, and the books that were sent down to Seth (Sheeth), Idris, and Abraham.[30] The Qur'an invites believers to affirm the following statement: "We believe in God, and the revelation given to us and to Abraham, Ishmael, Isaac, Jacob, and the Tribes, and in that given to Moses, Jesus, and that given to all the prophets by their Lord. We make no distinction among any of them, and to Him we submit."[31]

Jews and Christians in the Qur'an: The People of the Book

The Qur'an refers to Jews and Christians with the honorific title "the people of the book" (ahl al-kitab). Muslims believe that both of these communities received scriptures from God. The followers of all three traditions uphold common beliefs and practices such as faith in God, the Day of Judgment, and doing good deeds.[32] The Qur'an also permits Muslim men to marry women among the people of the book and to consume food prepared by these people.[33] Due to this qur'anic embrace, Jews and Christians have mostly enjoyed religious freedom in Muslim-majority societies until modern times. They were called protected religious minorities (dhimmis). However, especially from the nineteenth century forward, these religious minorities experienced limitations of their freedom, especially in postcolonial

---

29. Quoted in Nasr et al., 1031.
30. Diyanet İşleri Başkanlığı, Hadislerle Islam, 1:541.
31. Qur'an 2:136.
32. Qur'an 5:69.
33. Qur'an 5:5.

Muslim societies and mainly because of those societies' painful experiences with Western powers.[34]

The Qur'an addresses the people of the book more than thirty times and affirms that Moses received the Torah (Tawrat) and Jesus received the Gospel (Injil). Muslim scripture refers to the sacred texts of Judaism and Christianity with reverence: "We revealed the Torah, wherein is guidance and a light, by which the prophets who surrendered (unto God) judged the Jews, as did the rabbis and the scholars, in accordance with God's Scripture as they were bidden to preserve and to which they were witnesses."[35] In another verse, the Qur'an points to the sacred text revealed to Jesus: "And in their footsteps, We sent Jesus the son of Mary, confirming the Torah that had come before him. We sent him the Gospel, wherein is a guidance and a light, and confirmation of the Torah that had come before him and a guidance and an admonition to those who are mindful of God."[36] The Qur'an refers to the scriptures of Jews and Christians as sources of guidance.

In Islamic tradition, the term *scripture* specifies words divinely revealed to the prophets that were written down and recorded. In short, scripture is the direct word of God sent to the messengers by angels.[37] The Qur'an takes this understanding of scripture as its departure point when it engages the scriptures of Judaism and Christianity. While praising Jews and Christians as the people of the book, the Qur'an does not shy away from criticizing these communities and their sacred texts. In light of this, one of the words that the Qur'an employs is *tahrif*, which is usually rendered as "distortion" or "alteration": "They distort the meaning of the Word and have forgotten a good part of the message that was sent to them."[38] Another word the Qur'an uses to criticize other scriptures is *baddala*, which means "change" or "substitute": "But the wrongdoers substituted a different word from the one they had been given."[39]

Muslim scholars offered differing interpretations concerning these words employed by the Qur'an. Three major positions emerged as a result. First, either the entire text or a sizable portion of Jewish and Christian scriptures was distorted.

---

34. Ronald L. Nettler, "People of the Book," Oxford Islamic Studies Online, accessed April 18, 2020, http://www.oxfordislamicstudies.com/article/opr/t236/e0628.
35. Qur'an 5:44.
36. Qur'an 5:46.
37. Saeed, *Qur'an*, 45.
38. Qur'an 5:13.
39. Qur'an 2:59.

Second, the distortion happened both in the text and on the level of interpretation. Third, only the meaning of the sacred texts was altered, not the actual text. Advocates of this last view argue that the distortion is related to misinterpreting and twisting of the words of scripture.[40]

The following chapter explores the fifth article of faith, belief in the hereafter, which is one of the major themes of the Qur'an and the teachings of the Prophet Muhammad.

---

40. Saeed, Qur'an, 143–59. See also Muhammet Tarakçı, "Tahrif," in İslam Ansiklopedisi (Ankara: TDK, 2010), 39:422–24.

10 Death, Resurrection, and the Hereafter

Mahommah Baquaqua was born in 1824 into a noble Muslim family in Djougou, Benin, in West Africa. As a young man, Mahommah was sold to European traders and eventually taken to Brazil. In 1847, he traveled on a ship transporting coffee to New York, from where he was able to escape with the help of abolitionists. On his journey from West Africa to New York, Mahommah had been owned by many different slave masters.[1] Under them, he suffered such brutality that he attempted to drown himself during his captivity in Brazil. Referring to the abuses and cruelties he endured in the hands of one of his masters, Mahommah wrote, "But the day is coming when his power will be vested in another, and of his stewardship he must render an account; alas what account can he render of the crimes committed upon the writhing bodies of the poor pitiless wretches he had under his charge; when his kingship shall cease and the great accounting be called for; how shall he answer?"[2] In his statement, Mahommah was pointing to the day of judgment. In times of suffering and grief, he found hope in the Islamic theology of the hereafter and the accountability it promises.

Belief in life after death has been part of many religious creeds, and Islam is no exception. It is one of the six articles of faith in Islam. Perhaps no religious scripture is concerned with life after death as much as the Qur'an. One can find almost no page in it that does not reference the hereafter. Descriptions of heaven and hell are quite vivid in Muslim scripture. Interestingly, belief in God and the hereafter are often juxtaposed in the same verses. And the Qur'an presents faith in the hereafter as a common belief of Islam, Christianity, and Judaism.[3]

1. For more information about Baquaqua, see Mahommah Gardo Baquaqua and Samuel Moore, *Biography of Mahommah G. Baquaqua, a Native of Zoogoo, in the Interior of Africa* [. . .] (Detroit, MI: Geo. E. Pomeroy, 1854), https://docsouth.unc.edu/neh/baquaqua/summary.html.
2. Quoted in Kambiz GhaneaBassiri, *A History of Islam in America* (Cambridge: Cambridge University Press, 2010), 91.
3. Qur'an 3:114.

The Qur'an on the Resurrection of the Body

We know from the Qur'an that the Meccan polytheists did not believe in life after death.[4] They rejected the Prophet's message of resurrection and accountability on the day of judgment, arguing, "there is nothing beyond our first death, and we shall not be resurrected."[5] The Qur'an explains their view as claiming that "there is no life but our worldly life. We die and live, and nothing destroys us except time."[6] The Meccans also challenged the Prophet by calling him to bring their ancestors back to life if his argument of resurrection and accountability were true.[7] The Qur'an responds that they have no knowledge of the hereafter and only follow their own desires. It is God who gives life, causes people to die, and gathers them on the day of resurrection.[8]

In other passages of the Qur'an, the disbelievers of Mecca get more specific in their view of the resurrection: "What! When we and our forefathers have become dust, shall we really be raised from the dead? We have heard such promises before, and so did our forefathers. These are nothing but tales of the ancients."[9] In another verse, the Qur'an relates their accusatory question, "Who can give life to the bones when they are decayed?"[10]

Engaging with the disbelievers' arguments against belief in resurrection and accountability on the day of judgment, the Qur'an provides its own answers. One response is that it is possible for God to resurrect the dead given that he is the Almighty (al-Qadir). To challenge the argument that decayed bones could not be brought to life, the Qur'an points to the creation of humankind:

> Does not man not see that We [God] created him from a sperm? Yet behold! He is an open opponent. And he makes comparisons for Us, and forgets his own creation. He says, "Who can give life to the bones when they are decayed?" Say, "He will give them life Who created them for the first time, for He is well-versed in every kind of creation. It is He who made

4. Qur'an 16:38.
5. Qur'an 44:35–36.
6. Qur'an 45:24.
7. Qur'an 45:25.
8. Qur'an 45:26.
9. Qur'an 27:67–68.
10. Qur'an 36:78.

fire for you from the green tree, and behold, you kindle from it." Is not He Who created the heavens and the earth able to create the like of them? Yes, indeed. He is the All Knowing Creator. When He wills something to be, His way is to say, "Be!" and it is! So, glory be to Him in whose Hand lies the dominion of all things. It is to Him that you will be returned.[11]

The Qur'an also alludes to spring as evidence of resurrection: "Look, then, at the imprints of God's mercy, how He gives life to the earth after its death. This same God is the one who will give life to the dead. He has power over all things."[12] In another place, the Qur'an points to signs of resurrection in creation: "And how We send blessed water down from the sky and grow with it gardens, the harvested grain, and the lofty date palms with ranged clusters, as a provision for God's servants; and We give new life with it to land that is dead."[13] The passage concludes that similarly, "this is how the resurrection of the dead will be."[14] The Qur'an also indicates that resurrection is as easy as the creation of one being: "Your creation and your resurrection are only as the creation and resurrection of a single soul."[15]

Theology of the Hereafter

Muslim theologians approach the subject of the hereafter through God's attributes, which require both resurrection and human accountability. God is the One Who Creates with Wisdom and Purpose (al-Hakim), and therefore, nothing is created in vain. God creates humans who reflect his own attributes. If human lives concluded with death alone, this would contradict his wisdom, and human life as such would be a waste. Why would the most precious and most intelligent creature of creation die to no avail? Moreover, humans desire eternity; they long to live forever. God has equipped human nature with this desire. If God is the Almighty, the Loving, and the Compassionate One toward creation, why would he not fulfill the human desire for eternity? Similarly, one of God's names is the Just (al-'Adl), which refers

11. Qur'an 36:77–83.
12. Qur'an 30:50.
13. Qur'an 50:9–11.
14. Qur'an 50:9–11.
15. Qur'an 31:28.

to the divine notion of harmony, order, and balance in both this world and the next. While humans long for justice and are encouraged to strive toward it, there remains much injustice in this world. Those who commit major crimes against their fellow humans often get away with their injustices. Many leave this world without ever being held fully accountable. There are people who are born into suffering. People often face injustice despite being good natured and innocent. Is this consistent with God's justice? From an Islamic perspective, the hereafter and human accountability on the day of judgment will rectify those injustices and bring balance and order to these disturbances of God's creation. Those who have promoted goodness in this world will eventually be rewarded, and those who have caused evil and suffering will be held accountable and face their rightful punishment—unless they have sought forgiveness and repentance. Considering that injustice often happens in secret, the Qur'an repeatedly emphasizes that God sees everything and that there is nothing that is outside of his knowledge: "He knows what is in the heavens and the earth; He knows what you hide and what you disclose; God knows well the secrets of all hearts."[16] In one of the hadiths, the Prophet said, "On the day of judgment a sheep without horn will take its right from a sheep with horn"[17] The Qur'an highlights that even if people get away with their injustices here on earth, they will eventually have to face the ultimate judge who awaits them in the hereafter. Since the divine attributes are reflected in this world only in a dim and limited manner, God's name the Just One (al-'Adl) and many others of his qualities will be fully revealed in the afterlife.

Death as a Creation of God

According to Islamic eschatology, this world will end (qiyama), leading to the hereafter. God will resurrect everyone from the dead and gather them on the day of judgment. Human beings will then be accountable for their actions—good or bad. For each individual, however, the end of this world begins with one's own death. Remembering death in this world is an important way of being mindful of the hereafter and planning accordingly. The Qur'an repeatedly reminds people of their ultimate destiny—namely, death: "Every soul shall taste death. We test you

16. Qur'an 64:4.
17. Al-Tirmidhi, *Jami' al-Tirmidhi*, book 37, hadith 2605.

with evil and with good, and to Us you will be returned."[18] In another verse, the Qur'an points out that "death will overtake you no matter where you may be, even inside high towers."[19] Nevertheless, death is seen as a sign of God's creation or the manifestation of his name the Bringer of Death (al-Mumit). It is also part of God's design. Death and its timing are willed and assigned by God: "We have decreed death upon you. We would not be outstripped."[20]

Like life, God creates death. It comes as no surprise, then, that Islamic theology often depicts death positively. It is not a departure but rather a step forward to a new beginning. Whenever Muslims hear of the death of a loved one, they invoke the qur'anic phrase "We belong to God and to Him we shall return."[21] The poet Rumi (d. 1273) wrote about his future death and funeral in a way that eloquently captures the Islamic approach to death:

> On the day of (my) death when my coffin is going (by),
> Don't imagine that I have (any) pain (about leaving) this world.
>
> Don't weep for me, and don't say, "How terrible! What a pity!"
> (For) you will fall into the error of (being deceived by) the Devil, (and) that
>   would (really) be a pity!
>
> When you see my funeral, don't say, "Parting and separation!"
> (Since) for me, that is the time for union and meeting (God).
>
> (And when) you entrust me to the grave, don't say,
> "Good-bye! Farewell!" For the grave is (only) a curtain for
> (hiding) the gathering (of souls) in Paradise.
>
> When you see the going down, notice the coming up. Why should
> there be (any) loss because of the setting of the sun and moon?

18. Qur'an 21:35.
19. Qur'an 4:78.
20. Qur'an 56:60.
21. Qur'an 2:156.

*It seems like setting to you, but it is rising. The tomb seems like a
prison, (but) it is the liberation of the soul.*

*What seed (ever) went down into the earth which didn't grow
(back up)? (So), for you, why is there this doubt about the human
"seed"?*

*What bucket (ever) went down and didn't come out full? Why
should there be (any) lamenting for the Joseph of the soul because
of the well?*

*When you have closed (your) mouth on this side, open (it) on
that side, for your shouts of joy will be in the Sky beyond place
(and time).*[22]

God would not have taken Prophet Muhammad's life if death were not beautiful, as another poet put it.[23] While it appears that a seed dies and disintegrates, in reality, it yields life. Likewise, the death of humans should be regarded not as destruction or an end but rather as "the sign, introduction, and starting point of perpetual life."[24]

Muslims still mourn death but do so with the conviction that death is not an end; it is a new beginning. The Prophet's own experience reflects this philosophy. He had seven children, and six of them died before him. When the Prophet's son Ibrahim died in infancy, his companions saw him weeping. They asked him, "Do you mourn the dead too?" The Prophet answered that in the face of the death of our loved ones, "the eyes will weep; the heart gets sad. However, we will invoke the words that are pleasing to our Lord." The Prophet then turned to his dead son: "If there was no hope in death, and if it were not the destiny of everyone, and if those were left behind would not be united with those who die, we would be in even more grief. We exceedingly mourn your death."[25]

22. Jalaluddin Rumi, "On the Day of My Death," in *Diwan-e Kabir*, trans. Ibrahim Gamard, accessed May 17, 2020, http://www.dar-al-masnavi.org/gh-0911.html.
23. Necip Fazıl Kisakürek, *Çile* (Istanbul: Büyük Doğu Yayınları, 2014), 298.
24. Bediuzzaman Said Nursi, *The Letters* (Istanbul: Sözler, 2001), 284.
25. Diyanet İşleri Başkanlığı, *Hadislerle Islam* (Istanbul: Diyanet Yayınları, 2014), 7:549.

Contemplating Death and the Hereafter

Contemplating death and the hereafter is an essential aspect of Islamic spirituality. A companion of the Prophet was asked about a common supplication that the messenger would address to God. He answered that Muhammad would pray, "Oh God, give us goodness in this world and the hereafter and protect us from the hellfire."[26] The Qur'an relates that one of the prayers of Abraham was, "Our Lord, forgive me, my parents, and the believers on the Day when the Reckoning shall take place."[27] Moses prayed in this manner: "And ordain for us good in this world and in the Hereafter. We turn repentant to You."[28]

Islamic spirituality aims to maintain a balance between this world and the hereafter. The Prophet said, "For a believer the highest concern is the concern for both this world and the hereafter."[29] While Islam does not encourage an ascetic or monastic life by which believers will retreat from eating, drinking, sleeping, and marriage, it discourages them from being overly attached to this world. In other words, the work of this world should not come at the expense of one's relationship with God or their work for the hereafter. The Qur'an explains, "Men whom neither merchandise nor sale can divert from the remembrance of God, nor from regular prayer, nor from the practice of regular charity: Their only fear is for the Day when hearts and eyes will be overturned. That God may reward them according to the best of their deeds and add even more for them out of His grace, for God provides for whomever he pleases without measure."[30] That is why the following statement has become a mantra among Muslims: work for this world as if you will never die, and work for the hereafter as if you will die tomorrow.

Even today, whenever individual or communal prayer takes place among Muslims, the hereafter is remembered. Invoking death is regarded as being mindful of God and the impermanence of the world. Once people internalize the idea that everything but God is subject to departure and death, they will refrain from attaching their hearts to ephemeral things.

---

26. Al-Naysaburi, *Sahih Muslim*, book 48, hadith 37.
27. Qur'an 14:41.
28. Qur'an 7:156.
29. Ibn Majah, *Sunan Ibn Majah*, book 12, hadith 2226.
30. Qur'an 24:37–38.

Death is also mentioned in the story of Joseph, which the Qur'an calls "the best of stories."[31] At the end of the narrative, Joseph asks God to make him die in righteousness.[32] When a happy story ends with a reminder of death and separation, it generally diminishes the reader's joy and makes the story more painful for them. But in the qur'anic account, death is mentioned when Joseph is at the peak of happiness and joy. Having been betrayed by his brothers and sold into slavery, he has risen to an important rank and, in the end, is reunited with his family. The fact that Joseph remembers death demonstrates his belief that there is a greater happiness beyond this worldly life. The end of the story causes readers no sorrow; rather, it "gives good tidings and adds further joy."[33] Constantly remembering death prevents people from being heedless of God's glory and too attached to the things of this world.[34]

The story of the prophet Abraham in the Qur'an can be read in a similar fashion. In the story, Abraham is searching for his Lord.[35] When night falls, Abraham sees a star and says, "This is my Lord." But when the star sets, he says, "I do not love things that set." Abraham then sees the moon and says, "This is my Lord." But when it too disappears, he realizes it also cannot be his Lord. Upon seeing the sunrise and sunset, he reasons the same way. Abraham's search results in this conclusion: "I turn my face toward Him who created the heavens and the earth. I am not one of the polytheists."[36] The gist of the story is that the heart cannot be attached to those things that are subject to death and departure. When people are attached to such things, they cannot help but be disappointed. Loving things that are subject to death is not worthwhile because those things are not, in reality, beautiful. The heart is created to be the mirror of the love of God; to love things that are eternal precludes the love of ephemeral things.[37]

Death and the Formation of a Virtuous Character

Although it has become less common in modern times, building a virtuous character through the remembrance of death has long been part of religious traditions. For

31. Qur'an 12:3.
32. Qur'an 12:101.
33. Nursi, *Letters*, 335.
34. Nursi, 335.
35. For the related story, see Qur'an 6:74–79.
36. Qur'an 6:79.
37. Nursi, *Words*, 228.

example, the Latin phrase "memento mori" (remember that you must die) was a mantra in medieval Christianity—an important practice in building good character. Such practices have been equally important in the Islamic tradition. The hadith collections usually include a book of *janaiz*, devoted to the subject of death. The Sufi tradition also takes the remembrance of death as a significant element of its spirituality and of the formation of a virtuous character. The last—and longest—book of al-Ghazali's *Ihya' al-'Ulum ad-Din* is dedicated to death and the hereafter.

Muslims consider remembering death to be a means of forming a virtuous character. It can be an important way to attain sincerity. Pretentiousness and excessive attachment to possessions are obstacles to sincerity. The reality of death keeps believers from pretentiousness and protects them from the traps of their own egos. This is why Muslims often recite qur'anic verses like "Every soul shall taste death" and "Truly you will die one day, and truly they too will die one day," as contemplating death is a significant part of their spiritual life.[38] Constantly thinking of one's own death brings the faithful to an ideal state of sincerity. It leads to a joyful life—a life without remorse or regret at the end. Instead, pondering one's end leads the believer to appreciate life and live it to the fullest.

For Muslims, the remembrance of death not only fosters self-contemplation and gratitude but makes people humbler and more sensitive toward fellow humans. When people contemplate the ephemera of this world and think about their mortality, they can be more thoughtful toward each other. In his *Denial of Death*, cultural anthropologist Ernest Becker points out a direct correlation between refusing to face our mortality and fostering conflict. He asserts that when humans face their mortality, the world becomes a better place.[39] As Becker says, "Man's natural and inevitable urge to deny mortality and achieve a heroic self-image are the root causes of human evil."[40]

Contemplating death might also be an important cure for the often destructive emotions of enmity and jealousy. A person whose heart is full of enmity and jealousy toward a rival because of the worldly skills and blessings that rival has should realize that the beauty, strength, rank, and wealth their rival possesses not only are transient and temporary but also might be burdensome.[41]

---

38. Qur'an 3:185; 39:30. See also Nursi, *Flashes*, 217.
39. See Ernest Becker, *The Denial of Death* (New York: Free Press, 1997).
40. Ernest Becker, *Escape from Evil* (New York: Free Press, 1985), xvii.
41. Nursi, *Letters*, 315.

Death Rituals

Like adherents of other religions, Muslims practice specific death rituals. In the last moments of their lives, Muslims invoke the testimony of faith (*shahada*). Those around the deathbed should encourage the individual to say, "There is no God but God, and Muhammad is His messenger." In the presence of the dying person, Muslims usually recite the Qur'an, especially chapter 36, "Surat al-Yasin." Before burial, close relatives (ideally) wash the dead body, wrap it in a simple white shroud, and then say a prayer. Based on a prophetic hadith advising Muslims to hasten the funeral rites, it has become an important tradition in Islam to do the washing and the burial as soon as possible.[42]

Attending a funeral service is a communal obligation. However, if enough members in the Muslim community fulfill the obligation, Islamic law allows the remaining Muslims to not attend. In one of the hadiths, the Prophet lists the attendance at a funeral of a believer as a fundamental responsibility owed to one another.[43]

The funeral prayer usually includes a recitation from the Qur'an, especially the first chapter, "Al-Fatiha," and proclamation of "God is great" as well as some other supplications for the deceased and the congregation. Then the one leading the prayers asks the congregation to forgive the dead person for any wrongdoing, after which the congregation proceeds to the graveyard, often with people carrying the coffin together on their shoulders. In the grave, the head is laid in the direction of the Kaaba. Then the mourners close the grave with soil. In the cemetery, the congregation is involved not only in digging the grave but also in helping move the body into the grave. As in orthodox Judaism, cremation is impermissible in Islam due to the sacredness of the body.

Muslims believe that after burial, the angels of *munkar* and *nakir* will visit the dead person to ask questions about God and the Prophet. According to the tradition, the deceased will remain in the intermediate realm (*barzakh*) until resurrection on the day of judgment. One's condition in *barzakh* depends on that person's state of faith and good deeds at the time of death—it can be either a heavenly or hellish waiting room.[44]

---

42. Al-Naysaburi, *Sahih Muslim*, book 11, hadith 66.
43. Al-Bukhari, *Sahih al-Bukhari*, book 23, hadith 4.
44. Al-Tirmidhi, *Jami' al-Tirmidhi*, book 37, hadith 2460.

The community usually shows support to the mourners by offering condolences (ta'ziya). Part of the Sunna of the Prophet is also to offer food to the family of the deceased.[45]

Muslim Death and Burial in the United States

Distinctive death and burial rituals create a range of challenges for Muslims in the United States. First, few US funeral homes offer rituals according to Islamic practices, and some Muslims must perform the rituals in a non-Muslim funeral home. Another challenge is finding a burial place. Given that there is no crema-tion in Islamic tradition, acquiring Muslim cemeteries becomes crucial for the US Muslim community. While the number of Muslim cemeteries is increasing in the United States, many towns have resisted the establishment of a Muslim cemetery. As in the Jewish tradition, Muslims prefer a separate space of burial, but an allo-cated spot in a public section is permissible as well. In public cemeteries, it is not difficult to spot a Muslim grave. Usually, one can see a crescent moon with a star; verses from the Qur'an, especially the first chapter; or God's name the Everlasting (al-Baqi) on the gravestone. In fact, gravestones have played a significant role in studies on the history and diversity of Muslims in the United States.[46] One can also visit many graves of fallen Muslim Americans with the crescent moon and star in Arlington National Cemetery.[47]

The deaths and burial rituals of two prominent US Muslims, Malcolm X (d. 1965) and Muhammad Ali (d. 2016), provide a window into Muslim death rituals in the United States. Both were buried according to Islamic rituals. After his assassina-tion in 1965, Malcolm X's body was taken to Unity Funeral Home in Harlem, which normally would have prepared the body according to Christian practices. Upon the request of the Muslim community, however, the funeral director allowed a Muslim to prepare Malcolm X's body for burial according to Islamic rituals. His body was washed with a special holy oil and then wrapped with the traditional white linen

---

45. Mustafa Çağrıcı, "Taziye," in İslam Ansiklopedisi (Ankara: TDK, 2011), 40:203.
46. See Ronald R. Stockton, "Muslim Gravestones in Detroit: A Study in Diversity," Journal of the Asso-ciation of Gravestone Studies 24 (2018): 52–85.
47. Robin Wright, "Humayun Khan Isn't the Only American Hero," New Yorker, August 15, 2016, https://www.newyorker.com/news/news-desk/humayun-khan-isnt-the-only-muslim-american-hero.

shrouds known as *kafan*. Muslims recited some passages of the Qur'an over his body prior to the burial.[48]

Muhammad Ali died in 2016. His funeral was broadcast live on many major news channels. The Islamic rituals were practiced from the last moments of Ali's life through to his burial. US Muslim leader Imam Zaid Shakir was with Ali during his last moments and recited the Qur'an in the presence of family members. As a reporter described it, after he was removed from life support, Imam Zaid had been "watching the pulse in Ali's neck, watching it surge with life after he started breathing on his own and then watching it slowly ebb, and now he leans over and with his mouth close to Ali's right ear, he sings, 'There is no God but Allah, and Muhammad is his messenger.'" For the Islamic washing rituals, Ali's corpse was taken to the Bunker Family Funeral Home, which a Mormon family in Arizona owned. Unlike the typical Islamic ritual prior to burial, his body was embalmed in a manner that was compatible with Islamic teaching, without alcohol or formaldehyde. In the funeral home, a Muslim washer did the ritual and washed the corpse three times, "as tradition prescribes, the first time with soap; the second time with the ground lotus leaves, which foam like soap when he adds water; and the third time with camphor and perfume." Ali's body was then covered "with three sheets, stretching from his shoulders to his knees, from his waist to his feet, and then from head to toe."[49] The following verses from the Qur'an were recited at Ali's funeral:

> As for those who say, "Our Lord is God," and remain on the right path, the angels descend upon them saying, "Do not fear, and do not grieve; be happy with the good news of Paradise, which you have been promised. We are your protectors in the Hereafter, where you will have whatever you desire and whatever you ask for, a gift of welcome from the Most Forgiving, Most Merciful One." Who is better in speech than someone who calls people to God, does righteous deeds, and says "Truly, I am among those who submit"? Good and evil are not equal. [Prophet], repel evil with what is better, and your enemy will become a close friend, but only those who

---

48. Alex Haley, *The Autobiography of Malcolm X* (New York: Grove Press, 1965), 448.
49. Tom Junod, "The Greatest, at Rest," ESPN, accessed April 18, 2020, http://www.espn.com/espn/feature/story/_/id/19409912/the-planning-muhammad-ali-funeral.

are steadfast in patience, only those who are blessed with great righteousness, will attain such goodness.[50]

Both Malcolm X's and Muhammad Ali's funerals were interfaith in nature, and people from many different religious traditions celebrated their legacies.

In the next chapter, I conclude this part of the book with the sixth article of faith: belief in predestination and how it relates to the problem of evil.

---

50. Qur'an 41:30–35.

11 Predestination, Good, and Evil

On February 10, 2015, Deah Barakat; his wife, Yusor Abu-Salha; and his sister-in-law, Razan Abu-Salha, were brutally murdered by a neighbor in their Chapel Hill, North Carolina, home. All three were students and involved in charity work. Deah was a second-year student at the University of North Carolina (UNC) School of Dentistry. Yusor had just finished her degree at North Carolina State University (NCSU) and had been accepted to the same school as Deah. Razan was an undergraduate majoring in architecture at NCSU. Their families believed their children had been victims of a hate crime and that the perpetrator was motivated by his animosity toward Muslims. In June 2019, the perpetrator pleaded guilty to three counts of first-degree murder and was sentenced to three consecutive life terms without the possibility of parole. While the families of the victims did everything in their power to bring the murderer to justice, they also found comfort in their faith. Deah's brother recited two verses from the Qur'an in his court statement: "Do not say that those who are killed in the way of God are dead; they are alive, but you are unaware of it. Happy with what God has given them of His grace; and they feel pleased with the good news, about those left behind them who could not join them, that there shall be no fear for them nor shall they grieve."[1] Deah's mother remarked that what had happened to her son was an ugly crime, but she also said, "I believe that God is wise and He let this happen. I accept God's wisdom and I don't question it. I am sure there is some good for me coming out of [this tragedy]. I believe Deah did not die; only his state of being changed. He was among us, but now he is in heaven. Knowing that gives me a sense of relief."[2] Echoing her brother and mother, Deah's sister pointed out that while nothing could make up for her family's loss, much good had come out of their tragedy. NCSU established a scholarship in their honor. The UNC School of Dentistry created an annual "Deah Day" dedicated to their memory. Every year on that day, the entire

---

1. Qur'an 2:154; 3:170. See "Farris Barakat (Deah's Brother) Court Sentencing Statement 6/12/2019," Our Three Winners Foundation, posted June 24, 2019, https://www.youtube.com/watch?v=YU-gU1BwX6w.
2. For Deah Barakat's mother's remarks, see "Family of Deah Shaddy Barakat, One of Three Muslims Killed in Chapel Hill," Anadolu Agency, posted March 5, 2015, https://www.youtube.com/watch?v=3e9riCU9vpg&frags=pl%2Cwn.

school, including clinics, closes, and all students do community service to honor Deah and Yusor's charity work. In addition, students raised $500,000 that created an endowment for a refugee project Deah and Yusor were working on.[3] This case exemplifies the Muslim understanding of predestination, good, evil, and suffering.

Perhaps no theological issue in the world's religions has been more contentious than the question of predestination and its relation to the role of God in human actions and to the problem of evil and suffering. God is known as all powerful, all knowing, and all benevolent, especially in Judaism, Christianity, and Islam. If God predestines people to have certain fates, then how can they be accountable for their actions in this world and in the hereafter? If God is all powerful, do humans have free will? If God is omniscient and already knows what people will do, how can they be tested by God? If God is all benevolent, why does he not intervene, especially when innocent people face injustice and suffering? Like members of other religious traditions, Muslims have also been dealing with these questions.

In this chapter, we explore the belief in predestination and the problem of evil and suffering in Islamic theology. We first engage with some verses in the Qur'an and then look at different theological views concerning the notion of predestination. Finally, we explore the issue from the perspective of the divine names of God. The last section offers various ways of finding meaning in good and bad. Before we turn to the notion of predestination in Islam, however, it is important to note that some Muslim scholars prefer the expression *measuring out*, as they believe this better captures the Islamic approach to human action in relation to God than the word *predestination*.[4]

Belief in predestination is the sixth and final article of faith in Islam. The tradition first establishes the other articles of faith and then builds the belief in predestination on them, as it is one of the most difficult areas in Islamic theology. In one of the hadiths, the Prophet emphasized not only the belief in "measuring out" but also "the good and the bad side of it." Human beings, as such, will experience good and evil in this world. However, they should always maintain faith that both good and evil come from God. Whether what reaches them is benefit or loss, they are to accept it with thankfulness and have hope in God's mercy.[5]

---

3. For Deah's sister's talk, see "Dr. Suzanne Barakat Addresses the Parliament in a Moving Keynote," Parliament of the World's Religions, posted December 6, 2016, https://www.youtube.com/watch?v=j9NlSUhO7OU&frags=pl%2Cwn.
4. Sachiko and Chittick, *Vision of Islam*, 104.
5. Sachiko and Chittick, 113.

The two most common concepts that appear in Islamic theology in the context of predestination are *qadar* and *qada*. The word *qadar* (literally, "power") comes from the Arabic root *q-d-r*, which means "to decide," "measure out," or "judge." But as a term, it generally means that God knows everything in the past and future through his eternal knowledge. He is all knowing, and nothing exists outside of his knowledge. The word *qada* means "to execute," "create," or "fulfill." Put simply, *qada* is the execution of *qadar*. According to *qadar*, God knows and has written down everything that will occur. Through *qada*, God creates and ordains what is in the *qadar*. Sometimes, these two concepts are used interchangeably. In emphasizing God's power over creation, phrases like "What God wills" (*ma sha Allah*), "God willing" (*in sha Allah*), and "There is no might nor power except in God" (*la hawla wa la kuwwata illa billah*) have become part of the daily language of Muslims around the world.

Measuring Out in the Qur'an

The Qur'an emphasizes that God creates with measure: "We have created all things in proportion and measure. We have treasures of everything. We send it down only in well-known measure."[6] The Qur'an also stresses that there is nothing outside of God's knowledge: "With Him are the keys of unseen: None but He knows them. He knows all that is in the land and sea. No leaf falls without His knowledge, nor is there a single grain in the darkness of the earth, or anything, fresh or dry, that is not written in a clear Record."[7] The prophet Abraham's supplication in the Qur'an depicts God's involvement in people's lives: "[God is] who created me. It is He who guides me; He who gives me food and drink; He who cures me when I am ill; He who will cause me to die and then bring me to life again."[8]

Theological Schools on the Measuring Out

If God knows everything and is in control of everything, what role do humans play in their actions, whether good or bad? Islamic theological schools have taken three main positions on predestination, or measuring out.

6. Qur'an 54:49; 15:21.
7. Qur'an 6:59.
8. Qur'an 26:78–81.

First, based on various qur'anic verses and hadiths, some Muslim theologians have argued that every human action is predetermined, and thus humans have no power over what they do. Human beings do not have free will either. Like leaves in a strong wind, they cannot control their actions. This approach was represented by a theological school known as Jabriya, whose first representative was Jahm bin Safwan (d. 745). In addition to believing that all human activities are predestined, adherents of this school argued that if humans were the creators of their movements, then they would be able to create in the same way as God. However, only God can create, and humans are only the products of creation. Among God's attributes is that he is all knowing, and his knowledge is eternal. Everything then depends on his knowledge, and nothing can change.

The Jabriya approach had political implications, and it is therefore not surprising that others disagreed with this theological interpretation. Having the right answer for human actions in relation to God was important. In the civil wars during the Umayyad dynasty (661–750 CE), for example, many companions of the Prophet died at the hands of fellow Muslims. If human actions are foreordained, then believers must accept that Muslims who kill and are killed act as part of a plan foreordained by God. Other questions have revolved around what to make of the condition of someone who commits a major sin, especially a ruler. If humans are predestined to behave in a certain way and have no power over their actions, then believers should not revolt against the injustices of a ruler. Those who have argued in favor of this theological idea point to verses in the Qur'an to justify their positions: "God is the Creator of all things and He is the Guardian over everything. God knows what every female carries and how much their wombs diminish or increase—everything with Him is measured. Whomever God guides is on the right path, and whomever God leads to stray is a loser. Yet you do not wish unless God wishes. God is full of knowledge and wisdom."[9]

When it was founded, the second school, Qadariya, disagreed with almost everything the Jabriya campaigned for. The Mutazilites later expanded on the Qadariya view, which emphasized human free will and power in relation to God. Unlike representatives of the Jabriya school, they argued that humans control their own actions, and their movements cannot be attributed to God. At the heart of this

9. Qur'an 39:62; 13:8; 7:178; 76:30.

theological position is the question of justice in relation to God. Advocates of this school stress that humans are accountable because they enjoy freedom in their actions; they are the creators of what they do, whether good or bad, and they will eventually face punishment or reward for their choices. Attributing human acts to God is inconsistent with God's justice and incompatible with the idea of the world as a testing place for humans.

Mutazilites argued that if human actions are predestined, as the Jabriya maintained, then human accountability would seem pointless, and belief in a day of judgment would be unnecessary. Predestination implies that God forces certain actions on his creation. This would contradict the idea that God is just. The Mutazila school's view of predestination has had political implications as well. According to their interpretation, rulers can be held accountable for their injustices, and their crimes and sins cannot be interpreted as divinely predestined. The Mutazila school was especially favored by the Abbasid dynasty (750–1258). Like the Jabriyas, they also justified their position through verses in the Qur'an: "Whoever does evil will be requited for it and will find no protector or helper apart from God. They said, 'Our Lord, we have wronged ourselves: if You do not forgive us and have mercy, we shall certainly be lost.' We showed him the way, whether he be grateful or ungrateful."[10]

A third position that offers a middle way was originally put forward by the Ashari and Maturidi, which later became the official theological schools of the Sunni, who today make up more than 80 percent of Muslims. The founders of both schools were initially members of the Mutazila school but later parted ways. They disagreed with the Mutazilites concerning their view of human actions. The Ashari and Maturidi explained their position through the doctrine of acquisition (kasb). God is the creator of every action, but humans are the ones who acquire them by choosing them with their free will. Therefore, humans are accountable for their actions. God wants humans to opt for good, but they have the freedom to choose evil. In this sense, humans are not the creators of their actions, but because they desire or wish for a particular action, God creates it.

The Asharite and Maturidi schools also distinguished between what is determined and what is known. In this regard, one should understand divine determining as a form of knowledge. According to Muslim scholar Colin Turner, "The knowledge

10. Qur'an 4:123; 7:23; 76:3.

of the knower depends on the thing which is known; the thing which is known is not, and cannot be, dependent on the knowledge of the knower." For advocates of these schools, therefore, people's actions are not determined according to God's knowledge. Rather, because God is all knowing, he foresees people's will and choice. To elaborate this view, Turner provides the following example: "My knowledge that X is a thief is dependent on my having seen him steal, or on my having heard about his stealing from someone else; his being a thief is not, and cannot, be dependent on the fact that I know he has stolen something." Turner then points out that this person is "a thief regardless of whether I know he is a thief, and the fact that I know he is a thief has no effect whatsoever on his having become a thief, his being a thief now or the continuation of his thieving in the future." Likewise, Turner continues, what is known by God "does not depend for its existence on Divine knowledge: it is not God's knowledge of a thing which brings it into existence, or effects changes in its existential status, it is God's will in conjunction with His power." He concludes that "compulsion, therefore, is not something that can be predicated on knowledge, which is simply the awareness on the part of the knower of the thing which is known. Therefore, it is meaningless for anyone to assert that a man enters hell because God has always known that he would, in the same way that it is meaningless for me to assert that it is my knowledge that X is a thief that has made him steal from other people and end up in prison."[11] In this sense, the Asharite and Maturidi schools differed from the Mutazilites by emphasizing that humans are not the creators of their actions—God is. They also differed from the Jabriyas by noting that humans have free will when they choose to opt for what is good or what is evil.

Muslim theologians often turn to the following story to understand the positions of each theological school concerning predestination, human action, and God. Let's imagine X fires a rifle, and because of this action, Y is wounded and dies. Here the question is raised: "Since Y's death was determined by God to be at such-and-such a time, what was the fault of the man who fired the rifle through his own choice? For if he had not fired it, Y would still have died."[12] In addition, "If God had known from pre-eternity that X, whom He created, would enter hell, and if all things had been governed by divine determining, then the inescapable fact

---

11. Colin Turner, *The Qur'an Revealed: A Critical Analysis of Said Nursi's Epistles of Light* (Berlin: Gerlach, 2013), 375.
12. Turner, 377.

would have been that X had been 'destined' for hell from the outset. How, then, could X be said to have had free will, given that God knew before X was born that he would end up in hell?"[13] According to the Jabriya, even if X had not fired the gun, Y would still have died. They believed people are not the creators of their own actions. The Mutazilites maintained that if X had not fired the gun, Y would not have died because people are the creators of their own actions. The Asharites and Maturidis argued that If X had not fired the rifle, we do not know whether Y would have died or not.[14]

Predestination in Relation to Good and Evil

In Islam, predestination is often discussed in relation to the problem of evil and suffering. The Qur'an frequently refers to the evil, suffering, and calamities that people experience, all of which are part of their trial and examination in this world. Qur'an 90:4 explicitly states that humans were created in suffering. The word in Arabic that points to the suffering of people in this verse is *kabad*. According to some Qur'an commentaries, *kabad* pertains to hardship, suffering, pain, trial, and distress.[15] In other verses, the Qur'an specifies the forms of suffering and notes that God is testing people with "fear and hunger, and loss of wealth, lives, and crops."[16] The Qur'an also stresses human weakness and ignorance and indicates that because they possess inadequate knowledge, people cannot comprehend the wisdom behind their suffering and trials.[17] According to the Qur'an, people may dislike something that is good for them or like something that is bad for them.[18]

The Islamic theological position on suffering in relation to humans is well captured in the qur'anic story of the prophet Moses and an unidentified man known as Khidr in Islamic literature.[19] According to the Qur'an, God asked Moses who was the most knowledgeable among people. When Moses answered, "Me," God revealed that there was a person more knowledgeable than Moses at the place

13. Turner, 375.
14. Turner, 375.
15. See Muhammad bin Ahmad al-Qurtubi, *Jami' Ahkam al-Qur'an*, Altafsir.com, accessed April 18, 2020, https://www.altafsir.com. See also Muhammad Asad, *The Message of the Qur'an*, Islamic Bulletin, accessed April 18, 2020, http://muhammad-asad.com/Message-of-Quran.pdf.
16. Qur'an 2:155.
17. Qur'an 22:73; 33:72; 2:216.
18. Qur'an 2:216.
19. This story is narrated in chap. 18 of the Qur'an, "Sura al-Kahf."

where two seas met. He told Moses to go there and find the servant of God, Khidr. After Moses found Khidr, he asked if he could accompany Khidr in order to acquire his knowledge. Khidr replied, "You would not be able to be patient with me while traveling." When Moses assured him that he would be patient, Khidr responded, "How could you be patient in matters beyond your knowledge?"

Humbled, Moses answered, "God willing, you will find me patient. I will not disobey you in any matter."[20]

They agreed to travel together, but Khidr again advised Moses, "If you follow me then, do not question anything I do before I mention it to you myself."

They set off for their venture. First, they took a boat. While on the boat, Khidr made a hole in it. Moses got frustrated and asked, "How could you make a hole in this boat? Do you want to drown its passengers? What a strange thing to do!" Khidr reminded him of their agreement that Moses needed to be patient. Moses apologized for his forgetfulness. Farther along in their journey, Khidr killed a young boy they encountered. Angrily, Moses said, "How could you kill an innocent person? He has not killed anyone! What a terrible thing you do."

Khidr replied, "Did I not tell you that you would never be able to bear with me patiently?"

Moses responded, "From now on, if I question anything you do, banish me from your company."

Their journey continued. Moses and Khidr arrived at a town and asked for food and hospitality from its inhabitants. They were refused. When Moses and Khidr were about to leave the town, they saw a ruined wall, and Khidr rebuilt it. Moses was disquieted and once again questioned Khidr's motives. At this point, they parted ways. But before they took their departures, Khidr revealed to Moses the wisdom behind his actions.

In the first case, the boat was owned by some needy people who, with its earnings, were feeding their families. In the direction the boat was moving, there was a king who was seizing all solid boats. He would not, however, seize a boat that had a hole. In the second case, the young boy Khidr had killed would in later life have become a criminal and committed many atrocities. In the third case, the wall was owned by two orphans in the town, and a treasure for them was buried

20. Qur'an 18:69.

underneath it. He built the wall so that when the orphans reached maturity, they would own it.

Obviously, the acts committed by Khidr seemed horrifying—full of suffering, fear, and concern. But the story reflects the Qur'an's approach to evil and suffering. In Moses, we see that humans are ignorant compared to God. Because their knowledge is limited, they are unable to understand the larger picture of the evil and suffering around them, reflecting the qur'anic instruction, "What you see as evil might be good for you."[21]

God, Evil, and Suffering

Evil and suffering are also related to the manifestation of God's names (asma al-husna). This world and the humans who live in it are limited in many ways, but they are unique configurations and manifestations of the divine names. To explain why God allows suffering, an analogy to fashion designers and models might be helpful. Once models are hired, they have no say in the clothes they will wear. It is a designer's right to try various styles on the model; a model cannot say, "I do not want this dress." Let's imagine there is a beautiful designer dress that a fashion model likes. If the designer decides to try another dress on the model, the model cannot decline it if she dislikes it. The designer can only produce and decide on the best dress after trying many dresses on the hired model. These tests will eventually reveal the best of the designer as well as the model. Likewise, each creature can be considered God's fashion model. Without changes in our situation—such as sickness, death, or suffering—there is no way for people to know God.[22] It is through these alterations that one becomes acquainted with God's attributes, which are embodied in creation.

One of God's names is the One Who Heals (al-Shafi). If there is no illness, there is no way to discern that God is the healer—a necessary step toward deep experiential knowledge of God. Healing is closely related to mercy and compassion. Through illness, one may come to know God as the Giver of Mercy (al-Rahim) or the Almighty (al-Qadir). One of God's names is the Giver of Life (al-Muhyi). But life requires death—out of which new life may come. That spring brings new life

---

21. Qur'an 2:216.
22. Nursi, *Mektubat* (Istanbul: Söz, 2009), 271–72.

following the death brought by winter is a good illustration of this. Both life and death equally mirror God's names because each represents a different aspect of God's creative process. God is also the Most Generous (al-Karim) and the Provider (al-Razzaq). These names of God "require" the existence of the needy.[23] That God is generous and all providing has no meaning unless there are creatures who call on God to meet their needs.

Seeking Meaning in Evil and Suffering

Through suffering, humans progress and can move toward perfection. Without upsets, turbulence, or illnesses, life is static and monotonous, and people cannot evolve morally, spiritually, and intellectually. Islamic theology teaches that suffering may bring one closer to God and draws considerable attention to the suffering of the prophets, including Muhammad himself. Without suffering, we are unlikely to appreciate what we have or what is beautiful. Without sickness, we are unlikely to value health. Without poverty and hunger, we may not be able to appreciate wealth and surfeit. Without death, we cannot understand the importance of life. Without trials and tribulations, it would be difficult to imagine not only personal progress and gratitude but also material gains outside of one's self, such as in human rights and medicine.

Muslims' understanding of God has never been limited to theology. In order to have solid faith and truly know God, Muslim scholars often emphasized practice and worship. In the following chapters, I explore the idea of worship and spiritual practices of Islam based on its five pillars.

23. Nursi, Lem'alar, 216.

Part 4

Spiritual Practice

Pillars of Islam

12 The Profession of Faith

Shahada

The chapters in this part of the book concentrate on faith in practice as described by the five pillars of Islam—practices required for all Muslims. The pillars of Islam are the most comprehensive way of worshipping, remembering, and being close to God.

Before we turn to the first pillar, the profession of faith (*shahada*), let's begin with an introduction to worship in Islam and the five pillars the Prophet discussed in the hadiths. The pillars obligate Muslims to (1) believe that there is no god but God and that Muhammad is his messenger, (2) do five daily prayers, (3) give alms, (4) make the hajj, and (5) fast during the month of Ramadan.[1] The hadiths on Islam, or submission, assert that God requires active worship. Faith and practice go hand in hand. The Qur'an asks, "Do people think they will be left alone on saying, 'We believe,' and they will not be tested?"[2] Echoing this verse in one of the hadiths, the Prophet pointed out that belief in God necessitates worship.[3] In this regard, both inner and outer aspects of faith are significant, which has implications for ways of worshipping God in heart, words, and actions. Worship thus involves all the human faculties.[4]

The Qur'an states that God created humans so they could worship him: "I created jinn and humankind only that they might worship me [*liya'budu*]."[5] Worship is a way of being mindful of God.[6] Many Qur'an exegetes maintain that the purpose of creation is above all to know, love, and remember its creator by worshipping him. However, they also emphasize that God does not force people to worship. He rather leaves them with the free choice to acknowledge him or not. Muslims regard worship as a way of knowing God. In fact, some of the commentaries even point out that the word *liya'budu*, or "to worship me," also includes the notion of

---

1. See, for example, Al-Naysaburi, *Sahih Muslim*, book 1, hadith 12.
2. Qur'an 29:2.
3. Al-Naysaburi, *Sahih Muslim*, book 1, hadith 24.
4. Nursi, *Işaratu'l I'jaz* (Istanbul: Söz, 2009), 43.
5. Qur'an 51:56.
6. Qur'an 2:21.

"knowing me." They often link the meaning of this verse to a well-known *hadith al-qudsi*: "I was a hidden treasure, and I loved to be known; so I created creation in order to be known."[7]

Unsurprisingly, significant portions of the Qur'an, the hadith collections, and Islamic law are concerned with worship. If worship is one of the most important signs of Islam, what then is the best form of worship that is pleasing to God? In this regard, Muslim scholars take even simple rituals very seriously, for pleasing God even in a minor matter is critical for them. A case in point is one of the requirements concerning the five daily prayers. The Qur'an points out that hands should be washed up to the elbows.[8] One can interpret the original Arabic reference in the Qur'an in two ways: the elbow can be either included or excluded. Muslim scholars have dedicated volumes to understanding the best way of performing this seemingly simple washing ritual before the prayer.

One should also note that Islamic worship is not limited to its five pillars. However, these rituals are considered to be the all-encompassing, normative manner of worshipping God, and they make up the essence of all other forms of worship. Through them, Muslims thank, remember, and glorify God. Once believers orient their lives toward God through the five pillars, all other daily work and ordinary acts are considered as worship. Being good to your neighbor, having intimate relations, raising children, and studying are worship, as are contemplation and offering supplications and invocations. Even ordinary habits or acts of daily life such as working, eating, drinking, and sleeping are forms of worship. In Islam, no dichotomy exists between the sacred and the profane.

Muslim scholars also speak of "negative" forms of worship. If believers remember God, contemplate their own weakness, and sincerely seek refuge in God during moments of hardship, difficult periods are considered a form of worship as well. Those who rely on God in challenging times will be rewarded. Illness exemplifies this type of negative form of worship. When moments of illness are taken as opportunities to patiently contemplate the self in relation to God, it becomes a period of worship and deep spirituality.[9]

---

7. Lumbard, Commentary on *Surat al-Dhariyat*, Nasr et al., Study Qur'an, 1280.
8. Qur'an 5:6.
9. Nursi, *Lem'alar*, 34.

Humans are not alone in worshipping God. The Qur'an asserts that the entire creation worships, thanks, and glorifies God, each creature in its own language: "Have you not seen [Prophet] that everything in the heavens and earth worship God: the sun, the moon, the stars, the mountains, the trees, and the animals? So do many human beings."[10] Everything in the realm of creation stands in relationship with God: "The seven heavens and the earth and everyone in them praise Him. There is nothing that does not celebrate His praise, though you do not understand their praise: He is most forbearing, most forgiving."[11] Another significant aspect of Islamic worship is sincerity (*ikhlas*). In this regard, the key motivation to worship God is to do it solely for his sake and to attain his love.[12]

The five pillars of Islam can be compared with the sacraments in the Christian tradition. Sacraments are, in a way, ritual practices through which the followers of Christianity "receive blessing from God."[13] While they are the visible practices of the tradition, they also mark the spiritual grace bestowed upon Christian believers. Like the pillars of Islam, sacraments are a way to remember and connect with God. In this regard, Christian theologians speak of "sacramental consciousness," which is interpreted as "an awareness of the presence and activity of God in and through the things of the world."[14] One of the major differences between Islam and Christianity, however, is the fact that the sacraments are administered by an ordained minister, whereas in Islam, the practices are mainly performed individually.

I now explore the first pillar of Islam, the profession of faith: *shahada*.

The First Pillar: *Shahada*

José Ernesto Ferman is a Latin American Muslim. Born in 1990 to a Salvadoran family in San Jose, California, he grew up in Washington, DC. While José was raised in a Catholic household, he lost his faith in college. However, he was still deeply spiritual and wanted to explore different religious traditions. Right after graduation, he began working for a museum in DC where he befriended Muslim colleagues. His

10. Qur'an 22:18.
11. Qur'an 17:44.
12. Nursi, Işaratu'l I'jaz, 196.
13. Gail Ramshaw, *What Is Christianity? An Introduction to the Christian Religion* (Minneapolis, MN: Fortress, 2013), 81.
14. Dennis M. Doyle, *What Is Christianity?* (New York: Paulist, 2016), 165.

friendship with Muslims led him to explore Islam. José wanted to begin with the scripture. One of his colleagues suggested a local mosque where he could obtain the Qur'an. During his visit, he had the opportunity to observe the noon prayer. Two things struck him. One was the diversity of people in the mosque. There were many races and colors. The other was the way Muslims stood shoulder to shoulder in worship and then prostrated themselves together before God. The form and the egalitarian nature of the prayer touched his heart. For him, it was simple but powerful. José was also surprised to see that even the security guard joined the community in prayer. He then thought that the prayer must be essential in the tradition. José left the mosque with a copy of the Qur'an. After a week of reading portions of the scripture, he returned to the mosque to take classes. After three weeks of studying Islam, he told his teacher he wanted to become a Muslim. The first thing the teacher did was to teach José how to do ritual washing (*wudu*) before the prayer. The teacher then told him to come back on Friday, the day of congregational prayer in Islam. Right after the prayer, José made his profession of faith in Arabic (*shahada*) before hundreds of Muslims, which officially made him a Muslim.[15]

According to Islamic theology, every human is created with a natural inclination (*fitrah*) toward faith and is thus *muslim* in the most general sense. One can officially be part of the religion of Islam by formally reciting the *shahada*: "There is no god but God, and Muhammad is His messenger." The *shahada* is one of the phrases Muslims repeat throughout their lives. When a child is born into a Muslim family, it is traditional to recite the call to prayer (*athan*) in the newborn's ears. Muslims recite the *shahada* during their five daily prayers. When believers are about to die and depart from this world, family members, an imam, or a chaplain will make sure they end the last moments of their lives professing the *shahada*.

Islamic theology also discusses the *shahada* in the context of salvation. Traditional Muslim scholars from the four Sunni schools of jurisprudence argued that in order to have sufficient faith in God, one also needed to believe that Muhammad was his messenger. In addition, the *shahada* was known as the apparent line between faith (*iman*) and unbelief (*kufr*). It was on the basis of the *shahada* that many Muslim scholars discussed the fate of others as concerns heaven and hell. While they had diverse opinions concerning *iman* and *kufr*, the discussion centered

---

15. Based on José Ernesto Ferman, interview with the author, December 23, 2019, Ocean City, MD.

on the question of whether one accepted the Prophet Muhammad as a messenger of God. Al-Ghazali (d. 1111) spoke of three categories of non-Muslims who lack belief in the message of Islam. In the first category are those who have never heard about the Prophet Muhammad and his message. In the second are those who have been exposed to the Prophet's message clearly and without any distortion. In the third group are those who have heard about the Prophet's message but have not been exposed to the true character of the Prophet and have received the message in a distorted or insufficient manner. Al-Ghazali pointed out that God will forgive the first and third groups for not believing because they have not been exposed to the message properly.[16]

Professing the *Shahada* in the United States

The first pillar of Islam receives particular attention in the Western context, given both that Muslims are a minority and that many were raised in a faith tradition other than Islam. Approximately one in five adult Muslims in the United States is a convert.[17] For these people, the first stage of entering the new religion is to make the *shahada*. Tradition dictates that to convert to Islam, one must recite the *shahada* in front of two witnesses—a remarkably simple process.

While there are assorted reasons for conversion, about 9 percent of Muslim converts in the United States came to Islam through marriage to or a relationship with a Muslim.[18] This is partly related to the approach to interfaith marriages in Islamic law. Muslim legal scholars have come to a consensus, based on the Qur'an, that a Muslim man can marry a Jewish or Christian woman, but a Muslim woman cannot marry a Jewish or Christian man. In fact, all legal schools also hold the position that neither Muslim men nor women are to marry someone who does not believe in God. When it comes to Muslims living in non–Muslim majority countries, most legal schools have held the position that it is reprehensible (*makruh*) for a Muslim

16. For more details about al-Ghazali's view on the fate of non-Muslims, see Abu Hamid al-Ghazali, *On the Boundaries of Theological Tolerance*, trans. Sherman A. Jackson (Oxford: Oxford University Press, 2002).
17. For a study on Muslim populations in America, see Besheer Mohamed, "New Estimates Show U.S. Muslim Population Continues to Grow," Pew Research Center, January 3, 2018, https://tinyurl.com/56v97n87.
18. For a study on converts to Islam in America, see Besheer Mohamed and Elizabeth Podrebarac Sciupac, "The Share of Americans Who Leave Islam Is Offset by Those Who Become Muslim," Pew Research Center, January 26, 2018, https://tinyurl.com/z6934cy3.

man to marry a Christian or Jewish woman, even though Christians and Jews are considered to be the people of the book. Here, what is at stake is how to raise children. Raising them as Muslims is of primary importance, and having two Muslim parents to provide them with a strong faith foundation is key. In a non–Muslim majority country, the concern is that mothers will influence their children in a stronger way than fathers, and their children may therefore not be fully raised as Muslim if their mother is not Muslim. Based on this argument, some legal scholars have gone so far as to say it is impermissible in a non-Muslim country for a Muslim man to marry a non-Muslim woman, including a Jewish or Christian woman.

Considering that love recognizes no boundaries, including religious ones, how do Muslim scholars deal with the increasing reality of interfaith marriages in today's world? Naturally, many Muslim women fall in love, marry, and have relationships with people of other faiths or no faith. Muslim scholars found the solution in the *shahada*. As long as the non-Muslim man or woman professes the *shahada* in front of two Muslims, this person is considered a Muslim. A lack of practice of any aspect of Islam would not disqualify the person from being a Muslim. It does not matter whether the person said the *shahada* sincerely in his heart, as the law is concerned with the outward activity of speech rather than intentions—a realm that is only accessible to God.[19]

19. Sachiko and Chittick, *Vision of Islam*, 39.

13 The Five Daily Prayers

Salat

Aisha is a US Muslim who currently lives in Chicago.[1] Born in India, she lived in the United Kingdom for a number of years before moving to the United States in 2004. Aisha is in her second year of law school and has already interned at several law firms. She was raised in an Indian Sikh family but became Muslim in her late teens. Salat, or the five daily prayers, is a fundamental component of Aisha's spirituality. For Aisha, salat provides five times a day to start anew. When she was young and felt overwhelmed, her father would tell her to think about life in thirty-minute increments. Breaking her day into manageable chunks let her regain control over the hours that loomed ahead of her. After she became Muslim, Aisha transferred this advice to salat, partitioning her day and tackling its challenges in the segments of time between her prayers. Whenever the day feels like it is running off course, salat lets her seek counsel with her Lord and restart. She feels renewed after every prayer.[2]

Praying at work, however, is often difficult for Aisha. Finding a private bathroom or even just a sink in which to perform wudu, or ablution—lest your boss walk in and catch you with your foot in the sink—is only the first of many hurdles. She enters every office space or meeting place with anticipatory anxiety, mapping out in her brain where the nearest bathroom is and what seems like the least disruptive space in which to pray. Because Aisha does not cover her head in public, remembering to bring a scarf with her is also important. In addition to finding the right space for salat, finding the time to pray in a busy workday is also a challenge. It can appear disruptive to abruptly leave a meeting, and she always fears she might seem rude or disinterested in the conversation. However, the blessings that praying at work brings to Aisha far outweigh the challenges. Leaving her desk multiple times a day to clear her mind, even when her workaholic tendencies resist, is liberating. In a profession as demanding as the law, Aisha sometimes

1. Aisha is a pseudonym.
2. This case is based on Aisha, email interview with the author, February 23, 2020.

feels that all that keeps her from burning out is her *salat*. Billable hours, bonus amounts, forced smiles while networking—these all fade as she wraps her scarf tight, closes her eyes, and remembers that she has someone greater to report to. To Aisha, *salat* is a blessing because it reminds her who she is—a Muslim, a servant of God in constant submission to him alone—before she claims to be anyone or anything else. *Salat* is disruptive. It undermines her backbreaking daily routine and the nonstop flow of the capitalist workday. With every "Allahu akbar," or "God is great," invoked during the postures of prostration, bowing, and kneeling down, Aisha remembers that God is greater than anything else she does or any roadblock she might face.

Salat (literally, "connection") is the second pillar of Islam and an essential element of Islamic spirituality and worship. In addition to the formal *salat*, various forms of prayers exist in Islam such as supplication (*duas*), remembrance of God with various religious phrases (*dhikr*), contemplation of God through his creation (*tafakkur*), and recitation of the Qur'an. This chapter mainly concentrates on the five daily prayers.

Foundations of *Salat*

Worship is a major theme of the Qur'an, and *salat* is at the heart of Islamic worship. Besides its classical meaning, *salat* has various other connotations noted in the Qur'an: supplication, seeking God's forgiveness, or places of worship.[3]

The five daily prayers became an obligation for the Muslim community during the last years of the Prophet Muhammad's time in Mecca. Not long before his emigration to Medina in 622, the Prophet ascended to heaven during his famous night journey (*mi'raj*). The archangel Gabriel took him from Mecca to Jerusalem and then to heaven; the miraculous journey marks the Prophet's direct encounter with God. It was also during this time that the Prophet met with all the other prophets, including Jesus and Moses, who prayed behind him in the sacred mosque of Jerusalem. This gesture has been understood as a sign confirming his prophethood, indicating that he is the "seal of all prophets," as the Qur'an states. During the Prophet's famous journey, God gave him and his followers the gift of the five daily prayers. Initially,

---

3. Qur'an 9:103; 33:43; 33:56; 22:40.

God required fifty prayers a day, but Moses encouraged Muhammad to ask God to reduce the number, and God relented, cutting the number to five.[4]

The Qur'an presents *salat* as a key trait of believers who are mindful of God.[5] It describes the believers as those who perform their *salat* continuously and properly.[6] Those who live in awareness of God model themselves after the prophets. The Qur'an often refers to the prophets' *salat* and particular supplications. For example, Zachariah received the good news of having a son by the name Yahya (John the Baptist) while he was praying in the sanctuary of the temple.[7] The prophet Abraham prayed that God would make him and his offspring among those who persevere in prayer.[8] When the infant Jesus miraculously spoke in support of his mother, Mary, he referred to prayer as well.[9]

The Qur'an also points out that the daily prayers are required for believers at prescribed times.[10] As to the exact times, it mentions morning, noon, late afternoon, evening, and late evening.[11] The Qur'an also refers to the different postures performed during prayers such as standing, bowing, and prostrating.[12]

The five daily prayers are also an important component of the Sunna, or example of the Prophet Muhammad. Major chapters in hadith collections are dedicated to this key ritual of Islam. While the Qur'an references prayer, the Prophet remains the prime model for performing them properly. Muslims believe that the archangel Gabriel himself taught the Prophet how to perform the *salat*.[13] And this is why the Prophet instructed believers to take him as a model in establishing the five daily prayers.[14] Various hadiths refer to the five daily prayers as one of the most spiritually rewarding forms of worship and the central pillar of Islam.[15] Muslims regard prayer to be the believer's minor ascension (*mi'raj*) to the divine realm.[16] In a hadith addressing his companions, the Prophet told them to imagine a river flowing in

4. Ibn Ishaq, *Life of Muhammad*, 186–87.
5. Qur'an 2:3.
6. Qur'an 8:3; 7:173.
7. Qur'an 3:39.
8. Qur'an 14:40.
9. Qur'an 19:31.
10. Qur'an 4:113.
11. Qur'an 24:58; 11:114; 17:78; 2:238; 30:17–18.
12. Qur'an 22:77; 3:191.
13. Al-Bukhari, *Sahih al-Bukhari*, book 59, hadith 32; al-Naysaburi, *Sahih Muslim*, book 5, hadith 214.
14. Al-Bukhari, *Sahih al-Bukhari*, book 10, hadith 28.
15. Al-Tirmidhi, *Jami' al-Tirmidhi*, book 1, hadith 4, and book 40, hadith 11.
16. Major *mi'raj* refers to Muhammad's ascension to heaven.

front of one's house. He then asked whether any dirt would remain on the body if a believer would wash himself in the river five times a day. The companions affirmed that anybody would come out pure and clean. The Prophet asserted that, similarly, the five daily prayers function together like a river. *Salat* cleanses the believer from daily sins and faults.[17] The Prophet also said that the highest act of love for God is prayer performed at the prescribed time.[18]

Prayer was central to prophetic spirituality. The Prophet divided his daily routine into three parts. The first part revolved around prayer and recitation of the Qur'an, the second was reserved for social relations, and the third he dedicated to rest. His daily schedule was based on the five daily prayers, and most of the time, he would perform them in the mosque with his community. He also spent most of his nighttime in devotion. According to a hadith reported by the Prophet's wife Aisha, Muhammad would get up during the night and pray until his feet became swollen. When Aisha asked, "Oh Prophet of God! Why do you force yourself to worship so much when God has forgiven your past and future sins?" he would answer, "Should I not be a grateful servant of God?"[19] As defined by the Prophet, formal prayer in Islam is the most comprehensive expression of love and gratitude toward God.

Form and Structure of *Salat*

Based on both the Qur'an and the prophetic example, Muslims turn in the direction of the Kaaba to perform the daily prayer five times a day: dawn (*fajr*), noon (*dhuhr*), afternoon (*asr*), sunset (*maghrib*), and night (*isha*). Dawn prayer begins at the break of day and ends just before sunrise. Noon prayer begins when the sun is at its high point, or zenith, and ends when the shadow of an object becomes the length of the object itself, which then begins the time of afternoon prayer until just before sunset. Sunset prayer is offered during the time between sunset and the disappearance of twilight. Night prayer can be performed any time between twilight's disappearance and dawn's onset. However, Muslims commonly do it before midnight.

---

17. Al-Bukhari, *Sahih al-Bukhari*, book 9, hadith 7.
18. Al-Naysaburi, *Sahih Muslim*, book 1, hadith 162.
19. Al-Bukhari, *Sahih al-Bukhari*, book 65, hadith 4837.

Each prayer consists of cycles (*rakaat*). One cycle includes the following postures: standing, bowing down, standing again, prostrating oneself with the forehead and nose touching the floor, sitting, prostrating oneself again, and then moving to the final sitting position. The dawn prayer has two required (*fard*) cycles, the noon and afternoon prayers have four each, the evening prayer has three, and the night prayer has four. There are also recommended (*sunna*) cycles in addition to the required ones. Prayer is performed in silence and requires no clerical leader.

Prior to prayer, believers need to be in a state of ritual purity, which requires an ablution. The hadith collections include sections on ritual purity. Also, the books of Islamic law typically begin with rulings about ritual purification. Minor ablution (*wudu*) usually entails washing the hands up to the elbows, then the mouth, nose, face, head, and feet up to the ankles. There is also a major purity ritual (*ghusl*), which requires the entire body to be washed. Muslims perform this ritual after sexual intercourse and wet dreams. Women are required to complete a major purity ritual after their menstrual period and postpartum bleeding. It is also common among Muslims to perform *ghusl* before congregational Friday prayer. On exceptional occasions when water is not available to perform ablution, Muslims can then refer to the ritual of dry ablution (*tayammum*), which involves putting the palms on clean earth, dust, sand, stone, or a wall and then wiping the face and forearms symbolically.

Another requirement of prayer is the dress code for both women and men. While women cover their entire bodies except for their faces and hands, men are required to cover their shoulders and the area between the navel and the knees. It is also common for Muslim men to cover their heads while praying.

The Content of Prayer

Muslims generally pray in silence, but when they pray in congregation, the imam, or leader, recites the Qur'an out loud during dawn, sunset, and night prayer. Prayer is the glorification of God (*tasbih*), the proclamation of God's greatness (*takbir*), and the expression of gratitude (*shukr*) and love.

The language of prayer is Arabic—specifically, qur'anic Arabic, which is a particular form of the language. Any Muslim knows a significant amount of the Qur'an by heart. The most common phrases recited during the postures are "God is great,"

"Glory be to my God," and "All praise is due to God." The common portion of the Qur'an that is recited in each cycle is the first chapter, "Al-Fatiha" ("The Opening"): "In the name of God, Most Gracious, Most Merciful! Praise be to God, Lord of the Worlds, Most Gracious, Most Merciful, Master of the day of Judgment. You alone do we worship, and from You alone do we seek help. Guide us to the straight path, the path of those whom You have blessed, not of those who incurred Your wrath or have gone astray."[20] This part is followed by reciting verses from the Qur'an based on the believer's personal choice. During the sitting postures, Muslims recite a fixed expression praising God and asking him to send blessings upon the Prophet Muhammad. The prayer ends with salutations to the left and right by reciting the formula of "Peace and blessings of God be upon you." Since Muslims believe that angels join them during prayer, this greeting is also directed to them—the unseen community of worshippers.

Mosque and the Call to Prayer

The Arabic word for mosque is *masjid*, which literally means "the place of prostration." The mosque has never played as central of a role in Islam as the church has in Christianity; Islam has no priests, and mosques were never institutionalized under an authorized hierarchy. Believers are not required to do their five daily prayers in a mosque. The earth is considered sacred and, as such, a place of worship.[21] Muslims can perform their prayers wherever they want. In this regard, Muslims can carry out most of their religious duties in their homes. What matters most in praying is ritual purity: the place of prayer needs to be clean, since the forehead is put to the ground. In order to meet this standard, Muslims usually pray on a prayer rug or mat.

While praying in a mosque is not obligatory, the Prophet did strongly encourage Muslims to offer their prayer in community. Communal prayers were a significant element of the Prophet's spirituality. It became the established habit of the Prophet to perform his daily prayers, including dawn and night prayers, with the community in the mosque. In one of the hadiths, the Prophet said, "A prayer that is done communally is twenty-seven times more rewarding than the one done individually."[22]

20. Qur'an 1:1–7.
21. Al-Sijistani, *Sunan Abu Dawud*, book 2, hadith 99.
22. Al-Bukhari, *Sahih al-Bukhari*, book 10, hadith 46.

If two Muslims are gathered, they are encouraged to pray together, with the older person leading the prayer. If three Muslims are present, the person best able to offer a beautiful recitation of the Qur'an should guide the prayer. In another hadith, Muhammad said, "Whoever leaves his or her house with the intention of going to the mosque, for each of his/her steps there is a reward."[23] While prayers can be offered at any spot that meets the purity requirements, the mosque has played a key role in establishing the prayers communally since the early years of Islam.

From the outside, a mosque can usually be identified by a dome, a minaret, and a place of ablution. The call to prayer (adhan) is chanted from the minaret by the one who calls to prayer (muezzin). This practice dates from the Prophet's time. Both minaret and adhan are marks of Islamic societies. In seventh-century Arabia, Christians had a clapper or bell, while Jews had a horn to mark the sacred time. For Muslims, the human voice became the defining characteristic. Initially, the call to prayer was done from the rooftop. However, once minarets became part of the architecture of mosques in Muslim societies, muezzins began to recite the call from them. In most Muslim majority countries, the call to prayer is broadcast live during the prayer times. The muezzin calls the believers to prayer with the following formula in Arabic: "God is greatest, God is greatest, God is greatest, God is greatest. I bear witness that there is no deity but God. I bear witness there is no deity but God. I bear witness that Muhammad is the Messenger of God. I bear witness that Muhammad is the Messenger of God. Hasten to prayer. Hasten to prayer. Hasten to success. Hasten to success. God is greatest, God is greatest. There is no deity but God." For the dawn prayer, the line "Prayer is better than sleep" is added. In the Shiite tradition, the adhan formula also includes the phrases "Come to the best of actions" and "Ali is the vicegerent [wali] of God."

A prominent element inside a mosque is the mihrab, a niche in the front wall marking the direction of prayer, which is toward the Kaaba in Mecca. Another feature is the pulpit (minbar), which is located to the right (when looking toward the pulpit) of the mihrab. This is where the leader of the congregation stands to deliver a sermon during Friday or holiday (eid) prayer. Mosque interiors are simple, with no seats or pews. Instead, a carpet or large mat is usually installed for sitting and prostration. Muslims take off their shoes when they enter the mosque. Given

23. Al-Naysaburi, Sahih Muslim, book 5, hadith 54.

that one of the postures of the prayer is prostration, the cleanliness of the carpet or mat is important.

Congregational Friday Prayer: Juma

An aspect of Islam that is similar to the Sunday service in the Christian tradition or the Sabbath service in the Jewish tradition is the Friday (Juma) prayer. The Qur'an enjoins the believers to take a break from their worldly affairs in order to participate in the Friday congregational prayer: "Believers! When you are called to the congregational prayer, hasten for the remembrance of God and leave off business—that is far better for you, if only you knew."[24]

However, unlike in the Christian and Jewish traditions, Friday is not a day of prescribed rest. The Qur'an allows the believers to continue their work after prayer: "Then when the prayer is completed, disperse in the land and seek the bounty of God. Remember God often so that you may succeed."[25] However, many modern Muslim nations including Egypt, Iraq, Qatar, Jordan, Saudi Arabia, and the United Arab Emirates still observe Fridays as part of their weekend.

While Muslim men are required to observe Friday prayer, women are free to decide to attend Friday prayer or not. Many women opt out, since around the world, women often need to tend to their children or other important duties. Still, in many Muslim countries, women attend Friday prayers if they can. The prayer includes a sermon delivered by an imam, followed by two cycles of prayer. In addition to the Friday prayer, the funeral prayer and the holiday prayer are also offered communally. There are two major holidays in Islam. The first one is Eid al-Fitr, which is celebrated at the end of the month of Ramadan. The other one is Eid al-Adha, which marks the end of the annual hajj pilgrimage and commemorates the prophet Abraham's intention to sacrifice his beloved son.

Spiritual Dimensions of *Salat*

The ritual of five daily prayers is the most comprehensive form of worship in Islamic piety, and Muslims regard it as the index of all kinds of prayers. *Salat* involves

24. Qur'an 62:9.
25. Qur'an 62:10.

heart, tongue, and body. It also includes the other pillars of Islam: the profession of faith, fasting, alms, and pilgrimage. During *salat*, the believer repeatedly utters the *shahada*. Since it is not permissible to eat or drink during prayer, it is a form of fasting. As the body with all its special faculties is dedicated to God, *salat* is also a form of charity—surrendering and giving your body to God. During prayer, believers turn to the Kaaba along with millions of fellow Muslims. In this regard, it is an imaginary form of the pilgrimage.

Salat is a daily spiritual reorientation toward God. In a way, prayer responds to the qur'anic teachings of "I created humankind only that they might worship Me" and "Glorify God in the evening, in the morning—praise is due to Him in the heavens and the earth—in the late afternoon, and when the day begins to decline."[26] The times of the prayer are determined according to the astronomical positions of the sun in its daily movements. Accordingly, they vary from one place to another. In light of this, through the five daily prayers, Muslims around the world are praying twenty-four hours a day without cessation.

The beginning of each prayer time overlaps with major cosmic transformations, such as the change of day into night, thus mirroring divine power, grace, and blessings. By practicing ritual prayer, believers acknowledge these constant transformations in the universe as part of the divine work and offer glorification, thanks, and praise to the creator. The time of prayer also gives believers the opportunity to reflect on not only the manifestations of God in the universe but also the self. A daily cycle of the prayer is a reminder for people to reflect on the seasons in relation to their life span. The time of the morning prayer, between dawn and sunrise, reminds the believers of the early spring stage of life, beginning with conception in their mother's womb. The noon prayer, which begins when the sun reaches its zenith, is akin to midsummer and the prime of youth. The time of the afternoon prayer resembles the fall season and old age. The time of evening prayer, sunset, reminds believers of the departure of many creatures, including humans, from this world. It is the time when they can reflect on their own death and resurrection. The time of the night prayer resembles the winter season, when all beings are put to rest in a white shroud. This is the time when everything is shut down and humans are reminded of their accountability after death. The dawn prayer of the

26. Qur'an 51:56; 30:17–18.

next day is a new cycle, new life, and new resurrection. It reminds the believers of the hereafter.[27]

Salat is an invitation from God to be in his presence five times a day. Rumi (d. 1273) said that people who are full of love for God should always look forward to the time of prayer, as *salat* is a time of union with the divine. Rumi then said that believers should make clear their intention, glorify God, and stand still in prayer. During prayer, they should free themselves from all worldly affairs and the self. When it is time for prayer, people should rush to stand before God, as this is the way of salvation.[28] By accepting the invitation, the believers acknowledge the constant blessings they are receiving from God. They also recognize their weakness and shortcomings. Human needs are endless, and God's compassion and generosity are similarly infinite. By bowing down and prostrating themselves in deep humility during prayer, believers seek refuge in God and place their trust in him.[29]

During prayer, believers prostrate themselves before the divine with great love and admiration. The Prophet said that the believer is closest to God during prostration. With this fundamental act, believers acknowledge their lowliness compared to God's sovereignty over all things. Human beings are weak, while God is almighty. They are the sustained because God is the sustainer.

According to the Qur'an, *salat* protects the believers from evil conduct.[30] It mentions the deep sense of peace and tranquility that comes from being occupied with the remembrance of God.[31] In Islamic piety, *salat* is one of the most effective ways of remembering God, since it is enacted five times throughout the day. *Salat* can also have a positive impact on the mental well-being of Muslim believers. Particularly during trying times such as illness, *salat* becomes a source of strength.

Social Dimensions of *Salat*

I have had the opportunity to offer the five daily prayers in various places around the world including Turkey, Egypt, Estonia, Tanzania, Jordan, Syria, Germany, the

---

27. Nursi, *Words*, 51–52.
28. Ali Fahri Doğan, "Tasavvuf Ehlinin Namaz Hakkındaki Görüşleri ve İki Örnek," *Bingöl Üniversitesi İlahiyat Fakültesi Dergisi* 1 (2013): 69–95.
29. Nursi, *Words*, 52.
30. Qur'an 29:45.
31. Qur'an 13:28.

Netherlands, and the United States. Observing the five daily prayers in various contexts was not a strange experience for a traveling Muslim like me for two main reasons. First, the form and content of the prayer are mainly based on the Qur'an and the prophetic example, or Sunna. Second, the language of the prayer is Arabic. These aspects make *salat* a unifying force for Muslims around the world.

Even if they pray individually, knowing that millions of their fellow Muslims join them in prayer creates a sense of spiritual solidarity and deepens the bonds of faith. From the early years of Islam, one of the appealing aspects of its message was that everyone is equal before God: "The most noble of you in the sight of God is the most righteous of you."[32] Believers stand shoulder to shoulder, foot to foot, on the same line to glorify, praise, and thank God in prayer regardless of their rank, status, and race.

Even sharing grief and happiness is centered on *salat*. The funeral prayer is usually offered following one of the daily prayers at a mosque. Weddings also can take place in the mosque after the observance of the prayer. Daily prayers at the mosque are occasions for believers to socialize and exchange news.

Salat in the United States

Salat in the United States dates back to colonial and antebellum times. Many slaves brought to the New World belonged to the religion of Islam. Omar bin Said, for example, a Muslim from Senegal, was captured and enslaved in the early 1800s and brought to South Carolina to be sold. Like many other Muslim slaves, Omar was an observant Muslim in his home country. In his memoir, he noted, "Before I came to the Christian country—my religion was the religion of Mohammed, the Apostle of God—may God have mercy upon him and give him peace. I walked to the mosque before daybreak, washed my face and head and hands and feet. I prayed at noon, prayed in the afternoon, prayed at sunset, prayed in the evening."[33] Like Omar bin Said, many of the Muslim slaves in the nascent and still-expanding United States continued to practice the five daily prayers whenever they had a chance. In his

32. Qur'an 49:13.
33. Omar bin Said, "*Oh Ye Americans*": *The Autobiography of Omar ibn Said, an Enslaved Muslim in the United States*, 1831. National Humanities Center Resource Toolbox, The Making of African American Identity, vol. 1, 1500–1865, 2007, http://nationalhumanitiescenter.org/pds/maai/community/text3/religionomaribnsaid.pdf.

memoir, Job Ben Solomon—an Islamic scholar who was brought to Kent Island, Maryland, in the 1730s as a slave—remarked that he would regularly withdraw into the woods for his daily prayer.[34]

Considering that Muslims in the United States are a minority, their experience of *salat* is distinct. In this sense, the most important aspect of practicing *salat* in the United States is finding an appropriate place for washing rituals and prayer. Many Muslims have to find a space at their workplace, since their work hours overlap with the times of *salat*. The practice of *salat* creates a different dynamic in public spaces. Being performed five times a day makes *salat* a more visible practice compared to the rituals of other US religious traditions.

In addition, Muslims must do washing rituals (*wudu*) before the *salat*. Washing the feet is part of the ritual and may require a designated space. Consider a Muslim making an ablution in a regular public bathroom. This may even require putting the feet into the sink to meet one of the requirements of the ablution. This creates a bizarre scene for those unfamiliar with this ritual. In addition, it may not be comfortable for Muslims, especially older ones, as the sinks are too high to make an ablution. This is why there is a special place designated for ablution in Muslim countries and many international airports.[35]

Because they are still religious minorities in the United States, many Muslims practice their *salat* in interfaith prayer spaces such as chapels in airports, in hospitals, and on university campuses. These interfaith setups give Muslims the opportunity to acquaint themselves with people of other faiths and their practices. Perhaps because of not having enough space, many places of worship, such as churches and synagogues in the United States, host Muslim communities so they can observe their weekly congregational Friday prayer. The All Dulles Area Muslim Society (ADAMS) Center, one of the largest Muslim congregations in the United States, for example, uses space in churches and synagogues in the Washington, DC,

34. Job Ben Soloman, "A Slave about Two Years in Maryland": Some Memoirs of the Life of Job, the Son of Solomon, the High Priest of Boonda in Africa . . . Compiled by Thomas Bluett, 1734, Excerpts. National Humanities Center Resource Toolbox, Becoming American: The British Atlantic Colonies, 1690-1763, 2009, http://nationalhumanitiescenter.org/pds/becomingamer/growth/text5/diallo.pdf.
35. A good example is the modern *wudu* place at the Frankfurt Airport. Among the universities that installed ablution places in the United States are George Mason University, George Washington University, Miami University, University of Michigan–Dearborn, Elon University, and Eastern Michigan University. Among the airports, one can mention San Francisco International Airport, Orlando International Airport, and Kansas City International Airport.

area for prayer services. Muslim communities who cannot afford to have their own space are often welcomed at churches and synagogues for their prayers and events.[36] The Immanuel Church on the Hill, an Episcopal church in Alexandria, Virginia, has been hosting a primarily Pakistani Muslim community for more than a decade. This community performs their Friday prayer at the community hall of the church every week as well as their *tarawih* prayer every day during the month of Ramadan. Similarly, Fairlington Methodist Church in Arlington, Virginia, has been hosting the Muslim community for Friday prayer in their fellowship hall for more than thirty years. When the ADAMS Center was looking for a larger venue to offer the Friday prayer for its members, the Northern Virginia Hebrew Congregation opened its doors to the Muslim community. The US capitol has been hosting Friday prayer for many years. Also, fire departments in Virginia have been accommodating the Muslim community with space to offer their weekly Friday prayer for a number of years.

While Muslims enjoy great freedom and support in the United States, they have also experienced challenges. In some cases, the community has faced objections to requests for zoning permits needed to build a mosque. In these situations, some of the cases have been taken to the courts. Bernards Township in New Jersey is a good illustration. In 2015, following thirty-nine public hearings over four years, the planning board of the town denied the Muslim community's application to build a mosque. In response, the community filed a lawsuit against the town and eventually won the case in 2017. To settle the suit, the town's administration agreed to pay the Muslim organization $3.25 million and give permission to the community to build a mosque at its original proposed location. As part of the settlement, the officials of Bernards Township agreed to train all members of its planning board and township committee in diversity and inclusion, with an emphasis on Islam and Muslims.[37]

Another interesting case of practicing *salat* in the United States occurred at Duke University. In 2015, the university announced that on Fridays, right before Muslim congregational prayer time, the community could have an amplified call to

36. The Immanuel Church on the Hill in Alexandria, Virginia, has been hosting a primarily Pakistani Muslim community for more than a decade now. This community establishes its Friday prayers at the church's hall every week and their *tarawih* prayers every day during Ramadan.
37. See Mike Deak, "N.J. Officials to Pay $3.5M to Settle Mosque Lawsuit," *USA Today*, May 31, 2017, https://www.usatoday.com/story/news/politics/2017/05/31/mosque-lawsuit-settlement/357349001/.

prayer (*adhan*) from the bell tower of the university's chapel. The decision sparked major controversy at the university and nationwide. While those who supported the gesture regarded it as an expression of religious freedom and pluralism in the United States, others saw it as a promotion of sharia in the disguise of religious pluralism. The university quickly reversed its decision.[38]

In other places, Muslims and their supporters have faced criticism for setting aside places for washing rituals. At Minneapolis Community and Technical College, for example, the college's Muslim students were doing their *wudu* in a regular bathroom. When one of the students slipped and hurt herself during the ritual, the college's administration decided to build a more appropriate space for them. Some members of the college community, however, opposed the decision, arguing that the school was favoring a particular religious group, which was unconstitutional. After a legal briefing, the college's board concluded that installing the washing baths would not violate the constitution.[39]

38. For more details about the story, see Sari Horwitz, Susan Svrluga, and Pamela Constable, "Muslim Call to Prayer Sounds at Duke University, but Not from Chapel Tower," *Washington Post*, January 16, 2015, https://tinyurl.com/4ap87bmk.
39. See Tamar Lewin, "Some U.S. Universities Install Foot Baths for Muslim Students," *New York Times*, August 7, 2007, https://www.nytimes.com/2007/08/07/world/americas/07iht-muslims.4.7022566.html.

14 Almsgiving

Zakat

Taalibah Hassan is an African American Muslim who currently serves as vice president of the Muslim Association of Virginia. A biology teacher by profession, she has been an active member of this mosque community since the 1990s. In 2008, Taalibah hosted a refugee family from Iraq in her home. Seeking ways of raising money to support the family, she realized that her mosque community needed to be more organized for charity work. Taalibah, along with some other board members of the mosque, formed an alms (*zakat*) committee to distribute donations to those who are in need. Before this initiative, if anyone in the community needed financial support, the members simply took up a collection for that person after one of the communal prayers. The committee now has an application form. Once the application is approved, the person is qualified to receive *zakat* funds.

Muslims who are unable to pay their rent or utilities or to arrange a funeral for a family member may apply for these funds if they are unemployed or simply have a low income. As is the case in many mosques in the United States, Taalibah's community has a donation kiosk divided into three sections: general, *zakat*, and special donations. Donations received in the form of *zakat* are distributed to the poor throughout the year. In addition, the committee has a support plan during the two major Islamic holidays to make sure that those in need have enough funds to celebrate these special occasions with their loved ones, including the offering of traditional gifts. Her mosque also has a food bank and is part of a food aid program.[1]

Charitable giving to those in need is among the most important aspects of all world religions. Islam is no exception. Its third pillar is *zakat*, which Muslims regard as a form of worship. *Zakat* literally means "to purify." While there are many other forms of charity, *zakat* is an obligation for all Muslims who are financially able. Muslims understand financial ability to be having personal or family wealth above the minimum standard, known as *nisaab*.[2] In other words, Muslims are required to

---

1. This section is based on Taalibah Hassan, telephone interview with the author, February 15, 2020.
2. Qur'an 2:219.

pay *zakat* if their net assets exceed the *nisaab* threshold once the cost of basic living expenses and debt are deducted. Two and a half percent of anything accumulated above the *nisaab* amount is given to the needy as *zakat*. The amount constituting *nisaab* in the United States for 2019, for example, was calculated as being $3,849. *Zakat* is paid on the earned income of a full lunar year.

The Qur'an explains that "alms are meant only for the poor and the needy, for those who collect them, for those whose hearts are to be reconciled, for the cause of God, for travelers in need, and for those in bondage and in debt."[3] Priority is given to people who live nearby. *Zakat* is not given to one's parents, grandparents, children, grandchildren, or spouse. Muslims are simply obligated to take care of the members of their own immediate families.

In addition to the alms required for *zakat*, Islam encompasses other concepts that are related to charity. For example, *infaq* (literally, "spending") is a type of charity given without the expectation of reward or benefit. The Qur'an establishes some principles for this form of pious giving: People should not give to show off. While it is fine to make a public donation, it is better to make it in private.[4] Additionally, people should not "follow up after their gifts with reminders of their generosity or hurtful words."[5] As the Qur'an explains, "A kind word and forgiveness is better than a charity followed by hurtful words."[6]

Another concept related to charity is *sadaqa*, which has various forms. One is continuing charity (*sadaqah jariyah*). In one of the hadiths, the Prophet said that with death, there are only three ways for a person to receive a spiritual reward: through a charity that continues to give (e.g., building a school, mosque, fountain, or bridge), through a legacy of knowledge that is beneficial to people (e.g., establishing a scholarship or foundation), or through giving the world a righteous child.[7] In other words, *sadaqah jariyah* is building or contributing to something that benefits people in an ongoing way. The charity for breaking the fast (*sadaqah al-fitr*) is another form of offering, which is a required donation given to the poor before the celebration at the end of Ramadan. The head of the family pays this charity on behalf of each member of the family. The amount for each family member in 2019, for example, was ten dollars.

---

3. Qur'an 9:60.
4. Qur'an 2:271.
5. Qur'an 2:262.
6. Qur'an 2:263.
7. Al-Nawawi, "Forty Hadith."

The expectation to perform *sadaqa* is not limited to the wealthy. In one of the hadiths, the Prophet said that every Muslim should give *sadaqa*. His companions asked what should happen if one was not financially able to give to charity. The Prophet then said that if one worked, that was a form of charity. Because work could be beneficial to others, one's own work might be an opportunity to give *sadaqa*. The companions then asked what should happen if one was unable to work. The Prophet replied that one could still help those who were in need. They responded by asking what to do if this were not possible. The Prophet then said that just avoiding bad deeds was a form of *sadaqa*.[8] In another hadith, the Prophet said that making peace between two people is charity, helping someone ride their animal is charity, saying nice words is charity, taking the steps made to go to the communal prayers is charity, and removing things in people's way is charity.[9] Feeding your family is charity, having sexual intercourse with your spouse is charity, showing the way to someone who is lost is charity, assisting a disabled person is charity, planting a tree is charity, and so on. Indeed, simply smiling is charity.[10]

Theological and Social Dimensions of *Zakat* and Charity

Perhaps the most important theological dimension of *zakat* and charity in Islam is that believers give from what God provides them.[11] God created humans, their faculties, and their senses. The body is considered to be held in trust for God. In this regard, it is God who gives. The Qur'an refers to those who are unwilling to give to charity and accept God as the provider: "Among them are those who made a covenant with God, saying, 'If God gives us some of His bounty, we shall give charity and be among righteous'; yet when He did give them some of His bounty, they hoarded it and turned away disobediently. Because they broke their covenant with God, because they lied, He requited them with hypocrisy in their hearts until the Day they met Him."[12] Qarun (Korah), a biblical figure whom the Qur'an also

---

8. Al-Naysaburi, *Sahih Muslim*, book 12, hadith 70.
9. Al-Naysaburi, book 12, hadith 72.
10. Al-Tirmidhi, *Jami' al-Tirmidhi*, book 27, hadith 62; al-Sijistani, *Sunan Abu Dawud*, book 5, hadith 36.
11. Qur'an 2:4.
12. Qur'an 9:75–77.

mentions, represents this mindset. According to tradition, when he was asked not to be arrogant because of what he had, Qarun's answer was that he had earned what he had because of his knowledge.[13]

Islamic tradition urges believers to work as much as they can. In one of the hadiths, the Prophet remarked, "I seek refuge in God from poverty."[14] In another one, he asked his followers to earn by working with their hands instead of receiving help from others.[15] Muslims accept that despite hard work and for reasons often out of their control, many people still cannot achieve a decent living. For this reason, the wealthy are invited to support the needy. While believers are strongly encouraged to work hard for themselves and their families, the challenges of poverty might be seen as an opportunity for the wealthy to help the poor and be in solidarity with them.

The Qur'an often indicates that affluence is a great test for believers, as the wealthy are often attached to their property. Their wealth might come at the expense of their relationship with God. They may forget that this world is impermanent. Zakat is, in a way, accepting and acknowledging that all they are given is from God. It may also loosen their attachment to their physical possessions.

By giving zakat and sadaqa, believers purify their assets.[16] In one of the hadiths, the Prophet said that the zakat of the body is fasting, and the zakat of wealth is giving to the needy. Just as fasting purifies one's body, zakat purifies one's wealth.[17] Charity also provides purification for believers from "the defilement of sin and disobedience to God."[18] It is a form of thankfulness for what God has given.

The Qur'an repeatedly points out that those who give to charity for the cause of God will eventually benefit from it both in this world and in the hereafter. The Qur'an explains that "the likeness of those who spend their wealth in God's way is as the likeness of a grain which grows seven ears, in every ear a hundred grains. God multiplies for whom He wills. God is All-Embracing, All-Knowing."[19]

For those who do not give to charity from what has been given to them, the Qur'an warns of severe punishment: "Those who withhold what God has given them

13. Qur'an 28:78.
14. Ahmad bin Shu'ayb al-Nasa'i, *Sunan al-Nasa'i*, Sunnah.com, accessed February 2021, https://sunnah .com/nasai, book 50, hadith 34.
15. Al-Bukhari, *Sahih al-Bukhari*, book 34, hadith 25.
16. Qur'an 9:103.
17. Ibn Majah, *Sunan Ibn Majah*, book 7, hadith 1817; al-Bukhari, *Sahih al-Bukhari*, book 65, hadith 4661.
18. Caner K. Dagli, Commentary on *Surat al-Tawbah*, Nasr et al. Study Qur'an, 533.
19. Qur'an 2:261.

out of His grace should not think that it is better for them; on the contrary, it is worse for them. Whatever they greedily withhold will be hung around their necks on the Day of Judgment. The heritage of the heavens and the earth belongs to God. God is aware of what you do."[20] In another verse, the Qur'an states, "God does not like arrogant, boastful people, who are miserly and who order other people to be the same, concealing what God has given them from His Bounty. We [God] have prepared for the disbelievers a humiliating punishment. And for those who spend their wealth to show off, and who do not believe in Him or the Last Day. Whoever has Satan as his companion has an evil companion indeed!"[21] The verse concludes, "What harm would it have done them were they to believe in God and the Last Day, and spend part of what God has provided for them? God knows them well."[22]

Taking care of the needy is a major challenge in all modern societies. One of the most pressing questions is the role of the state in caring for the poor. Because Islamic theology accepts that even people who work hard may still be unable to earn a decent living, Muslims believe these people deserve the support of both the state and those who are better off than they are. Supporting a fellow human is a form of compassion and solidarity. Muslims understand that when some in society are in desperate economic need and there is no care for them, crime and chaos may result. A hand needs to be extended to these individuals and their families so that they can rise. In this sense, *zakat* might even be a means of bringing peace and security to a society. In a way, it is a peaceful bridge between the rich and the poor. Unfortunately, modern individualism can lead people to be indifferent at best and judgmental at worst to those who are in poverty. Many have this mentality: "Once I am full, what is to me if others die of hunger?"[23] The Islamic concept of charity helps offset this mindset.

The Tradition of *Waqf*

The institution that has embodied the practice of charity in Muslim societies for centuries is endowment (*waqf*). Mosques, seminaries, and Sufi lodges have

20. Qur'an 3:180.
21. Qur'an 4:36–38.
22. Qur'an 4:39.
23. Nursi, *Signs of Miraculousness*, 52.

been endowed by charities through *waqf*. In addition, *waqf* endowments support institutions—soup kitchens for the poor, hospitals, mental health facilities, and accommodations for travelers—that benefit the community.[24] For example, thousands of people can benefit from soup kitchens on a daily basis.[25]

While traveling from Cairo to Damascus in the fourteenth century, Ibn Batuta (d. 1377) listed among the services provided by the *waqfs* helping people make the pilgrimage, financially supporting girls of poor families who were about to get married, freeing captives, providing food and clothing for travelers, helping people return to their countries, building sidewalks, and cleaning streets.[26] Today, many charitable organizations continue to function as *waqf* in Muslim communities, including in the United States. Unfortunately, with colonialism and the rise of modern nation-states, the institution of *waqf* has lost much of its independence and impact.

Zakat in Muslim Countries

Because there is enormous potential to accommodate the needs of the poor through *zakat* and *sadaqa*, almost all Muslim-majority countries have state institutions collecting *zakat*, and some of them have laws on this form of charity. Countries like Saudi Arabia, Qatar, Kuwait, and Bahrain collect *zakat* instead of income tax from their Muslim citizens. Non-Muslims pay income tax instead.

Among Muslim countries that have been successful in collecting *zakat* through state agencies are Malaysia and Indonesia. In 2010, Malaysia collected $443 million in *zakat*, and Indonesia collected $166 million.[27] Even the United Nations High Commissioner for Refugees (UNHCR) is seeking ways to receive *zakat* from Muslims to support refugees. Today, more than fifty million refugees are scattered around the world, most from Muslim-majority countries. Naturally, the Muslim community can be a source of resources for those refugees. The UNHCR consulted with prominent

24. Gábor Ágoston and Bruce Masters, eds., *Encyclopedia of Ottoman Empire* (New York: Facts on File, 2009), 590.
25. Bahaeddin Yediyıldız, "Vakıf," in *İslam Ansiklopedisi* (Ankara: TDK, 2012), 42:481.
26. Yediyildiz, 480.
27. For more information, see "A Faith-Based Aid Revolution in the Muslim World?," *New Humanitarian*, June 1, 2012, https://www.thenewhumanitarian.org/report/95564/analysis-faith-based-aid-revolution-muslim-world; and Mervan Selcuk and Sakir Gormus, *Zekâtın Kurumsallaşmasının Seçilmiş İslam Ülkeleri Tecrübeleri Çerçevesinde Analizi* (Istanbul: ICPESS, 2016), https://www.pesa.org.tr/single-post/2016/12/23/icpess-2016-proceedings-bildiriler-kitab%C4%9B1.

Muslim scholars and organizations about *zakat* for refugees; most agreed that the UNHCR is eligible to collect and distribute *zakat*.[28]

Some Muslims have pointed to the mismanagement of *zakat* and *sadaqa* funds. Islamic finance experts point to the potential for using charitable donations from Muslims as a means of dealing with poverty. Unfortunately, the reality is that as Muslim wealth increases, so does poverty. It should be otherwise. Because of financial mismanagement, however, *sadaqa* and *zakat* funds are sometimes not as effective as they should be.[29]

Zakat and Charity in the United States

Many charitable Muslim organizations and mosques seek to collect and distribute US Muslims' *zakat* and *sadaqa*. Usually, the websites of these organizations have guidelines about how to calculate your annual *zakat*. Charitable donations are a bridge to those who are in need. The Zakat Foundation of America, for example, provides hot meals to underserved communities during Ramadan, allocates fresh meat to needy families during the holidays, distributes food packages and other necessities to communities in need of support year-round, supplies backpacks filled with educational tools to families in need at the start of the school year, shields the most vulnerable in the society from the cold through winter kit distributions, supports refugees, and offers wellness services and workshops to community members. The foundation also sponsors international programs funded by *zakat* from Muslims. Among the services these programs offer are sending essential water and food to the less fortunate, especially during the month of Ramadan; repairing damaged infrastructure; providing temporary shelter in the form of tents; and supporting a child with food, clothing, education, and health care. In addition, the organization has *sadaqah jariyah* programs such as constructing water wells in Africa and building schools or mosques.[30]

Muslims in the United States have been seeking nontraditional ways of channeling *zakat* funds. A case in point is the Believers Bail Out (BBO) project. Initiated

28. For the fatwas, see Musa Furber, UNHCR *Zakat Collection and Distribution*, Tabah Report no. 1, May 2017, https://unhcrzakatfatwa.com/.
29. "Faith-Based Aid Revolution?"
30. See the Zakat Foundation of America, accessed May 17, 2020, https://www.zakat.org/en/what -we-do/.

by a number of Muslim scholars and activists in 2018, the project aims to bail out Muslims who are in pretrial detention or US Immigration and Customs Enforcement (ICE) custody.[31] Over two million people are incarcerated in US prisons. One-fourth are being held in pretrial detention. They are behind bars without being convicted of any crime. The overwhelming majority of these prisoners are people of color, including Muslims, who cannot afford bail. According to a study from 2019, the median bail amount for felonies in the United States is around $10,000.[32] The BBO asks Muslims to support the project through their *zakat*, as the Qur'an points out that in addition to providing assistance to the poor and the needy, the *zakat* fund can be used to free those who are held captive.[33] In its first two years, the organization raised $250,000 in *zakat* and *sadaqa* funds and was able to bail out more than twenty Muslims.[34]

31. For more information about the project, see the BBO's website, accessed April 18, 2020, https://believersbailout.org.
32. Wendy Sawyer and Peter Wagner, *Mass Incarceration: The Whole Pie 2019*, Prison Policy Initiative, March 19, 2019, https://www.prisonpolicy.org/reports/pie2019.html.
33. The project's website makes a reference to Qur'an 9:60.
34. See more at https://believersbailout.org/.

15 Ramadan Fasting

Susan Douglass is a US Muslim who grew up in Cleveland, Ohio. She earned a PhD in world history from George Mason University and currently serves as an education outreach coordinator at the Center for Contemporary Arab Studies of Georgetown University. Susan has been fasting during the month of Ramadan since 1974. For her, Ramadan is the most intimate spiritual practice after the five daily prayers. The other pillars of Islam are performed in public, but fasting is between oneself and the creator. If we make a mistake and eat or sip water, and catch ourselves, Douglass points out, it is immediately apparent that we are aware of the divine presence as the observer of our deed. Concerning her experience of fasting in the United States, Susan mentions that generally, Americans are aware of what Ramadan fasting is; however, many still think that it is unimaginable to neither eat nor drink anything during the day.

Susan finds it challenging to maintain the predawn meal (*suhoor*) and prayers and then wait until well into the evening while working a full-time schedule. But even so, after a few days, she finds that it gets easier. For her, attending meals to break the fast (*iftars*) with friends, family, and community is the best way to pass the month, trying to avoid the petty errors of daily life and ending the month with the entire community gathered together. One of her favorite events with family during the month of Ramadan in Washington, DC, was the communal iftar gathering held on the National Mall between the Washington Monument and the Capitol Building.

Fasting is an ancient practice that not only Muslims but also the adherents of many religions—including Hindus, Buddhists, Jews, and Christians—have and continue to follow. We read in the book of Exodus that Moses fasted for forty days and forty nights on the mountain, abstaining from both food and water.[1] After this fast, he received the Ten Commandments from God.[2] During Yom Kippur (Day of Atonement), many Jews fast for almost twenty-five hours. For them, it is a time

---

1. Exodus 34:28. Scriptures taken from the Holy Bible, New International Version®, NIV®. Copyright © 1973, 1978, 1984, 2011 by Biblica, Inc.™ Used by permission of Zondervan. All rights reserved worldwide. www.zondervan.com The "NIV" and "New International Version" are trademarks registered in the United States Patent and Trademark Office by Biblica, Inc.™
2. Deuteronomy 9:9.

of repentance and spiritual reflection. Jesus also fasted for forty days and forty nights while in the desert before his temptation by the devil.[3] Christians believe this spiritual experience made him resilient against the devil. During the Lenten season, in commemoration of Jesus's fasting, Christians abstain from eating certain foods, especially meat.

Fasting is also a key component of Islamic spirituality. While there are various practices of recommended fasting in the Islamic calendar, fasting during the month of Ramadan is required for Muslims, and it is one of the five basic pillars of Islam.[4] The fast of Ramadan is the most frequently observed ritual among Muslims. It is also the most private compared to other Islamic practices. The first pillar, the *shahada*, is usually recited publicly. Similarly, the five daily prayers, pilgrimage to the Kaaba, and alms are outward, visible rituals. Some might perform these rituals insincerely or in order to show off; however, fasting is only known to God and the believer. Muslims understand fasting to be a special form of worship. According to one of the hadith traditions, God said, "Fasting is for me, and I will reward it."[5]

The fast of Ramadan became required for the Muslim community in the second year of the Prophet Muhammad's immigration from Mecca to Medina, in 622 CE. During this period, Muhammad received the revelation in which the reasoning for fasting was outlined: "O you who believe, fasting is prescribed for you, as it was prescribed for those before you, so that you may become righteous."[6] The first part of the verse reminds believers that fasting has been part of other revealed traditions before Islam. The second explains the reason for the fasting—to be mindful of God or to increase one's God-consciousness.

Muslims fast during the month of Ramadan, the ninth month of the Islamic lunar calendar. Unlike the solar calendar, the lunar calendar is based on the moon's cycles. Because one lunar cycle takes a little more than 29 days, the months of a lunar calendar alternate between 29 and 30 days. Twelve lunar cycles is about 354 days. It falls, therefore, behind the Gregorian calendar about 11 days each year. Because of the lack of added or catch-up days as in the Gregorian calendar, the months of the lunar calendar cycle through all the seasons of the Gregorian calendar and

---

3. Matthew 4:2; Luke 4:2.
4. Al-Naysaburi, *Sahih Muslim*, book 1, hadith 21.
5. Al-Bukhari, *Sahih al-Bukhari*, book 97, hadith 193.
6. Qur'an 2:183.

complete one cycle every thirty-three years. The month of Ramadan in the lunar calendar, therefore, cycles through the entire year. Because of this, Muslims will fast during all four seasons over the course of thirty-three years. During the summer months, the daily fasting period can be long. In 2018, for example, Ramadan began in mid-May and ended around mid-June. Depending on the exact location, the fasting hours ranged from sixteen to nineteen hours in Canada and the United States. While in Iceland the daily fasting period was around twenty hours, for Muslims in Argentina it was around ten hours. In addition, fasting can be challenging in countries like Morocco and the United Arab Emirates, as the temperature can rise to over one hundred degrees Fahrenheit in the summer.

As the month in which the Qur'an was revealed to the Prophet Muhammad, Ramadan is also the holiest month of the year in the Islamic calendar.[7] It is also the only month that the Qur'an mentions by name.[8] The Qur'an notes that this month includes the most sacred night of the year, the Night of Power (Laylat al-Qadr).[9] Muslims regard the month of Ramadan, and this night within it, as the most spiritually rewarding time of the year. Ramadan is an occasion to cultivate spirituality and seek forgiveness from God. Fasting in the month of Ramadan is a unifying element in Muslim societies, as its rules and etiquette are clearly defined by the Qur'an, the Sunna of the Prophet, and Muslim scholars.

The first day of fasting during Ramadan begins with the sighting of the new moon. In one of the hadiths, the Prophet Muhammad said, "When you catch sight of the new moon (of the month of Ramadan), begin to fast, and end your fasting when you see the new moon of (the month of Shawwal, or the tenth month in the Islamic calendar)."[10] Here, it is also important to note that determining the first day of Ramadan has been a contentious issue within Muslim societies because of disagreement concerning whether the moon is visible. This disagreement becomes a particularly divisive issue when some Muslims fast while others celebrate the end of fasting, known as Eid al-Fitr. In some Muslim societies, the sighting of the moon is calculated based on astronomical science, while in others, believers follow the hadith that says the moon should simply be sighted by reliable individuals.

7. Qur'an 2:185.
8. Qur'an 2:185.
9. Qur'an 97:3.
10. Al-Bukhari, *Sahih al-Bukhari*, book 30, hadith 10.

Although some Muslims in the United States follow the tradition of their country of origin regarding the first and last day of fasting, the majority follow their local mosque's or religious organization's decision.

The daily fasting period extends from dawn to sunset. During this time, Muslims abstain from food, drink, and sexual intercourse. The Ramadan fast is an obligation for every Muslim who is mentally fit, is physically healthy, and has reached puberty. The Qur'an, however, exempts those who are unable to fast due to health issues, travelers, and pregnant, lactating, or menstruating women.[11] One can either make up missed days after Ramadan or feed a hungry person as compensation.[12]

Muslim Life during Ramadan

Fasting in the month of Ramadan is a hallmark of Muslim societies. Anyone visiting a Muslim-majority country during this time will observe a real difference in daily life compared to other months of the year. Mosques draw bigger crowds, businesses have reduced working hours, and many stores and restaurants are closed during the day. The streets are quieter than usual. As one traveler observed in Egypt, "The feeling of being at the market of Khan el-Khalili (in Cairo) during *iftar* is indescribable. Hundreds begin eating at the same moment when hearing the call to prayer, followed by locals playing *oud* (a type of Middle Eastern guitar)."[13] Another visitor reported, "During Ramadan, Saudi life slows down and many people become nocturnal. School hours are reduced and work schedules change, usually either being reduced to about five or six hours per day, or having people sleep during the day or work through the night. Many people take time off work but few travel abroad, preferring to spend time with their families nearby."[14] Silke Irmscher, who lived in Indonesia for many years, shared the following concerning the holy month: "Ramadan in Indonesia is a special time. Its atmosphere often reminds me of the Advent season in Europe. . . . Why? Just like in Advent, I feel that people take more care for

---

11. See Qur'an 2:184.
12. Qur'an 2:184.
13. "What It's like to Travel during Ramadan in Turkey, Morocco and the Middle East," *Peregrine Adventures* (blog), May 24, 2017, https://www.peregrineadventures.com/blog/24/05/2017/ramadan-travel-guide/.
14. Miles Lawrence, "My Fasting Experiment: Ramadan in Saudi Arabia," Al Arabiya News, July 1, 2016, http://english.alarabiya.net/en/blog/2016/07/02/My-fasting-experiment-Ramadan-in-Saudi-Arabia.html.

each other and also for themselves. They practice in holding back anger, exercise patience and show empathy for those who are around. Families spend more time together and rushing through life in the name of business becomes secondary. Not to mention the religious music and the chains of lights at mosques or shopping centers that create the same cozy atmosphere as does a Christmas tree."[15]

Because of its impact on Muslim societies, Ramadan is also an important theme in Islamic literature. A great deal has been written about Ramadan etiquette. In the literature, Ramadan is usually personified, and Muslims always look forward to welcoming this divine guest. According to one poet, "God bestowed upon us Ramadan as a guest / We should welcome it [fasting] wholeheartedly / We should be a good host until it [Ramadan] is with us / What if the guest would be welcomed [fasted] warmly by the old and young?"[16] Islamic literature also contains examples of poems expressing sadness about the departure of Ramadan. One poet wrote, "O friends let's cry / As the month of fasting is departing again / Let's grieve for this sad moment / As the month of fasting is departing again."[17]

Muslims start their days during Ramadan with the predawn *suhoor*, a nutritious breakfast that prepares them for the daytime fast. The Prophet strongly encouraged all Muslims to rise for this meal, reportedly saying, "There is a lot of blessing in it."[18] Muslims then break their fast at sunset with dates or water followed by a meal called iftar. During iftar, the din in Muslim cities quiets, and the streets empty. In most cases, iftar meals are communal, as the Prophet Muhammad encouraged. According to one tradition, he said, "Whoever shares an iftar meal with a fasting fellow Muslim, this person will get the spiritual reward of the fast of two people. Nothing will be reduced from the spiritual reward of the person receiving the meal."[19] In another tradition, the Prophet said, "Share your iftar meal with those who fast. Share your food with good people so that the angels can be with you."[20]

During the month of Ramadan, Muslims offer a special prayer called *taraweeh* (literally, "rest and relaxation") in addition to the five daily prayers (*salat*) and communal

15. Silke Irmscher, "10 Facts about Ramadan in Indonesia," CulturEnery, June 9, 2016, https://www.culturenergy.com/11-facts-about-ramadan-indonesia/.
16. Halit Dursunoğlu, "Klasik Türk Edebiyatında Ramazan Konulu Şiirler," A.U. *Türkiyat Araştırmaları Enstitüsü Dergisi*, no. 22 (2003): 20–21.
17. Dursunoğlu, 18.
18. Al-Bukhari, *Sahih al-Bukhari*, book 30, hadith 32.
19. Al-Tirmidhi, *Jami' al-Tirmidhi*, book 8, hadith 126.
20. Diyanet İşleri Başkanlığı, *Hadislerle Islam* (Istanbul: Diyanet Yayınları, 2014), 2:423.

Friday prayer. After iftar during Ramadan, Muslims often do their night prayer (isha) and the taraweeh at a mosque. Typically lasting around one hour, the taraweeh usually consists of twenty cycles of standing, bowing, prostrating, and sitting. The movements include recitations of the Qur'an as well as special supplications and invocations. In many mosques, including those in the United States, the imam will recite one-thirtieth of the Qur'an during each each taraweeh prayer. In this way, the entire Qur'an will be recited by the end of the month. In some places, during summer when sunset comes late, the taraweeh may end around midnight. In this regard, fasting significantly shapes Muslims' schedules throughout the month. Considering that many Muslims go to bed after midnight because of the taraweeh prayer and get up almost an hour before dawn, it should come as no surprise that working hours are reduced in many Muslim-majority countries and that many Muslims use their vacation leave during Ramadan in places like the United States and Canada.

Many Muslims observe the last ten days of Ramadan as a spiritual retreat known as itikaf. The Qur'an references this practice, and it is part of the Sunna of the Prophet Muhammad.[21] During this third period of Ramadan, the Prophet himself would withdraw to the solitude of his mosque (masjid al-nabawi) in Medina and dedicate his time to worship and prayer.[22] Following this prophetic example, many Muslims participate in quiet retreats in a mosque during the last ten days of Ramadan. During this same time, Muslims perform a required act of charity known as sadaqa al-fitr to help the less fortunate prepare for Eid al-Fitr, which celebrates the end of Ramadan.

Spiritual and Social Dimensions of Ramadan Fasting

Many sources report on how the Prophet Muhammad observed the month of Ramadan. He would break his fast by eating an uneven number of dates. If he had no dates, he would break it with water. The Prophet spent a sizable portion of his Ramadan days in worship and prayer. We are also told that Prophet Muhammad was generous during the month of Ramadan, giving charity and support to the needy.[23] The Prophet also recited the Qur'an during the night, at which time

---

21. Qur'an 2:187.
22. Al-Bukhari, Sahih al-Bukhari, book 33, hadith 1.
23. Diyanet İşleri Başkanlığı, Hadislerle Islam, 2:446.

the archangel Gabriel would come to him and listen. Their way of reciting the Qur'an to each other is known as *muqabala*, a tradition that is widely practiced among contemporary Muslims as they recite the Qur'an to each other communally during the month.[24] By following the example of the Prophet Muhammad, Muslims seek to use Ramadan fasting to rejuvenate their relationship with God, to reconnect to their personal spiritual life, and to reemphasize their social connections and charitable obligations.

Fasting to Be Mindful of God

During Ramadan, Muslims aim to renew their relationship with the Creator. While believers constantly receive blessings from God, they sometimes forget the true source of these blessings because of the distractions of their busy lives. Often people claim ownership of what they have, whereas in reality, everything they possess is owned and given by God alone. Fasting makes believers ever mindful of all the blessings and bounties bestowed upon them. Before breaking the fast, Muslims gather around the dinner table. They do not touch the food in front of them until the call to the prayer (*adhan*) is heard. Each individual Muslim, along with millions of fellow believers, acknowledges that all the blessings, including food, are from God and belong to him. Fasting thus is a collective way of being thankful and grateful to God.[25]

Beyond making the believer mindful of their dependence on God, abstaining from food is a way of drawing closer to God. In Islamic theology, God is the One Who Provides (al-Razzaq). What he provides, nevertheless, comes through many hands. An apple passes through the hands of the farmer and the grocer on its way to the dinner table, but the real source of this blessing is al-Razzaq. And while people pay a price for what the farmer and grocer provide, they also make a "payment" to God. The form this payment takes is ultimately the gratitude that the Qur'an calls a mark of true faith (*iman*). Thankfulness toward God, expressed through sincere worship, should come naturally to a person. In other words, the only human and ethical response to receiving infinite bounties is gratitude. Fasting is an acknowledgment of God's blessings and a means to appreciate and understand the value of

24. Diyanet İşleri Başkanlığı, 2:396.
25. Nursi, *Letters*, 566.

what one receives.[26] A wealthy person whose stomach is always full is less likely to be aware of the value of a piece of dry bread. During Ramadan, however, God asks everyone to fast regardless of their wealth and rank so that they might appreciate God's blessings and be grateful for them.[27] When it is time to break the fast, a believer realizes that even a piece of dry bread is a divine bounty.[28] This existential gratitude liberates the believer from the constant desire to accumulate unnecessary goods. Individuals realize that they do not need much in order to live their lives. The fast of Ramadan teaches people to free themselves from consumerist thinking and to attain true liberation.

Fasting as a Means of Spiritual Discipline

Fasting helps the believer focus on the spiritual dimension of their personal life. It is a way to train oneself to more easily connect to the spiritual world. Perhaps this is one reason that so many religious traditions use fasting as a means to cultivate spirituality. Gandhi said, "Fasting is part of my being. I can as well do without my eyes, for instance, as I can without fasting. What the eyes are for the outer world, fasting is for the inner. . . . A genuine fast cleanses the body, mind and soul. It crucifies the flesh and to that extent sets the soul free."[29] In a similar vein, Rumi explained, "There's a hidden sweetness in the stomach's emptiness. We are lutes, no more, no less. If the sound box is stuffed full of anything, no music. If the brain and the belly are burning clean with fasting, every moment a new song comes out of the fire. The fog clears, and a new energy makes you run up the steps in front of you."[30] In another instance, Rumi said that "fasting blinds the body in order to open the eyes of your soul."[31]

In their normal states of constant activity, individuals may think of themselves as powerful and independent—a self-deception that can lead people to forget about their creator. With fasting, believers can reflect on their weakness and utter

26. Nursi, 458.
27. Nursi, 567.
28. Nursi, 458.
29. Mahatma Gandhi, "My Fasts," Mkgandhi.org, accessed May 17, 2020, https://www.mkgandhi.org/momgandhi/chap06.htm.
30. Quoted in William C. Chittick, *The Sufi Path of Love: The Spiritual Teachings of Rumi* (Albany: State University of New York Press, 1984), 157.
31. Quoted in Nevit O. Ergin and Will Johnson, *The Forbidden Rumi* (Rochester, VT: Inner Traditions, 2006), 79.

dependence on God. In fact, fasting is one of the most effective ways of disciplining the self. This becomes especially evident in one of the hadiths, in which God asked the ego (*nafs*), "Who are you and who am I?" The ego answered, "I am myself and you are yourself." God then punished the ego and threw it into the fire. But the ego still did not give up its selfishness and arrogance. God asked the same question again and received the same reply. So God continued to punish the ego. God then punished it with hunger and asked the same question. This time the ego replied, "You are my Compassionate Sustainer and I am your impotent servant."[32]

Fasting during Ramadan is not only about abstaining from food, drink, and intimate relations. The Prophet Muhammad said, "How many of those who fast get nothing from it but hunger and thirst!" The renowned theologian al-Ghazali identified three degrees of fasting. First is ordinary fasting, during which believers abstain from food, drink, and sexual satisfaction. Second is fasting with other faculties of the body (ears, eyes, tongue, hands, and feet, along with other senses). In this category, for example, fasting of the eyes means refraining from looking at anything that is bad or disapproved of. A fasting tongue means refraining from lying, backbiting, and abusive talk—the tongue should be busy remembering God and reciting the Qur'an—and fasting ears are closed to reprehensible talk. The Prophet said, "The backbiter and the listeners are together in sin."[33] Believers avoid overeating, do what is pleasing to God, and remain between fear and hope in their relationship to their creator. The third and highest level of fasting is the fasting of the heart from bad thoughts, worldly concerns, and anything that makes a believer unmindful of God.

The Qur'an was revealed to Muhammad during the month of Ramadan, and it is therefore during this time that Muslims engage the most with the divine words.[34] Fasting prepares Muslims to connect with divine words in the appropriate spiritual state. It is a fresh engagement. Muslims reactivate their relationship with the Qur'an as if it had just been revealed. During this month, Muslims recite the Qur'an individually and communally. The usual goal is to recite the entire Qur'an in the course of the month. Ramadan is also a busy time for those who know the entire Qur'an by heart (*huffaz*). Many mosques seek to hire a *hafiz* with a beautiful voice during

32. Quoted in Nursi, *Letters*, 473.
33. Al-Ghazali, *Ihyā' 'Ulūm al-Dīn*, 1:389.
34. Qur'an 2:185.

this month. In the United States, Canada, and European countries, if a mosque does not have a good reciter (*qari*), it may import one from a country like Egypt, Morocco, Turkey, or Saudi Arabia for the month of Ramadan. These *qaris* recite the Qur'an for the community after the daily prayers as well as during the communal prayers of *taraweeh*.

The month of Ramadan and the recitation of the Qur'an also have a significant impact on the use of certain internet applications. According to a survey conducted in Indonesia, Malaysia, and Singapore in 2016, the activity level of Qur'an and prayer-related apps increased significantly during the season of the fast. The same research also concluded that "entertainment apps, including music and audio, video, social, and communications, were all impacted to greater or lesser degrees, either experiencing negative growth or slowed growth trends" during the month in these countries.[35]

Ramadan is also the month during which rewards for virtuous deeds increase a thousandfold. The Qur'an refers to the Night of Power as "better than a thousand months."[36] In order to make the most of this spiritual opportunity, Muslims pray, fast, and engage with the Qur'an as much as they can.

While the main purpose of fasting is to be mindful of and thankful for God, it is also an opportunity for Muslims to exercise dietary discipline. People have various addictions, including smoking, coffee, and overeating. During Ramadan, people may fast up to sixteen hours a day. If they do not get up for the *suhoor* meal before dawn, their daily fasting is twenty-four hours. This discipline gives them the strength and courage to control their diet and live in a healthier way.

The Social Dimension of Ramadan

Ramadan is a time of community, solidarity, and charity. Muslims must make a charitable contribution known as *zakat al-fitr* during this month. The Prophet Muhammad even encouraged his followers to give their annual *zakat* at this time.[37]

---

35. For the study, see Rosa Rong, *Ramadan Report: A Survey of Mobile Internet User Behavior in Indonesia, Malaysia, and Singapore*, Cheetah Global Lab, IAB Southeast Asia and India, accessed April 18, 2020, http://iabseaindia.com/wp-content/uploads/2017/03/CheetahMobile_Ramadan _Report.pdf.
36. Qur'an 97:3.
37. Qur'an 2:185.

Fasting creates awareness among the rich to be mindful of and generous toward the poor. Everyone is encouraged to help their fellow humans during the month. It should come as no surprise that most mosques or Muslim organizations do their major fundraising during Ramadan. They know that the community is the most generous during these sacred days.

Ramadan in the United States

Ramadan is becoming a widespread part of US culture. According to a survey from 2017, 80 percent of US Muslims fast during this month.[38] It is highly likely that this practice began with Muslim slaves who were brought to the United States. Considering that about one-third of these slaves were adherents of Islam, they likely would have fasted given the opportunity. Perhaps not commonly known, the White House and the Department of State have hosted iftar dinners for the Muslim community since Thomas Jefferson was in office. In 1805, part of the month of Ramadan overlapped with the month of December. During one of those days, Jefferson received Sidi Soliman Mellimelli, a Tunisian envoy, at the White House. They were scheduled to have dinner an hour before the time of breaking the fast. After learning that his Muslim guest was fasting, Jefferson postponed the dinner until sunset. With this gesture, Jefferson not only accommodated the religious needs of his guest but made history by hosting the first iftar dinner at the White House.[39]

The month of fasting has also been at the center of interfaith engagement in the United States. Many mosques, synagogues, and churches host iftar dinners for people of all faiths during Ramadan. Muslims host their neighbors, Muslim and non-Muslim alike, for iftar dinner. If the month of Ramadan overlaps with the academic year, many colleges and universities host iftar dinners throughout the month to make their Muslim students feel at home.

On the day of *eid*, Muslims gather for a communal prayer known as *salat al-eid*. Because the Eid al-Fitr holiday draws a crowd, Muslims usually rent hotel ballrooms, stadiums, or school auditoriums for their *eid* prayers. For several years now, New

38. "Eight-in-Ten U.S. Muslims Say They Fast during Ramadan," Pew Research Center, July 24, 2017, https://tinyurl.com/52jm6esh.
39. Gaye Wilson, "Dealings with Mellimelli, Colorful Envoy from Tunis," *Monticello Newsletter* 14 (Winter 2003), republished as "Tunisian Envoy," Jefferson Monticello, https://www.monticello.org/site/research-and-collections/tunisian-envoy.

York City's iconic Empire State Building has been illuminated with green lights in celebration. In 2015, the New York City Department of Education recognized Eid al-Fitr as an official school holiday. Even school districts in less urban areas, such as Howard County, Maryland, have recognized the holiday on their calendars. In 2001, the US Postal Service issued a stamp honoring Eid al-Fitr. Calligraphy on the stamp reads "Eid Mubarak," or "Blessed Eid."[40]

Because of the possibility of overeating during iftar and generating excessive waste during Ramadan, many Muslim organizations in the United States make efforts to educate the community about having a "green" Ramadan. The motto of one such organization, aptly named Green Ramadan, is "Green your Ramadan with zero-trash *iftar* kits."[41] The same organization has also campaigned for a meatless Ramadan.[42] An Islamic organization in Chicago issued guidelines for the community during Ramadan to share food with one's neighbor, not waste food or water, plant trees, recycle materials such as plastic, and not use Styrofoam cups and plates. Ramadan sermons also urge the community to care for the environment, use energy-saving light bulbs, organize mosque cleanup days, and post signs around the mosque to "go green" for Ramadan.[43]

40. "Eid Greetings," US Postal Service, accessed May 17, 2020, https://store.usps.com/store/product/buy-stamps/eid-greetings-S_556204.
41. "About," Green Ramadan, accessed April 18, 2020, http://greenramadan.com/about/.
42. "#MeatLessRamadan with Nana Firman," Green Ramadan, May 15, 2018, http://greenramadan.com/tag/meatless/.
43. See Abdullah Mitchell, "Go Green This Ramadan," Council of Islamic Organizations of Greater Chicago, March 31, 2017, https://www.ciogc.org/5-31-17-go-green-this-ramadan-2/.

16 Pilgrimage

Hajj

While in prison as a young man during the 1940s, Malcolm X (d. 1965) was introduced to Islam through the teachings of Elijah Muhammad (d. 1975) and the Nation of Islam (NOI). In the context of racial segregation and discrimination in the United States, Malcolm X initially found the teachings of the NOI appealing. Elijah Muhammad taught that ancient civilizations had originated with the Black race. At some point in history, white people—believed by Elijah Muhammad to have been the creation of a rogue Black scientist named Yakub (Jacob)—had brainwashed and exploited Black people. The best example of this exploitation was when white men went to Africa, kidnapped Black people, and brought them to the West as slaves. Elijah Muhammad maintained that before the mischief of the devil race, the earth had been a peaceful place. After his release from prison, Malcolm eventually became one of the most public figures of the NOI in the United States.[1]

In 1964, with the support of an immigrant Muslim professor in New York, Malcolm X embarked on his hajj that introduced him to the diversity of Muslims. For him, it was shocking to see people of all colors honoring one God together. The scene on the airplane from Cairo to Jeddah astonished him: "Packed in the plane were white, black, brown, red, and yellow people, blue eyes and blond hair, and my kinky red hair—all together, brothers! All honoring the same God, Allah, all in turn giving equal honor to each other."[2] Malcolm also wrote about the pilgrimage sites: "There were tens of thousands of pilgrims, from all over the world. They were of all colors, from blue-eyed blondes to black-skinned Africans. But we were all participating in the same ritual, displaying a spirit of unity and brotherhood that my experiences in America had led me to believe never could exist between the white and non-white."[3] For him, the religious society that he was exposed to in Mecca was color-blind.[4]

---

1. Haley, *Autobiography of Malcolm X*, 152–69.
2. Malcolm X, quoted in Haley, 328.
3. Malcolm X, quoted in Haley, 344–47.
4. Malcolm X, quoted in Haley, 343.

After his hajj experience, Malcolm distanced himself from the teachings of the NOI concerning the white race. As Ossie Davis explained, "No one who knew him before and after his trip to Mecca could doubt that he had completely abandoned racism, separatism, and hatred."[5] Not long after his hajj journey, Malcolm wrote an article admitting that he had made "sweeping indictments of all white people, the entire white race, and these generalizations have caused injuries to some whites who perhaps did not deserve to be hurt."[6] But Malcolm also pointed out that his new perspective on race in the United States was the result of the spiritual enlightenment that he had received during his pilgrimage to Mecca. As a result, he noted, "I no longer subscribe to sweeping indictments of any one race."[7]

Hajj is the fifth pillar of Islam. Muslims perform it during the last month of the Islamic calendar (Dhul Hijjah) beginning on the eighth day and ending on the thirtieth day of the month. Because the hajj schedule follows the lunar calendar, it occurs eleven days earlier than it did the previous year. That is why the hajj period rotates through all the seasons.

Hajj is one of the largest pilgrimage gatherings. According to the Saudi government, in 2017, around two and half million people performed the hajj. For centuries, Muslims have been traveling on pilgrimage to Mecca, where the Kaaba, to which Muslims direct their face during the five daily prayers, is located. Many rituals performed during the pilgrimage are reenactments of events in the life of Abraham.

History of the Kaaba

The Kaaba dates back to the prophet Abraham (or Ibrahim, as Muslims call him). According to Islamic literature, following God's command, Abraham brought his concubine Hagar and son Ishmael to a deserted place and left them there. The Qur'an refers to this occasion as follows: "Our Lord, I [Abraham] have settled some of my offspring in a valley without cultivation, close to Your Sacred House, Lord, so that they may perform the prayer. Make people's hearts incline toward them, and provide them with fruits, so that they may be thankful."[8]

---

5. Ossie Davis, quoted in Haley, 454.
6. J. H. Clarke, *Malcolm X: The Man and His Times* (New York: Macmillan, 1969), 302.
7. Clarke, 302.
8. Qur'an 14:37.

Being left in an abandoned area with her son, Hagar put her faith in God and believed that God would not let them perish in the desert. Not long after Abraham's departure, Hagar and her baby were thirsty. She went back and forth many times between the two hills known as Safa and Marwa to find water.[9] Water then miraculously appeared on the surface of the ground near Hagar and Ishmael. Many years later, Abraham returned to the place where he had left his family. He told Hagar and Ishmael that God had asked him to build a house.[10] The family started to build the house, which came to be known as the Kaaba, or the House of God. The Qur'an mentions the effort it had taken for them to build the house: "When Abraham and Ishmael were raising the foundations of the House [they prayed], 'Our Lord, accept this service from us. You are the All Hearing One, the All Knowing One.'"[11] God refers to the Kaaba in the Qur'an as "my house."[12] The Kaaba has been a center of worship and devotion to the one God for centuries. The Qur'an refers to the house as "the first House [of worship] established for people was the one in Mecca, full of blessing and guidance for all kinds of beings. There are clear signs in it; it is the place where Abraham stood up to pray; whoever enters it attains security."[13]

According to Islamic sources, however, at some point, the devotions and rituals in the Kaaba began to deviate from the monotheistic tradition (hanif) of Abraham. People started to associate many gods with the God of Abraham, and the Kaaba became a place of idolatry. Islam both emerged from this monotheistic-turned-polytheistic environment and built upon it. Various religious groups performed many different rituals at the Kaaba before the coming of Islam. The Qur'an and the Prophet "modified and sanctified" some of these rituals.[14]

Hajj in the Life of Muhammad

Hajj became an obligation for the Muslim community during the Prophet's tenure in Medina.[15] Because of the conflict between the Muslim community and the Meccans, Muhammad's followers were unable to fulfill the duty of the hajj until

9. Qur'an 2:158.
10. Qur'an 22:26.
11. Qur'an 2:127.
12. Qur'an 22:26.
13. Qur'an 3:96–97.
14. Sachiko and Chittick, Vision of Islam, 19.
15. Qur'an 3:97.

after the conquest of Mecca in 630 CE. Once Meccan society had surrendered to the Muslim community, it became the Prophet's mission to reorient the rituals toward monotheism. From the time of the conquest onward, only Muslims have been allowed to visit the Kaaba.

Hajj was a key component of the Prophet's spirituality, and he encouraged his community to complete the duty of the hajj as soon as they had the means to do so.[16] The Prophet Muhammad did his hajj only once—in what is known as the farewell hajj. During this pilgrimage, the Prophet delivered his farewell sermon to thousands of Muslims. At the core of the message of this sermon were justice and equality. He reminded his fellow Muslim pilgrims that all humans came from Adam, who was created from dust. No person is superior to another because of their race or color. An Arab is not superior to a non-Arab; neither is a non-Arab superior to an Arab. A white person is not superior to a Black person; likewise, a Black person is not superior to a white person.[17]

Superiority in the eyes of God should be superiority in piety (taqwa). Muhammad also stated that men have rights over women; likewise, women have rights over men. Fellow Muslims should be mindful of each other's rights and should not wrong each other. The Prophet also reminded the pilgrims of their relationship with God. They should be mindful of God, worship him, practice the five daily prayers, fast during the month of Ramadan, perform their pilgrimage, and pay their alms. With the qur'anic verse "Today I have perfected your religion for you, completed My blessing upon you, and chosen for you Islam as your religion,"[18] Muhammad reminded his fellow pilgrims that revelation had come to an end and that his departure from this world would soon happen. He also stated that he entrusted them with two things: the Qur'an and his Sunna. If the believers followed them, they would be correctly guided.[19]

Hajj Rituals

Hajj is required of all Muslims who have reached puberty and who are sane, free, and have the financial means. It is an occasion for spiritual renewal. Before leaving

---

16. Al-Sijistani, *Sunan Abu Dawud*, book 11, hadith 12.
17. Bünyamin Erul, "Veda Hutbesi," 42:592.
18. Qur'an 5:3.
19. Erul, "Veda Hutbesi," 42:592.

for the pilgrimage, pilgrims ask their fellow Muslims to forgive them if they have wronged anyone. While Muslims perform many rituals throughout the pilgrimage, the required ones are to be in a sacred state (*ihram*), to make circumambulations around the Kaaba (*tawaf*), to complete the rapid walking between the hills of Safa and Marwa (*sa'y*), and to visit Mount Arafat.

In the state of *ihram*, Muslim pilgrims repeatedly recite in Arabic, "Labbayk, Allahumma Labbayk. Labbayk. La shareeka laka. Labbayk. Innal-hamda wan-n'imata laka wal-mulk. La shareeka lak" (I am at your service, O God. I am at your service. You have no partner. I am at your service. Praise and blessing belong to you and the kingdom too. You have no partner). There are designated places for *ihram* before the other rituals of the pilgrimage begin. To be in the state of *ihram*, male pilgrims wear two unstitched white sheets. With one piece, the male pilgrim covers the upper half of the body; with the other, he covers the lower part. Women cover the entire body except for the face. In the state of *ihram*, certain things are required, and other things are impermissible. The most important rule is that the fellow pilgrims are required to be mindful of their fellow humans, animals, and inanimate beings. They are not to harm anyone or anything. Based on the qur'anic injunction, having sexual intercourse, committing a sin, or being in conflict with a fellow human are prohibited.[20] In addition, pilgrims are not to cut the grass or damage the trees of Mecca, kill or even scare animals, or lay claim to what another person has lost. In this sense, everything is regarded as being under divine protection in the designated places of Mecca and Medina.

The second ritual is *tawaf*. As part of this practice, pilgrims circumambulate the Kaaba seven times. While Muslims usually turn to the Kaaba during the five daily prayers, during the hajj, they are in the presence of God. It is both a spiritual and an emotional occasion. As one pilgrim described it, "Upon entering the Kaaba, sorrows disappear; it feels like entering heaven. If you have arrived in the Kaaba, tears are trickling down your face like the rain. You recall your experiences, the many sins you have committed. Arriving in the Kaaba, the conscious heart is filled with compassion, not remembering profits and losses, greed and selfishness, forgetting jealousy."[21] Pilgrims circumambulate the Kaaba as if they are in worship. The

---

20. Qur'an 2:197.
21. Sheikh Daud, quoted in Venetia Porter and Liana Saif, *The Hajj: Collected Essays* (London: British Museum Research Publication, 2013), 218.

tawaf continues throughout the day except during the five daily prayers, when the pilgrims pause to pray in community. The *tawaf*'s starting point is the Black Stone (Hajar al-Aswad), which is located in the eastern corner of the Kaaba. This stone is traditionally regarded as sacred. Many pilgrims also perform two cycles of prayer during the *tawaf* near the place known as the station (*maqam*) of Ibrahim.

The other major ritual during the hajj is *sa'y*, which is performed to reenact Hagar's running back and forth between the hills of Safa and Marwa to find water for her son, Ishmael. The *sa'y* ritual is followed by drinking from the water of *zamzam* that miraculously appeared during Hagar's walks. After the *sa'y*, male pilgrims often shave their heads.

The next stage in the pilgrimage is gathering at Mount Arafat, located in the eastern part of Mecca. Millions of Muslims gather and pause before God at this location. The Prophet Muhammad gave part of his famous farewell sermon during such a gathering at Mount Arafat. On their return to the Kaaba from Arafat, the pilgrims have two more stations. One is a place called Muzdalifah, where pilgrims pass the night in tents. The scene looks like a vast tent city. As one pilgrim described it, "Muzdalifah is like a human homeless camp of spiritual refugees who have left their homes in search of God."[22] The other station is Mina, where the pilgrims reenact God's testing of Abraham. According to the story, Abraham asked God to bless him with a righteous son.[23] God gave him a "patient" servant, Ishmael.[24] God then asked Abraham to sacrifice his beloved son Ishmael, which became a major test of Abraham's faith in God. As the Qur'an relates the story, "When the boy was old enough to work with his father, Abraham said, 'O my dear son, I have seen in a dream that I must sacrifice you. What do you think?' He said, 'Oh my Father, do as you are commanded. You will find me, God willing, among those who are patient.'"[25] When the time came to do as God had commanded him, Abraham went to Mina to sacrifice his son. On the way, Satan tempted him to shirk his duty. He was torn—on one side was a divine command; on the other side was his beloved son. Abraham was able to resist Satan and threw stones at him. When Abraham laid down his son to fulfill the divine will,

22. Najah Bazzy, "Personal Reflections of a Hajjah and Others," in *Pilgrimage and Faith: Buddhism, Christianity, and Islam*, ed. Virginia C. Raguin and Dina Bangdel with Francis E. Peters (Chicago: Serindia, 2010), 332.
23. Qur'an 37:100.
24. Qur'an 37:101.
25. Qur'an 37:102.

God sent a ram to be sacrificed instead. Abraham and his son had passed the test.[26] Pilgrims reenact this story by throwing stones symbolically to avoid the temptation of Satan and surrender to God's will. At this stage, they sacrifice animals, which is a form of piety or a way of getting closer to God. According to the Qur'an, "It is not their meat nor their blood that reaches God, it is your piety that reaches Him."[27]

The final stage of the pilgrimage is to do the *tawaf* of the Kaaba again. In this stage, as if born again, the pilgrim seeks God's forgiveness and embarks on a new spiritual journey. Although it is not part of the official hajj rituals, many pilgrims include the city of Medina as part of their hajj journey to visit the site where Prophet Muhammad, along with many of his companions, is buried.

Eid al-Adha: The Festival of Sacrifice

The last several days of the pilgrimage season overlap with the second of the major Muslim holidays, the Festival of Sacrifice (Eid al-Adha). For the sake of God, Muslims around the world sacrifice animals during this festival. The sacrifice is considered a form of thanksgiving and social solidarity, as the meat of the animals goes to the needy and the poor. The festivities begin with communal prayer and a morning sermon in the mosque, followed by the animal sacrifice and meat distribution. From the dawn prayer the day before until the afternoon prayer on the fourth day of the celebration, Muslims recite the *takbir al-tashriq* after each daily prayer, either individually or communally. Recited in Arabic, the *takbir al-tashriq* can be rendered as "God is great. God is great. There is no God but him. And God is great. God is great. And to God belongs all praise."

In addition to the major hajj, Muslims perform the minor hajj (*umra*). Unlike the major hajj, the *umra* is not required and can be performed at any time of the year. The Prophet strongly encouraged his followers to do the *umra*. In fact, the prominent hadith scholar al-Bukhari (d. 870) dedicated one section of his collection to the virtues of making a minor hajj. Many Muslims do an *umra* in the last ten days of Ramadan. In one of the hadiths, the Prophet said an *umra* done during the month of Ramadan is spiritually equal to a major hajj.[28]

---

26. Qur'an 37:102–7.
27. Qur'an 22:37.
28. Al-Tirmidhi, *Jami' al-Tirmidhi*, book 9, hadith 132.

Spiritual Dimensions of Hajj

Hajj is both a spiritual and material journey and a time of spiritual renewal and rebirth. It requires believers to sacrifice their property, body, and time for God's sake. Hajj is an opportunity for believers to detach themselves from their worldly attachments. It is a means of reorienting themselves toward God.

Because pilgrims wear simple attire, it is not possible to distinguish a person's rank or status, which reminds everyone that they are equal in the eyes of God. This becomes especially evident on the plain of Arafat when thousands of pilgrims gather together as one human congregation. It is a remarkable experience of unity. In a way, the scene is the living embodiment of the qur'anic verse "People, We created you all from a male and a female, and made you nations and tribes so that you may come to know one another. Indeed, the most noble of you in the sight of God is the most righteous of you. God is all-knowing, all-aware."[29]

Chapter 22 of the Qur'an is named after the hajj. The chapter repeatedly points to the day of judgment (qiyama) and accountability before God. When Muslims die, they are wrapped in a white shroud before burial. The pilgrim's attire reminds believers that this world is impermanent and that the hereafter and accountability await. Gathering with many fellow humans reminds them of the gathering on the day of judgment. Al-Ghazali relates some of the rites of the hajj to the remembrance of death and resurrection. The pilgrim should contemplate the demanding journey to Mecca as it relates to the time of death and day of judgment. Separated from home and family, they should reflect on their eventual separation from this world. Being in the state of *ihram*, the believers should be reminded of their death, as what they wear resembles a shroud, and the gathering during the hajj is like the gathering of all humanity on the day of judgment. Al-Ghazali likens the moment of seeing the Kaaba to the excitement aroused by people's desire to experience paradise and union with God on the day of judgment.[30]

The hajj is also an opportunity for pilgrims to reset their manners. Satan, according to Islamic tradition, represents arrogance, pride, selfishness, and temptation. Pilgrims symbolically throw stones at Satan in Mina in order to keep themselves

29. Qur'an 49:13.
30. Abu Hamid al-Ghazali, *Inner Dimensions of Islamic Worship*, trans. Muhtar Holland (Leicestershire, UK: Islamic Foundation, 2006), 111–13.

away from these shortcomings and to turn to God unconditionally.[31] Following in Abraham's footsteps after he stoned Satan, the next stage is the animal sacrifice, which symbolizes detaching oneself from what one is attached to. Perhaps Abraham's trial was about being overly attached to his son Ishmael. The pilgrim's attachments can be to anything—rank, class, family, profession, property, and so on.[32] The ritual of sacrifice is an occasion for pilgrims to reflect on these worldly attachments.

While today one can travel to Mecca in a few hours, in the past, making the hajj meant hardship and separation from loved ones. Going to Mecca and returning home could take months, if not years. Many pilgrims would pay off their debts and say goodbye to their fellow Muslims in case they did not return, as many died on the hajj. The memoirs of prominent fourteenth-century Muslim traveler Ibn Battuta (d. 1377) illustrate this well. As Ibn Battuta related upon embarking on a hajj journey from the city of Tangier in what is now Morocco, "I set out alone, having neither fellow traveler in whose companionship I might find cheer, or a caravan whose party I might join, but swayed by an overwhelming impulse within me, and a desire long cherished in my bosom to visit these illustrious sanctuaries [of Makkah and Madinah]." Comparing his departure from home to birds that forsake their nests, Ibn Battuta wrote, "My parents being yet in the bonds of life, it weighed sorely upon me to part from them, and both they and I were afflicted with sorrow at this separation." Only after a long, arduous journey through many Muslim centers—including Algeria, Tunis, Cairo, and Damascus—did Ibn Battuta reach Mecca. During his journey to Tunis, two fellow travelers fell ill, one of whom died. Ibn Battuta also got sick. He prayed, "If God decrees my death, it shall be on the road with my face set toward the land of the Hijaz and Mecca."[33]

The risk of making the hajj was not only about the long distance traveled or the prolonged separation from family; it was also about one's personal health and safety. In 1865, for example, a major epidemic broke out during the hajj. The epidemic made its way to Mecca through pilgrims from Java and Singapore. By end of the hajj season, fifteen thousand of an estimated ninety thousand pilgrims had died of cholera.[34]

---

31. Al-Ghazali, 116.
32. Ali Shariati, *Hajj* (Costa Mesa, CA: Evecina Cultural and Education Foundation, 1993), 84.
33. Douglas Bullis and Norman MacDonald, "From Pilgrim to World Traveler: Tangier to Makkah," *Aramco World* 51, no. 4 (July/August 2000), https://tinyurl.com/mdshd9sd.
34. F. E. Peters, *The Hajj: The Muslim Pilgrimage to Mecca and the Holy Places* (Princeton, NJ: Princeton University Press, 1994), 301.

In fact, even in modern times, thousands of pilgrims have died during stampedes or accidents. As recently as 2015, for instance, more than two thousand pilgrims died during a stampede.[35] The same year, a crane collapsed and killed more than a hundred pilgrims.[36]

The sa'y ritual, which consists of running back and forth between the hills of Safa and Marwa, reminds believers that they should never give up hope in God. When Hagar was desperately looking for water in the desert, God rewarded her and Ishmael with the water, which is known as "zamzam water" today. Remembering Hagar and her son's case, believers are reminded that they should turn to God even in the most difficult situations. Pilgrims try to relate to her story, knowing that God, in many different ways, will eventually open a door to them. Hagar started her life as a servant, but because of her faith in God, all believers revere her.

One who completes the hajj receives the title of hajji. Hajjis are respected in the community as they aspire to be better Muslims in many different ways. Pilgrims continue their submission to God with even more honorable deeds and prayers after the hajj is completed.

Social Dimensions of Hajj

Hajj also has social dimensions. For centuries, Muslims from across the world—regardless of their status, race, or color—have traveled to Mecca to visit the house of God. Hajj transcends the artificial borders that separate humans, the arbitrary categories that lead to discrimination.[37] As much as it is a personal experience, hajj is also a collective practice. There is no individual identification, no man or woman, no Black or white. As Ali Shariati (d. 1977) wisely said, "It is the transformation of one person into the totality of a 'people.' All the 'I's' join and become 'We.'"[38]

When Muslims decide to go on hajj, people in the community visit them to say goodbye. Upon their return, the pilgrims are visited again by relatives and community members who wish to congratulate them, the hajjis. Those who visit usually receive gifts and a sip of zamzam brought from Mecca. In a way, a hajj gathering

35. "Hajj Stampede," BBC News, September 24, 2015, https://www.bbc.com/news/world-middle-east -34346449.
36. Jessica Elgot, "Mecca Crane Collapse," Guardian, September 11, 2015, https://tinyurl.com/59htkuyy.
37. Shariati, Hajj, 8–9.
38. Shariati, 27.

is a microcosmic gathering of the entire Muslim world. It is a major means of promoting the unity, solidarity, communication, and cooperation of the global Muslim community.

Hajj is one occasion when both Sunni and Shiite Muslims from all over the world perform rites together. It is the largest gathering that brings Sunni and Shiite Muslims together. However, Shiite Muslims sometimes face discriminatory treatment by Sunni authorities and local Sunni populations. Their experience of hajj has become even more difficult with Sunni Wahhabis controlling the holy cities.[39] Political conflicts have negatively impacted Sunni pilgrims as well. Shiite Savafid Iran, for example, shut down its border to pilgrims coming from South Asia several times between the sixteenth and eighteenth centuries.[40]

Muslim empires have used the hajj to unite their ethnically diverse subjects and often made significant investments in the hajj business. In many cases, states have even covered pilgrimage expenses. Rulers of the Mughal Empire, for example, sponsored hajj travels as a way to demonstrate their support of Islam to their subjects. When the Ottomans took control of the holy cities of Mecca and Medina in the early sixteenth century, they gained great prestige in the eyes of Sunnis. The Ottoman rulers also assumed the title of the Servant of the Holy Sanctuaries (*khadim al-haramayn al-sharifayn*), organized pilgrim caravans from Cairo and Damascus, and provided safety and security throughout the journey.[41] The title is currently held by the king of Saudi Arabia.

Hajj from the United States

Among US Muslims, hajj has long been an established practice. Hundreds of institutions organize tours to Mecca, and every year, thousands of Muslims travel from the United States to visit the house of God. For US Muslims, there is no restriction on the number of people who can make the hajj, but Muslim-majority countries have quotas, and they select their hajj candidates through a lottery. This means that for many Muslims, it can take years to make their hajj. For example,

39. Peters, *Hajj*, 172–73.
40. John Slight, *The British Empire and the Hajj: 1865–1956* (Cambridge, MA: Harvard University Press, 2015), 31.
41. Slight, 31–34.

although more than 2,000,000 Turkish citizens applied to make hajj in 2019, Turkey's quota for the year was 80,000.[42] The hajj quota for Indonesia in 2019 was 231,000—a very small number for a country with more than 220,000,000 Muslims (the most for any country in the world). The average time Indonesian Muslims must wait to make their hajj is around thirty-seven years. As of 2016, there were more than 3,000,000 Indonesians on the waiting list.[43]

While US Muslims enjoy great freedom to make the hajj, they also face challenges to doing so. Because the hajj season rotates through the Islamic calendar, with its date changing by eleven days every year, Muslims must perform the hajj during a particular window that changes annually, creating problems for them in countries where they are in the minority. In 2018, for example, Safoorah Khan, a Chicago middle school teacher, applied for an unpaid leave of absence to complete the hajj during the first three weeks of December. Her school denied the request because her proposed leave dates overlapped with the school schedule and claimed the requested leave was unrelated to her professional duties. Khan resigned in order to fulfill her hajj duty but filed a religious discrimination lawsuit against the school. The US Justice Department also filed a complaint against the school district, alleging that it had violated Khan's religious rights and compelled her to choose between her schoolwork and her religious beliefs. The Department of Justice and the school district eventually reached a settlement that resolved Khan's suit. According to the settlement, the Berkeley School District paid Khan $75,000 for lost pay, compensatory damages, and attorney's fees. The district was also required to develop an improved religious accommodation policy and to provide mandatory training to all the officials who were part of the decision-making process for religious accommodations.[44]

In the next chapters, I address some contemporary questions concerning the diversity of Muslims, Sufism, women, and jihad.

42. "2019 yılı hac kuraları çekildi," CNN Türk, December 28, 2018, https://www.cnnturk.com/turkiye/2019-yili-hac-kuralari-cekildi-iste-kura-sonuclari.

43. "Indonesians Have to Wait for 37 Years to Perform Hajj," Al Arabiya News, June 22, 2016, https://tinyurl.com/spxeerte.

44. "Justice Department Settles Religious Discrimination Lawsuit against Berkeley School District in Illinois," Department of Justice Office of Public Affairs press release, October 13, 2011, https://tinyurl.com/49ydfed4.

Part 5

Contemporary Questions

17 Unity, Divisions, and Diversity

In a tradition that dates back to the presidency of George Washington, in January 2017, the Washington National Cathedral hosted its fifty-eighth National Prayer Service for the inauguration of President Donald Trump and Vice President Mike Pence. Twenty-six religious leaders from different faiths participated in the service. One was Imam Mohamed Magid, executive director of the All Dulles Area Muslim Society (ADAMS) based in Sterling, Virginia.[1] In his brief presentation, Imam Magid recited two verses (in Arabic and in English) from the Qur'an that are widely recited in interfaith circles by Muslims in the United States. The first verse was, "People, We created you all from a male and a female, and made you nations and tribes so that you may come to know one another. Indeed, the most noble of you in the sight of God is the most righteous of you. God is all-knowing, all-aware."[2] And the other was, "Among His signs is the creation of the heavens and the earth, and the variations in your languages and your colors. Truly in that are signs for those who know."[3] With these verses, Imam Magid emphasized the value that Islam places on unity and diversity.

The death of the Prophet Muhammad was one of the most dramatic events in the history of Islam. He was the Prophet of God and the leader of the nascent Muslim community. Whenever a community member had a question about the meaning of a Qur'an verse or another issue, they would ask the Prophet and find satisfaction in his answers. But after the Prophet died, questions arose as to who should lead the community moving forward. Muslims wondered who was qualified to both interpret the Qur'an according to the will of God and be the spiritual and political leader of the Muslim community. Disagreements over answers to these questions fostered the first divisions to occur within the early Islamic community.

---

1. Daniel Burke, "Imam Delivers Message to Trump at Inaugural Service," CNN, January 21, 2017, https://www.cnn.com/2017/01/20/politics/trump-imam-magid/index.html.
2. Qur'an 49:13.
3. Qur'an 30:22.

The Sunnis

Following the Prophet's death, three dominant groups emerged from the disagreements over succession. The first argued that the community should come to a consensus about who should succeed him. Right after Muhammad died, some of his closest companions agreed that the most qualified leader after the Prophet would be Abu Bakr (r. 632–34). Abu Bakr had accepted the invitation to Islam without hesitation and had supported the Prophet during his most challenging times. Demonstrating his faith in this man who was both his friend and one of his first followers, the Prophet had asked Abu Bakr to lead communal prayers when he was bedridden before his death. When the news about Muhammad's ascension to heaven (mi'raj) spread, many doubted whether it had actually happened. However, Abu Bakr responded by proclaiming, "I believe that it did happen if Muhammad said so," earning him the moniker Abu Bakr al-Siddiq (the righteous one).[4]

When Muhammad emigrated from Mecca because of persecution, it was Abu Bakr who accompanied him. When the Meccans learned that Muhammad had fled the city during the night, they pursued him. They even surrounded the cave in which both Muhammad and Abu Bakr were hiding. When Abu Bakr became anxious, the Qur'an tells us that it was Muhammad who comforted him.[5] Abu Bakr was also Muhammad's father-in-law. The Prophet was married to his daughter Aisha, who herself was influential in many ways, including being the transmitter of many hadiths from the Prophet. The group that supported Abu Bakr's bid to become the first leader of the community after Muhammad (which he ultimately did) later became known as "the people of the Sunna and the community" (ahl al-sunnah wal jamaah), or those who follow the example of the Prophet and his community. Today, this group is known as Sunnis.

The Shiites

A second group maintained that the most qualified person to be the leader of the Muslim community after the death of the Prophet should be a blood relative. Ali bin Abi Talib was both the Prophet's cousin and his son-in-law. He was married to

4. Ibn Ishaq, *Life of Muhammad*, 181.
5. Qur'an 9:40.

Muhammad's beloved daughter Fatima—the only child of his who survived the Prophet. Ali became a Muslim at an early age and, like Abu Bakr, was one of the Prophet's first followers. He was known to be pious, courageous, and knowledgeable. Muslims who supported Ali as the first successor of Muhammad referred to several hadiths of the Prophet to affirm Ali's leadership. In his last sermon, the Prophet had told the community that he would leave them two things. If they followed them, they would remain on the straight path. These things were the Qur'an and the members of his family (*ahl al-bayt*). On their way from Mecca to Medina after the farewell pilgrimage, the Prophet and his followers gathered at a place called Ghadir Khumm. On that occasion, the Prophet declared, "For whomever I am his leader (*mawla*), Ali is his leader."[6] Members of the second group, which came to be known as Shias, interpreted this hadith as evidence that Ali should succeed the Prophet. The word *shia* means "party," and the name *Shiites* refers to the party or followers of Ali. It is important to note that Ali initially did not accept the leadership of Abu Bakr, who succeeded Muhammad, but eventually, Ali (r. 656–61) pledged allegiance to Abu Bakr and much later became the fourth caliph of the Muslim community.

The divide between the two groups grew wider over time, ultimately leading to two major civil wars within the early Muslim community after the death of the third caliph, Uthman bin Affan (r. 644–56). Uthman was first married to the Prophet's daughter Ruqayya. When she died, Uthman then married Umm Kulthum, Muhammad's other daughter. Uthman was from the prominent Umayyad clan and appointed a number of his relatives to high government positions. However, many Muslims were discontented with his leadership, and eventually, his troops mutinied, and he was assassinated.

Ali became the fourth caliph after Uthman's death and immediately set out to find Uthman's killer(s). The Prophet's influential wife, Aisha, along with some of his close companions, such as Talha bin Ubaidullah and Zubayr bin Awwam, demanded immediate justice for Uthman's death. But an entire group of rebels had claimed responsibility, and Ali believed that instead of assigning blame to the whole group, the state needed to take the time to find and punish the actual person or people who had committed the murder. Aisha and her supporters soon became impatient with Ali's more measured approach and rebelled against him, but Ali ultimately defeated their forces. Many Muslims died in this first civil war, including Talha

6. Al-Tirmidhi, *Jami' al-Tirmidhi*, book 49, hadith 4078.

and Zubayr. The war is known as the Battle of the Camel, during which the camel Aisha rode into battle died in the fighting.

After the Battle of the Camel, Ali also fought with Muawiya and his followers. Muawiya's parents had been among Muhammad's earliest and fiercest enemies. However, they embraced Islam after Muhammad entered Mecca in 630. Likely as a result of Muhammad's reconciliation efforts, Muawiya served as one of Muhammad's scribes until the Prophet's death. During Abu Bakr's caliphate, Muawiya became an important figure in the military. Under the second caliph, Umar bin al-Khattab (r. 634–44), Muawiya became the governor of Damascus. Muawiya's influence continued to grow, especially under Uthman, as they were both from the Umayyad clan. When Ali assumed the caliphate, among those who disavowed his leadership was Muawiya, who held Ali partially responsible for Uthman's murder and argued that the caliph had not done enough to find and bring the murderers to justice.

Muawiya's defiance eventually led to the second civil war, known as the Battle of Siffin, during which thousands of Muslims on both sides died. Having lost confidence in Ali's leadership, the conflict ended with an arbitration agreement instead of a decisive victory. A group of Ali's followers parted ways with him to form the Kharijites (literally, "the ones who leave"). The third group to emerge from the succession struggles after Muhammad's death, the Kharijites not only disagreed with Ali and Muawiya but also declared both Ali and Uthman, and anyone else who disagreed with them, to be unbelievers (*kafir*). Ali's forces killed most of the Kharijites; however, in turn, a Kharijite assassinated Ali in 661. He was buried in Kufa (today, Najaf in Iraq), which would become an important pilgrimage site, especially for Shiite Muslims. Today, a moderate form of Kharijism is present among a group known as the Ibadis in North Africa and Oman.

After Ali's death, his followers nominated Hasan, Ali's son, to be his successor in Kufa. At the same time, Muawiya was leading his army to Kufa. Hasan abdicated his leadership role, and Muawiya became the new caliph. Muawiya's leadership marked the establishment of the Umayyad dynasty (661–750). Prior to his death in 680, Muawiya designated his son, Yazid I (r. 680–83), as his successor. Simultaneously, Ali's followers had nominated Ali's son (and the Prophet's grandson) Husayn to lead the community, but only a few Muslims supported him. Husayn and his followers were brutally killed when they faced Yazid's army in Karbala, Iraq. While Yazid remains one of the most divisive and despised figures in the history of Islam,

Husayn is remembered as a great martyr. Every year, Muslims commemorate his death on Ashura, the tenth day of Muharram, the first month of the Islamic lunar calendar. Husayn's shrine in Karbala is a major pilgrimage site in the Shiite tradition.

According to a 2015 Pew Research Center survey, Muslims make up almost one-fourth (1.8 billion) of the global population.[7] The number of Muslims is projected to grow to nearly 2.8 billion in 2050, making up 30 percent of the world population.[8] The same research concludes that Islam will be the second largest religion in the United States by 2050 and the largest religious tradition in the world by 2070.[9]

The ten countries that had the largest Muslim populations at that time were Indonesia, India, Pakistan, Bangladesh, Nigeria, Egypt, Iran, Turkey, Algeria, and Iraq. While fewer than 20 percent of Muslims were living in the Middle East / North Africa in 2015, more than 60 percent of Muslims lived in the Asia-Pacific region.[10] Around 25 million (4.9 percent of the population) Muslims were living in Europe at the time of the survey.[11] The overwhelming majority (87–90 percent) of Muslims worldwide are from the Sunni tradition.[12]

Sunni Diversity

With the rise of modernity and progress in the West and the colonization of Muslim societies, a number of movements emerged from within Sunni Islam. Muhammad Ibn Abd al-Wahhab (d. 1792), for example, founded Wahhabism in response to what he perceived as the moral and political decline of the Muslim world in the eighteenth century. Like the Puritans of England, he believed that many unorthodox practices had entered into Islam in the course of history and proposed a return to Islam's origins. Emphasizing the unity of God (*tawhid*), Ibn Abd al-Wahhab believed that Islam should be purified from non-Islamic practices. Still practiced today

---

7. "The Future of World Religions: Population Growth Projections, 2010–2050," Pew Research Center, April 2, 2015, https://www.pewforum.org/2015/04/02/religious-projections-2010-2050/.

8. Pew Research Center, "Muslims," Pew-Templeton Global Religious Futures Project, accessed May 18, 2020, http://www.globalreligiousfutures.org/religions/muslims.

9. Bill Chappel, "World's Muslim Population Will Surpass Christians, Pew Says," NPR, April 2, 2015, https://tinyurl.com/5u9db65t.

10. Michael Lipka, "Muslims and Islam: Key Findings in the US around the World," Pew Research Center, August 9, 2017, https://tinyurl.com/2kzm9y39.

11. "Europe's Growing Muslim Population," Pew Research Center, November 29, 2017, https://www.pewforum.org/2017/11/29/europes-growing-muslim-population/.

12. "Sunni and Shia Muslims," Pew Research Center, January 27, 2011, https://www.pewforum.org/2011/01/27/future-of-the-global-muslim-population-sunni-and-shia/.

and especially influential in Saudi Arabia, Wahhabism opposes the popular cult of saints as well as the practice of visiting tombs and shrines. As such, the movement is opposed to many practices of the Sufi and Shiite traditions. The school is also known for literal interpretations of the Qur'an and the Sunna, and its followers refer to themselves as Muwahhidun (monotheists) or those who uphold *tawhid*.

Another group that emerged from within Sunni Islam is the Jamaat-i Ahmadiyya, a late nineteenth-century missionary and messianic movement founded in India by Mirza Ghulam Ahmad (d. 1908). Ghulam Ahmad claimed to be a renewer (*mujaddid*) of Islam, the seal of the saints (*khatam al-awliya*), and the messiah as well as the guided one (*mahdi*). He taught his followers that Jesus had survived the crucifixion, had traveled to India, and had died a natural death in Kashmir.[13] Some of his writings implied that he was a prophet of God.[14] The Jamaat-i Ahmadiyya split over the question of Ghulam Ahmad's prophecy. While the Lahori Ahmadis believed that Ghulam Ahmad was only a renewer (*mujaddid*) of Islam, the Qadiyanis maintained that he was also a prophet (*nabi*).

The Sunni mainstream has interpreted Ghulam Ahmad's teachings as rejecting the finality of Muhammad's prophecy. Both Sunni and Shiite Muslims regard the movement as heterodox. As a result, members of the Ahmadiyya movement have suffered marginalization, persecution, and discrimination, particularly in Pakistan. In 1974, the Pakistani parliament adopted a constitutional amendment that declared members of the group to be non-Muslim and criminalized their religious practices. Because of this unbearable situation, the community moved its headquarters from Pakistan to London in 1984.

Shiite Diversity

Shiites comprise between 10 and 13 percent of the Muslim world. They make up the majority of Muslims in Iran, Iraq, Azerbaijan, and Bahrain and a significant minority in Pakistan, India, Yemen, Kuwait, and Lebanon. The majority of the Shiite population belongs to Twelver Shiism, whose adherents believe in the succession of the twelve imams after the Prophet Muhammad. The first three imams are Ali bin Abi Talib (d. 661) and his two sons, Hasan (d. 670) and Husayn (d. 680). Zayn

---

13. Adil Hussain Khan, *From Sufism to Ahmadiyya* (Bloomington: Indiana University Press, 2015), 1–8.
14. Khan, 51–53.

al-Abidin (d. 713), the only surviving male descendent of Husayn, became the fourth imam. He was succeeded by his son Muhammad al-Baqir, who was designated as the fifth imam. Jafar al-Sadiq (d. 765), al-Baqir's son, became the sixth imam. The twelfth imam was Muhammad al-Mahdi (b. 869 CE). Twelver Shiites believe that Muhammad al-Mahdi went into occultation and will return in the future, along with Jesus, as the *mahdi* to restore faith and justice. The twelfth imam might appear to those who are in "an appropriate spiritual state."[15]

The Ismailis—also known as the Seveners—form the second major branch within the Shiite tradition. This Shiite group is named after Ismail, the eldest son of the sixth imam, Jafar al-Sadiq. Although his father had designated him as his successor, Ismail died first, after which Jafar al-Sadiq designated another of his sons, Musa bin al-Kazim (d. 799), the seventh imam. However, the Ismailis have continued to take Ismail as the seventh imam and his son Muhammad bin Ismail as the eighth. The Ismailis became influential within the Islamic world, both establishing the Fatimid caliphate and founding Cairo, which became a major science and art center, as their capital in the tenth century. The Fatimid dynasty took its name from the Prophet's daughter Fatima. Al-Azhar University, which remains a central institution for the study of Islam, was built by the Fatimids (the Prophet's daughter was referred to as Fatima al-Zahra [the luminous], and the name of the university draws from her honorific). The Ismailis ultimately split into several factions, including the Nizaris and the Musta'lis, over disagreements concerning the succession. Fatimid caliph Mustansir Billah designated his younger son, Musta'li, as his successor, instead of his older son, Nizar. After Mustansir Billah's death, some Ismailis continued to follow Nizar as their imam. Today, the forty-ninth hereditary imam, London-based Prince Karim Aga Khan, leads the Nizari Ismailis.

The third important group within the Shiite tradition is the Zaydis, which is named after Zayd bin Ali (d. 740). Unlike the Twelver Shiites, who recognize Muhammad al-Baqir as the fifth imam, the Zaydis take Zayd bin Ali, great-grandson of Ali bin Abi Talib, as their fifth imam. Unlike the Twelvers and Ismailis, the Zaydis do not recognize a hereditary line of imams. They also do not have the eschatological idea of a concealed *mahdi* who will return in the future. In this regard, they are theologically closer to the Sunni tradition. Today, many Zaydis live in Yemen.

15. Nasr, *Heart of Islam*, 73.

Unity in Diversity

While disagreements abound concerning the succession among Islamic groups, they also hold much in common. All Muslims agree on the text of the Qur'an and emphasize the importance of following the Prophet's example. Also, all the groups accept the qur'anic teachings of *tawhid*, prophecy, and the hereafter. Ritual differences are also minor among the schools of law in both the Sunni and Shiite traditions. Nevertheless, some dissimilarities exist. First, in mainstream Shiism, the imams are believed to be inerrant (*masum*). Second, Sunnis and Shiites follow different chains of hadiths. While adherents to one tradition might consider a particular hadith reliable, adherents to another tradition may consider that hadith unreliable. Furthermore, imams play a key role in hadith transmission only in the Shiite tradition.[16] Third, in addition to the *zakat*, which is a pillar for both traditions, in the Shiite tradition, followers owe imams a share of any inheritance they receive. Another difference is the acceptance of temporary marriage (*mutah*), which Twelver Shiites consider legal. *Mutah* is a short-term marriage contract between a man and an unmarried woman for a specified period of time agreed to by the parties. Scholars disagree about the minimum duration of the marriage. For some, the time period should be at least three days, while others require three months or one year.[17]

Religious Sects in the World of Islam

Various other religious sects exist within the Islamic world. One is the Druze, which is an offshoot of the Fatimid Ismailis that emerged in Cairo in the tenth century. Its followers took Fatimid caliph al-Hakim bin Amr Allah (r. 996–1021) as their imam. They call themselves Unitarians (al-Muwahhidun) because of their emphasis on monotheism. Today, there are around one million Druze that live mainly in Lebanon, Israel, and Syria.

Yazidis are another religious group. Followers of an ancient tradition that predates Islam, the majority of Yazidis live in northwest Iraq, although one can also

---

16. Farhad Daftary and Azim Nanji, "What Is Shi'a Islam?," in Cornell, *Voices of Islam*, 1:217–44, https://iis.ac.uk/what-shia-islam.
17. "Mutah," Oxford Islamic Studies Online, accessed May 18, 2020, http://www.oxfordislamicstudies.com/article/opr/t125/e1662.

find Yazidis in Syria and Iran. Predominantly Kurdish speaking, Yazidis have been harassed and have tended to live in isolated places because of their beliefs. The group became particularly well known in the West, as they were brutally persecuted and attacked by the so-called Islamic State or Islamic State in Iraq and Syria (ISIS) in 2014.[18] Many Muslims inaccurately believe that the followers of Yazidism worship the devil. A major figure in the Yazidi tradition is the archangel Melek Taus, who is often depicted as a peacock. The account of Melek Taus is similar to the story of Satan in the Abrahamic traditions. The angel initially rebelled against God but was eventually forgiven. Yazidis believe that Melek Taus continues to mediate between humans and God and also serves as a guide for humans in making decisions between good and evil.[19]

Another religious sect, Alawism, emerged as an offshoot of Shiism in ninth-century Iraq. Until modern times, the Alawites were known as the Nusayris after Muhammad bin Nusayr al-Namiri (d. 864), who is regarded as the founder of Alawism. The movement is known to be an eclectic tradition incorporating Shiite, Gnostic, Christian, and ancient pagan elements. One of the most distinctive doctrines of Alawism is the deification of Ali bin Abi Talib, the Prophet's son-in-law. Alawites make up more than 10 percent of the Syrian population. While they have been ostracized and persecuted by both Sunnis and Shiites in Islamic history, with the rise of the Assad family in Syria, this group has become more influential and is currently ruling over the Sunni majority. Since the early twentieth century, the Alawites have emphasized their association with the Twelver Shiites.[20] A significant number of Alawites live in Lebanon and Turkey. The Alawites of Turkey, however, have generally dropped many of the tenets of mainstream Shiism.

Bahaism is another tradition rooted in Shiism whose origins stem from the teachings of Siyyid Ali Muhammad. Born in Iran in 1819, he came to be known as the Bab (gate). In his early twenties, Siyyid Ali participated in the gatherings of Shaykis, a messianic movement. Upon becoming one of the leaders of the movement, Siyyid Ali declared himself to be the messianic figure whom they were all expecting. While

18. The group has also referred to itself as the Islamic State in Iraq and the Levant (ISIL). See, for example, "ISIS Fast Facts," CNN, last updated December 4, 2019, https://www.cnn.com/2014/08/08/world/isis-fast-facts/index.html.

19. Christine Allison, "The Yazidis," *Oxford Research Encyclopedia of Religion*, January 2017, https://tinyurl.com/ndtt5u78.

20. M. Kramer, "Syria's Alawis and Shiism," in *Shiism, Resistance and Revolution*, ed. M. Kramer (Boulder, CO: Westview, 1987), 237–54.

Siyyid Ali gained a number of followers, he and his supporters were brutally persecuted. Siyyid Ali was publicly executed in Tabriz in July 1850 by the order of the grand
vizier of the time. Iranian Mirza Husayn Ali Nuri (d. 1892), who became the successor
to the Bab, is known as Baha Ullah (Glory of God) by his followers. Baha Ullah revealed
that he was the messenger of God foretold by the Bab. He spent most of his life in
exile and in prison and eventually died in exile in Acre, Palestine, in 1892, during the
Ottoman Empire. Assuming leadership after his father's death, Baha Ullah's eldest
son, Abdul Baha, established the center of his community in Haifa (now in Israel),
where he passed away in 1921.[21] Shoghi Effendi, Abdul Baha's eldest grandson, was
another prominent figure in the Bahai tradition—he led the community until his death
in 1957. The followers of Bahaism believe all the aforementioned figures possessed
divine authority. Today, the Bahai community is led by the Universal House of Justice.
According to their official website, around five million people ascribe to the Bahai
faith. The countries with the largest Bahai populations are India, the United States,
Kenya, and Vietnam. Additionally, around three hundred thousand Bahais live in Iran,
where they constitute the largest religious minority group.[22]

At times, Islam is perceived as an intolerant religion. However, despite persecu-
tions and challenges, until very modern times, religious minorities have not only
survived but often thrived in the Islamic world. For them, living in the world of
Islam has never been more challenging than it is today, for a number of reasons.
The rise of modern nation-states in Muslim societies has contributed to the
increasing persecution of religious minorities, as unified nation-states tend to
frown upon religious diversity. In order to form a national religion, many modern
Muslim countries essentially nationalized or sponsored a particular form of Islam.
In other words, they actively promoted religious uniformity. Second, secularism
has been enforced from the top down in many Muslim countries at the expense
of religious freedom, especially for religious minorities. Egypt, Iran, Pakistan,
and Turkey are just some examples of this trend. With the movement toward
normative national religions, traditional religious institutions such as madrasas,
seminaries, and Sufi lodges have been dismantled. Third has been the impact of

21. "Bahai Religion: A Brief Summary," Bahai.org, accessed April 18, 2020, http://dl.bahai.org/bwns/
   assets/documentlibrary/643/BahaiReligionABriefSummary.pdf.
22. "Statistics," Bahai.org, accessed April 18, 2020, https://news.bahai.org/media-information/
   statistics/.

Western colonialism. Many modern Islamic movements emerged through seeking solutions to the problems of colonized Muslim societies. Painful experiences of modernity and secularism and a lack of democratic traditions are just some of the reasons for the existence of religious intolerance and extremism in many modern Muslim societies.[23]

Muslims in the United States

An estimated three to four million Muslims live in the United States today. No country reflects the diversity of Muslims as much as the United States, which has become a microcosm of the global Muslim population. The presence of Muslims in North America dates back to the early 1500s, when Muslims initially traveled to the continent during colonial expeditions. Documents from the sixteenth century mention such Muslim names as Omar, Ali, Hasan, and Osman. This should not be surprising, as Muslims were present on the Iberian Peninsula from the eighth century onward and ruled parts of it until the Spanish Inquisition began in 1478. The presence of Islam as a power on the peninsula officially ended in 1492.[24]

A more substantial Muslim presence in what would become the United States, however, began with the importation of slaves. Some scholars estimate that around 15 percent of the slaves brought from west and central Africa were Muslims, as there was a vibrant Muslim community in these regions. Among those slaves were African scholars and nobles. While Muslims were disconnected from Islam during the period of slavery on the North American continent, with the influence of Black US Muslim movements in the early twentieth century, Black Americans (re)turned to Islam in large numbers. According to a survey from 2017, Black Muslims make up 20 percent of the Muslim American population; around half are converts to Islam.[25] Nearly 40 percent of US Muslims are white. They include Muslims of European, Middle Eastern, and Persian backgrounds. While Asians, including those from South Asia, make up 28 percent of the Muslim

---

23. For more on religious minorities in the world of Islam, see Gerard Russell, *Heirs to Forgotten Kingdoms* (New York: Basic Books, 2015).
24. Jane I. Smith, *Islam in America* (New York: Columbia University Press, 2010), 51–52.
25. For the survey, see Besheer Mohamed and Jeff Diamant, "Black Muslims Account for a Fifth of All U.S. Muslims, and about Half Are Converts to Islam," Pew Research Center, January 17, 2019, https://tinyurl.com/25kferb4.

American population, Hispanics comprise 8 percent.[26] There are also Muslims of Native American background.[27]

Within the Muslim American community, several indigenous religious movements emerged as part of Islam in America. One was the Moorish Science Temple, which Timothy Drew, who changed his name to Noble Drew Ali, founded in 1925 in Chicago. The word *science* in the name of the organization referred to the mystical sciences serving to balance the material and spiritual worlds. In the context of racism and segregation in the United States, Drew Ali wanted to form a distinctive identity for the Black community. He taught his followers that African Americans were related to the Moors, natives of Morocco, and thus were Muslims. With his teachings, Drew Ali aimed to bring African Americans back to "their original religion, create a sense of community separate from whites, develop self-respect and self-love, follow a strict moral code, and encourage spiritual development."[28] Regarded as a prophet by his followers, Drew Ali drafted a sacred text known as the *Holy Koran of the Moorish Science Temple*, which was unrelated to the scripture of Islam, the Qur'an. In addition to chapters written by himself, Drew Ali's holy book included mystical selections from other texts, such as Levi Dowling's 1908 *Aquarian Gospel of Jesus the Christ*, an apocryphal biography of Jesus, as well as chapters from the Rosicrucian ethics manual known as *Unto Thee I Grant* and *The Infinite Wisdom*.[29] Although the movement initially gained a following among some Black Americans, it lost influence after Ali's death in 1929. Today, a small number of people still associate themselves with Drew Ali's teachings.[30]

Another indigenous Muslim movement, the Nation of Islam (NOI), emerged during the 1930s in the Jim Crow era of segregation in the United States. Founded by Wallace Fard (d. 1934, also known as Wallace Fard Muhammad), the movement drew on the tenets of Islam and Black nationalism. Fard believed that Islam was the original religion of Black people. In 1934, Fard suddenly disappeared, and his student Elijah Poole (later Elijah Muhammad) assumed leadership of the movement. Elijah

26. "Demographic Portrait of Muslim Americans," Pew Research Center, July 26, 2017, https://www.pewforum.org/2017/07/26/demographic-portrait-of-muslim-americans/.
27. GhaneaBassiri, *History of Islam in America*, 2.
28. Curtis, *Muslims in America*, 34–35.
29. GhaneaBassiri, *History of Islam in America*, 220.
30. For more information about the current state of the movement, see "Moorish American History," Moorish Science Temple of America, accessed April 18, 2020, http://msta1913.org/MoorishHistory.html.

Muhammad led the movement until his death in 1975. The movement grew rapidly and received national attention from the membership of major public figures such as Malcolm X and Muhammad Ali.

The theology Elijah Muhammad developed was inconsistent with mainstream Islam. For him, Fard was not only the Christian messiah but also the Muslim *mahdi*. This made Fard God in the flesh and Elijah Muhammad the messenger of God. Elijah Muhammad taught his followers that humanity originated from the Black race, which had developed a great civilization. Later on, an evil man known as Scientist Yakub "genetically engineered a race of white devils." As Edward Curtis points out, Elijah Muhammad wanted to "mentally resurrect black people and lead them back to Islam." He believed that God would eventually destroy white people and that the Black race would overcome the oppression whites had inflicted on them.[31]

Malcolm X was perhaps the best-known member of the NOI. In the early 1960s, Malcolm X met some immigrant Muslims who challenged the teachings of the NOI, claiming they were unorthodox. Seeking close ties with Malcolm X because of his influence, they also invited him to perform the hajj. Increasingly disillusioned with the NOI's leadership, Malcolm X accepted the invitation and, with the support of an Egyptian scholar, embarked on the hajj journey in 1964. The trip would mark a turning point in his life.[32] During his hajj experience, he came to the conclusion that many of the NOI's teachings and practices, including its view of the white race, were incompatible with the teachings of Islam. As pointed out in chapter 16, Malcolm X's pilgrimage transformed him in many ways. He cut ties with the NOI and rejected its teachings, particularly those related to race.[33]

Malcolm X was shot to death in 1965. Elijah Muhammad continued to lead the NOI until his death in 1975, after which his son W. D. Muhammad (d. 2008) assumed leadership of the community. He changed the name of the movement first to the American Society of Muslims and then to Mosque Cares and brought the majority of the members into mainstream Sunni Islam. Today, a small number of Muslims still associate themselves with the NOI under the leadership of Louis Farrakhan (b. 1933).

---

31. Curtis, *Muslims in America*, 37.
32. Curtis, 64.
33. Clarke, *Malcolm X*, 302. Also see GhaneaBassiri, *History of Islam in America*, 245–46.

18 Mysticism

Sufism

Born in 1982, Tyler is a US Muslim who grew up in Pittsburgh, Pennsylvania, and became a software developer. After converting to Islam from a Southern Baptist and Jehovah's Witness background, Tyler struggled to integrate his past practices into the dictates of his new religion. He wanted to more strictly follow the tenets of Islam but worried that the hustle and bustle of life was diminishing his discipline to do so. Research led Tyler to Sufism, Islam's spiritual tradition, which he believed could help him achieve the levels of practice he sought. Tyler soon found a spiritual guide in Shaykh Nuh Ha Mim Keller, an American who currently lives in Amman, Jordan. Tyler journeyed there and was initiated as a follower of the Shadhili Sufi order.[1]

Tyler and other adherents to the order follow set daily routines. Members complete a sequence of seven lessons that advance their spiritual growth. While these lessons teach no more than the normal practices of all Muslims, Sufis advocate specific means to successfully follow the practices. The first lesson is to pray all five daily prayers on time for forty days without missing any. This lesson also includes controlling one's anger for the same duration. What anger is, and the methods to control it, are explained through Sufi teachings.[2]

Sufis gather weekly for group remembrance of God (*dhikr*) and to listen to their spiritual guide's lessons on topics in Sufism. These weekly meetings take place all around the world and often rotate among members' homes. Adherents perform personal *dhikr* twice a day, morning and night. These and many other ritual Sufi practices have strengthened Tyler's connection to Islam and allowed him to deepen his relationship with God. He feels he benefits from not only qur'anic teachings and the sayings of the Prophet Muhammad but also practical implementations of that wisdom in the Sufi methods. He cannot imagine his life without Sufism.[3]

---

1. Tyler, interview with the author, February 8, 2020, Mclean, VA.
2. Tyler, interview.
3. Tyler, interview.

Sufism in Islam

Scholars debate the origin of the word *sufi*. The most common interpretation is that it originated from an Arabic word rendered as "wool" (*suf*). Sufis referred to the ascetics in the Near East who wore a simple garment made of wool.[4] They were known for their simplicity and sincerity in their faith. Sufis follow practices that date from the Prophet's time and place the foundation of their faith traditions in certain verses in the Qur'an. For their asceticism, for example, Sufis brought up the verses of the Qur'an emphasizing the hereafter over this world:

> Everything will perish except His [God's] Face.[5]

> The worldly life is nothing but an illusionary pleasure.[6]

> Short is the enjoyment of this world, the Hereafter is the best for those who do right.[7]

> Wealth and children are an ornament of the life of the world. But the good deeds that endure are best in the sight of your Lord for reward, and better in respect of hope.[8]

Islamic scholars believe that the development of Sufism was a reaction to the socio-economic status of Muslims after Muhammad's death. Not long after his departure, Muslims expanded their territories and enjoyed great power. Prosperity and selfishness were becoming more common in Muslim societies. Muslims' overinvolvement in world affairs would often distract them from their spirituality and efforts for the hereafter. As shown in the previous chapter, major disagreements over leadership led to civil wars, and many died in these conflicts. Questions and divisions abounded around the meaning of justice and how to live the faith sincerely. Society

---

4. Carl Ernst, *Sufism: An Introduction to the Mystical Tradition of Islam* (Boston, MA: Shambhala, 2011), 19–20.
5. Qur'an 28:88. One reading of this verse is that all things will pass away but God.
6. Qur'an 3:185.
7. Qur'an 4:77.
8. Qur'an 18:46.

was rife with theological and legal disagreements. Increasingly disillusioned, some Muslims emphasized detachment from the material world. In addition to following the teachings of the Qur'an and the Prophet, they stressed sincerity and the inner dimension of faith. Their way came to be known as Sufism (*tasawwuf*).

Sufism has been prominent in Islam, and it is widely believed that many people have come to Islam because the followers of Sufism are known for their piety, sincerity, simplicity, tolerance, and good moral character. Sufism emphasizes the inner or esoteric side of faith, stressing "inwardness over outwardness, contemplation over action, spiritual development over legalism, and cultivation of the soul over social interaction."[9] When it comes to theology, "Sufis speak of God's mercy, gentleness, and beauty far more than they discuss His wrath, severity, and majesty."[10] Known as a mystical dimension of Islam, Sufism is often misrepresented as a separate group within Islam, alongside Sunnis and Shiites. However, it is a form of spirituality within both traditions, and there are both Sunni and Shiite Sufis.

Sufis emphasize not only the simplicity of the Prophet's life but also his piety, manner of worship, and dedication to God. The Prophet ate little and never left the dining table with a full stomach. He always encouraged his companions to be mindful of God and to detach themselves from the love of this world. Instead of accumulating property, the Prophet gave away his possessions to the poor. Likewise, his closest companions lived a simple life and committed themselves to God.

The aim of Sufism is to bring about the perfect human (*insan-i kamil*)—in other words, to form an ideal spiritual and moral person. While the spiritual seeds of Sufism were present during the lives of the Prophet and his companions, the major terms that contemporary Muslims associate with Sufism emerged only after the second generation of Muslims (*al-tabiin*), the successors of the Prophet and his companions. From the twelfth century on, Sufism became institutionalized through the Sufi orders (*turuq*), which were established and quickly spread throughout Muslim societies to guide people on their spiritual journey in a more structured way.[11]

The process of becoming a Sufi requires a master (*shaykh*)—a spiritual father or mother—to guide the disciple (*murid*) on their journey into Sufism. The initiated consider each other as brothers and sisters. The *shaykh* provides guidance according

9. William C. Chittick, *Sufism: A Beginner's Guide* (Oxford: Oneworld, 2007), 23.
10. Chittick, 23.
11. H. Kamil Yilmaz, *Ana Hatlariyla Tasavvuf ve Tarikatlar* (Istanbul: Ensar, 2017), 23.

to each disciple's character, and the disciple commits to following the shaykh's spiritual instructions. In the case of a prospective male disciple, once he commits to the Sufi order of his choice and to the shaykh, the candidate goes to a Sufi lodge, where the shaykh determines if the person is ready (motivated and able) to join the order. Once the disciple passes this test, the procedure begins. The disciple makes a major ablution and then sits knee to knee with the shaykh, after which they hug. The shaykh then asks the disciple to repent of all sins and mistakes. If he has wronged someone, he should ask for their forgiveness. The disciple then pledges obedience to the shaykh on the spiritual journey. Along with other members of the order, the disciple attends the shaykh's spiritual gatherings (sohba) and rituals such as communal dhikr.[12] It is important to note that, from early on, many women have been drawn to Sufism and have joined Sufi orders. One of the most prominent women Sufis was Rabia al-Adawiyya (d. 801). However, Sufi orders have been and remain highly patriarchal in structure and hierarchy, and men dominate their ranks.

Members of Sufi orders gather in lodges for communal worship, invocations, and other rituals such as chanting and dancing. The Sufi lodges also serve as schools where disciples study both religious sciences and traditional medicine and the arts.

Disciples on the journey toward becoming the ideal human pass through numerous different spiritual stations—Sufi scholar Al-Qushayri (d. 1074) listed fifty—including repentance (tawba), solitariness (uzla), abstinence (wara), asceticism (zuhd), silence (samt), hunger (ju), abandoning desire (tark al-shahwa), humility (tawadu), opposing the soul or ego (mukhalafat al-nafs), contentment (qanaa), trust in God (tawakkul), thankfulness (shukr), patience (sabr), sincerity (ikhlas), remembrance of God (dhikr), manners (adab), prayer (dua), poverty (faqr), gnosis (marifa), love (mahabba), and yearning (shawq).[13]

Purifying the self (nafs) is one of Sufism's most important goals, and "The one who knows his self knows God" has become an important mantra in Sufi spirituality. Sufis regard the self as an enemy even greater than Satan. Dealing with the desires of the self is presented as the greatest jihad.[14] The Qur'an instructs believers that they should not claim their self to be pure.[15] Al-Ghazali (d. 1111), a prominent theologian

12. Yilmaz, 186.
13. Ernst, Sufism, 104.
14. Ernst, 104.
15. Qur'an 53:32.

who is also known for outlining the orthodox views within Sufism, dedicated one of his treatises to fighting the ego (*jihad al-nafs*) in his magnum opus, Ihya' 'Ulum al-Din. In this work, al-Ghazali highlighted the importance of jihad against the ego:

> Know that the body is like a town and the intellect of the mature human being is like a king ruling that town. Its armies are the external and internal senses and its subject are its organs. The ego that commands evil (*nafs ammara*), which is manifested in desires and anger, is like an enemy that contests him in his kingdom and fights to kill his people. The body thus becomes like a battleground and soul is its guard. If he fights against his enemies and defeats them and compels them to do what he likes, he will be praised when he returns to God's presence, as God said: "Allah favors those who strive with their wealth and lives a degree above those who stay behind" (Qur'an 4:95).[16]

In order to deal with the ego that distracts one from God and spirituality, Sufism encourages disciples to eat, sleep, and talk less than others. In many orders, disciples often seclude (*khalwah*) themselves on their spiritual journey. A typical Sufi lodge has a section called *khalwatkhana*, a dark space where the disciple stays for forty days. The idea is to detach oneself from the world and to contemplate God's blessings. Some Sufi scholars justify this seclusion with verses from the Qur'an, especially Moses's spiritual journey in the desert for forty days.[17] The Prophet pointed out in a hadith that "anyone who worships God sincerely for forty days, his heart is purified and his tongue will be the fountain of wisdom."[18]

The Sufi orders also speak of stages of the self (*nafs*). The *shaykh* encourages the disciple to be mindful of those stages. To purify the self, the disciple invokes a different name of God at each stage:

- *The commanding self* (nafs al-ammara): *The lowest level of the self. At this stage, the self always commands what is evil. It longs after its desires and embodies arrogance, jealousy, backbiting, discontentment, greed,*

---

16. Al-Ghazali, *Ihyā' 'Ulūm al-Dīn* (Cairo: al-Quds, 2012), 3:11.
17. Qur'an 7:142.
18. Yilmaz, *Ana Hatlariyla Tasavvuf ve Tarikatlar*, 196.

selfishness, *forgetfulness of God, and so on. For this step, the disciple invokes "La ilaha illa Allah" (There is no deity but God).*

- The *blaming self* (nafs lawwama): *At this level, when the self commits acts of sin and disobedience against the teachings of the Qur'an, it blames itself and turns to God again for repentance and forgiveness. At this stage, the name of God invoked is Allah.*
- The *inspired self* (nafs al-mulhama): *At this level, the self is inspired and can distinguish good from evil. The self has the ability to resist lust. At this stage, God's name He (Hu) is invoked.*
- The *contented self* (nafs al-mutmainna): *At this stage, the self is at peace. Most of the struggles on the spiritual path are now over, and the seeker is closer to the divine. In addition, the self embodies good traits such as humility, patience, and love. The disciple invokes God's name the Truth (al-Haqq).*
- The *surrendered self* (nafs al-radiyah): *The ego surrenders to the divine, not only in good and prosperous times but also during trials and challenges. At this point, God's name the Ever Living (al-Hayy) is invoked.*
- The *gratified self* (nafs al-mardhiyya): *At this level, not only is the self content and surrendering to the divine, but God is also pleased with the self because of the spiritual progress that has been made. For this spiritual stage, God's name the Self-Subsisting (al-Qayyum) is invoked.*
- The *complete self* (nafs al-safiyya or al-kamila): *At this level, the self has finally reached the ideal spiritual level, and the seeker acquires master status. For this final stage, God's name the Subduer (al-Qahhar) is invoked.*[19]

Today, there are over four hundred Sufi orders. The major ones are as follows:

- *Nakhshbandiyya*: Named after Muhammad Baha ud-Din Nakshband Bukhari (d. 1389), Nakhshbandiyya is one of the most common Sufi orders in Muslim societies, especially in Central Asia, Anatolia, and India. The order claims a direct link to the Prophet Muhammad through his

19. Yilmaz, 236–38.

companion and father-in-law Abu Bakr. Imam Ahmed al-Sirhindi of India
(d. 1624) played a significant role in its spread in South Asia. With the
influence of prominent figures like Abdullah Ali Dehlavi (d. 1824) and his
disciple Mawlana Khalid al-Baghdadi (d. 1827), the order has become the
most influential in modern Muslim societies. While in some orders the
invocations (dhikr) are performed out loud in a group or individually, the
members of the Nakhshbandiyya order do them in silence.

- Qadiriyya: This order was founded by Abdul Qadir Jilani (d. 1166), who
  descended from Ali bin Abi Talib. His work, Futuh al-Ghayb (Revelations
  of the unseen), is still widely read in Sufi circles. With many branches
  throughout the world, it has been one of the most influential orders among
  Muslims.

- Rifaiyya: Named after its founder, Ahmed Rifai (d. 1182), this order was
  influential during the reign of the Ottoman Empire. Today, members live
  mostly in Turkey, the Balkans, Egypt, Syria, Iraq, and Syria. Some followers also live in the United States.

- Suhrawardiyya: This order was founded by Diya al-din Suhrawardi
  (d. 1168) and is widespread in Iraq, Syria, Iran, Central Asia, India, and
  Anatolia. Prominent Persian poet Saadi Shirazi (d. 1291), who is known for
  his works Bustan and Gulistan, was a member.

- Chishti: Established by Muinuddin Hasan Chisti (d. 1236), this order was
  one of the first and is now one of the most common orders in India. It also
  played a key role in the spread of Sufism in South Asia and shaped the
  spirituality of Muslims in that region.

- Shadhili: This order was founded by Abul Hasan al-Shadhili (d. 1258) in the
  early twelfth century. Prominent Muslim philosopher and historian Ibn
  Khaldun (d. 1406) was a member of the Shadhili order. It has been influential in Africa, especially in places like Algeria, Tunisia, Morocco, and Egypt.

- Mawlawiyya: This order was founded by Jalal al-Din Rumi (d. 1273), who
  was born in what is now Balkh Province, Afghanistan. Pushed out by the
  Mongol invasion, Rumi eventually settled in today's Konya, a city in central Turkey. There, he penned his famous Masnavi, which remains one of
  the most read Sufi works. Aside from his writing, Rumi's legacy is his tolerance and love for others. His order became widespread in major centers

of the Ottoman Empire. Seclusion (cile) and dance (sema) are important components of the Mavlawiyya order. Seclusion lasts 1,001 days. On this spiritual journey of purifying the self, the disciples of the order seclude themselves in the Sufi lodge. By performing ordinary chores, they aim to dismantle the negative traits and tendencies of the self. After the seclusion period, the disciple is promoted to another rank. The sema is today known as the dance of whirling dervishes. During the rituals of the sema, Sufis play musical instruments like the nay and kudum.[20]

Sufism in Modern Times

While Sufism has been influential throughout Islamic history, it has also been controversial. Scholars of Islam such as Ibn Taymiyya (d. 1328) and Ibn Qayyim al-Jawziyya (d. 1350) criticized some of the practices of Sufism as incompatible with orthodox Islam and attempted to purge them from Muslim societies by reemphasizing the teachings and practices of the Prophet Muhammad and his companions.[21] The writings of Ibn Taymiyya and al-Jawziyya had a significant impact on what would become modern Salafism, a revivalist movement that emerged in the context of late nineteenth-century Western imperialism. By the early twentieth century, Muslim societies had become even more dependent on the West than in the nineteenth century. As a reaction to this predicament, the Salafi school, which emphasized the Qur'an and teachings of the Prophet as the only paths to Muslim progress and independence from colonialism, became more influential. The Salafi school had a significant impact on Hasan al-Banna (d. 1949), an Egyptian and the founder of the Muslim Brotherhood, as well as on Sayyid Abul Ala al-Mawdudi (d. 1979), a Pakistani who formed Jamaat-i Islami, an Islamic revivalist party.[22] In addition, some politically minded Muslims have regarded Sufism as an obstacle to their societies' progress. For example, Sir Muhammad Iqbal (d. 1938), a Muslim Indian poet and European-trained philosopher, saw European countries make progress in the areas of economy, technology, and government and wanted to offer solutions to the Muslim countries so that they could advance like the West. Although he was well versed in and often engaged with Sufi writings, he

20. For the major Sufi orders, see Yilmaz, 243–68.
21. M. Sait Özervarli, "Selefiyye," in *İslam Ansiklopedisi* (Istanbul: TDV, 2009), 36:400.
22. Özervarli, 402.

also criticized those aspects of Sufism that he believed promoted "fatalism, passivity, and a false notion of the absorption of humanity in unity with God," as Carl Ernst pointed out.[23] Another scholar who critiqued Sufism was Said Nursi (d. 1960). Like many modern Muslim scholars, Nursi was raised in a Sufi environment, and many of his teachers belonged to Sufi orders. However, Nursi believed that the teachings of institutional Sufism were insufficient to answer the questions concerning faith. He kept the essence of Sufism in his teachings, especially some of the spiritual practices, but left institutional Sufism. Some scholars refer to his approach as Neo-Sufism.[24]

Sufism is known to be peaceful and tolerant, and many Muslims and non-Muslims believe Sufism can be a solution to the violence people perpetrate around the world in the name of Islam. While Sufism is often presented as apolitical, Sufi institutions have played a significant role in resisting colonialism in Algeria, Libya, the Caucasus, and Sudan. Ironically, modern Muslim nation-states emerging from colonialism often dismantled, nationalized, or otherwise brought under control the Sufi institutions that had supported their creation in the first place.

Sufism in the United States

Many US Muslims practice Sufism. Perhaps one of the most notable features of Sufism in the United States is its diversity. Scholars believe that many Muslim slaves brought to the Americas from Africa were involved in Sufi spiritual practices, even if they did not officially belong to Sufi orders. Slavery disrupted those practices, as Muslim slaves were not free to attend Sufi lodges or receive spiritual guidance from their *shaykh*.

Sufism also entered the US spiritual landscape through both academic studies of Islamic spirituality and immigration. References to and English translations of the works of such Sufi masters as Saadi Shirazi (d. 1291), Rumi (d. 1273), Omar Khayyam (d. 1131), and Hafiz Shirazi (d. 1390) date from the early eighteenth century, often without explicit reference to Islam—the religious tradition to which they belong.[25]

23. Ernst, *Sufism*, 201.
24. M. Hakan Yavuz, "Nur Study Circles (Dershanes) and the Formation of New Religious Consciousness in Turkey," in *Islam at the Crossroads: On the Life and Thought of Bediuzzaman Said Nursi*, ed. Ibrahim M. Abu-Rabi' (Albany: State University of New York Press, 2003), 313n7.
25. Mehdi Aminrazavi, *Sufism and American Literary Masters* (Albany: State University of New York Press, 2014), 1.

The works of Sufi masters would later have a significant influence on the works of such giants of American literature as Ralph Waldo Emerson (d. 1882) and Walt Whitman (d. 1892). Rumi has been a perennial best-selling poet in America. United Nations Educational, Scientific and Cultural Organization (UNESCO) proclaimed 2007 as the International Year of Rumi, celebrating his legacy and acknowledging his tolerant and pluralistic form of Islam.

Immigrants brought institutional Sufism to the United States. Pir Inayat Khan (d. 1927) emigrated from India in 1910 and established the Chishti order. Today, there are many centers in the United States affiliated with his order. Another Sufi master was Bawa Muhaiyadeen (d. 1986), who came to the United States from Sri Lanka in 1971 and founded the Bawa Muhaiyadeen Fellowship in Philadelphia, which is affiliated with the Qadiri order.

Also worth mentioning is the Shadhiliyya-Miriamiyya group, which Swiss native Frithjof Schuon (d. 1998) founded. During one of his journeys to North Africa in 1932, he met Algerian Sufi master Ahmed al-Alawi (d. 1934). Schuon became al-Alawi's student and studied Sufism under his guidance. Moving to the United States in 1980, Schuon had visions of himself connecting with Mary and Jesus, who became the center of his spiritual practices. That is why Schuon's group is also known as the Path of Mary (Tariqa Miriamiyya). His teachings influenced many scholars of Islam, including Seyyed Hossein Nasr, Martin Lings, Titus Burckhardt, Victor Danner, and William Stoddart.[26]

Muslims who immigrated to the United States from places like Lebanon, Syria, Palestine, Pakistan, India, Yemen, Bosnia, Turkey, and Iran also brought their Sufi practices with them. Today, almost all Sufi orders present in Muslim societies have found homes in the United States, including Sufi groups affiliated with Shiite traditions such as the Nimatullahi order, Jafari Shadhili group, and Oveyssi-Shahmaghsoudi. In addition, a sizable number of US Muslims who practice Sufism are converts.[27]

---

26. Marcia Hermansen, "Hybrid Identity Formations in Muslim America: The Case of American Sufi Movements," *Muslim World* 90, nos. 1–2 (Spring 2000): 158–97, esp. 170.
27. Marcia Hermanson, "What Is American about American Sufi Movements?," in *Sufism in Europe and North America*, ed. David Westerlund (London: Routledge, 2004), 43.

19 Physical and Spiritual Struggle

Jihad

Amid the coronavirus pandemic around the globe in March 2020, a story from Iran made headlines in major news outlets. According to the news, the country's highest religious authority, the leader of the Islamic Revolution, Ayatollah Ali Khamenei, had declared the Iranian medical staff who lost their lives by contracting coronavirus while treating patients in hospitals as martyrs (*shahid*), a status that can only be attained through jihad. Those who sacrificed their lives caring for the people of Iran during the pandemic would be considered equal to Iran's fallen soldiers who defended the country during wartime. Like military martyrs, the families of fallen medical staff will now receive payments and benefits.[1] In this chapter, we examine the concepts of jihad and martyrdom in Islam.[2]

Jihad in Islamic Theology

Islam emerged during a time when violence was part of daily life. The virtue of courage in fighting was a central theme of pre-Islamic Arab literature. Referring to someone as "the son of war" was common. Those who died while fighting courageously for their people were glorified in poetry after death.[3] With the coming of Islam, the virtue of courage merged with the virtue of piety and became known as jihad.

Today, the term *jihad* is almost always reduced to a fixed meaning in popular literature and often used synonymously with "holy war" or "armed combat." While

1. Nassim Karimi and Amir Vahdet, "Iran to Call Dead Medical Staff 'Martyrs' as Virus Kills 291," AP News, March 10, 2020, https://apnews.com/12c49ab6a3f3dbc19fc1fc99dc9daa58.
2. This chapter is a revised version of my previously published work. Used by permission of Wipf and Stock Publishers, http://www.wipfandstock.com. For more details, see Salih Sayilgan, *An Islamic Jihad of Nonviolence: Said Nursi's Model* (Eugene, OR: Cascade Books, 2019), 43–52.
3. Michael David Bonner, *Jihad in Islamic History: Doctrines and Practice* (Princeton, NJ: Princeton University Press, 2006), 7–8.

seeing jihad as a fight on the path toward God became a dominant approach in some Muslim societies, the concept of jihad has always had larger implications.

The word *jihad* is derived from the Arabic verb *jahada*, which literally means "to endeavor, strive, or struggle." The term *ijtihad*, a key concept in Islamic law, comes from the same root, which means "independent judgment or reasoning in legal or theological questions." Likewise, the word *mujtahid* originates from the same verb. A *mujtahid* is a person who would conduct diligent reasoning concerning questions in Islamic law.

The Qur'an mentions the word *jihad* only twenty-four times—in most cases, in the context of spiritual struggle. While it is true that in the Qur'an, jihad implies a physical fight, the word in no way signifies "holy war." Instead, the Qur'an utilizes *qital* for "physical fight." "Holy war" does not exist as a concept in Islamic literature. Warfare or fighting is either just or unjust, but never holy. The Qur'an and Islamic law are concerned with preserving life, and in the qur'anic world, peace is always preferred to conflict.[4] On the basis of the Qur'an and the prophetic example, Muslim scholars concede that Islamic law gives priority to five universal objectives. One is the protection of life. The others are the protection of mind, religion, property, and offspring (as discussed in chapter 6).[5] In this regard, Islamic doctrine has never presented killing someone or taking one's own life as holy.

Jihad is one of the most comprehensive concepts in Islamic literature. In reality, it encompasses an entire way of life—living in a way that is pleasing to God. Meeting this goal requires struggle and submission. Following the teachings of the Qur'an and the Sunna of the Prophet Muhammad is jihad. Following through with the five daily prayers may be an important jihad for a believer, as it is not easy to do the prayers in a modern environment with so many distractions. Giving to charity might be another form of jihad. For a social worker, taking care of the needy is a form of jihad. The jihad of a firefighter is to save lives. For a student, seeking knowledge is a jihad. According to a hadith, the Prophet said, "On the day of resurrection, the ink of scholars will be compared with the blood of the martyrs on the scales, and the former will prove to be higher in status."[6]

---

4. Qur'an 4:128.
5. Hallaq, *Introduction to Islamic Law*, 26.
6. Al-Ghazali, *Ihyā' 'Ulūm al-Dīn*, 1:19 and 22. Also see Suyuti, *al-Jami' al-Saghir*, no. 10026, quoted in Nursi, *Lem'alar*, 278.

Patience (*sabr*) also became an essential component of jihad in Islamic literature. Both the Qur'an and hadiths urge believers to have patience in the face of challenges to their faith, persecution, and aggression. This becomes particularly evident in the Qur'an: "Say, '[God says], O My servants, be mindful of your Lord! For those who do good in this world there is good; God's earth is spacious. Those who patiently persevere will truly receive a reward without measure.'"[7] The point is that God will eventually reward the virtue of patience.

Perhaps the best example from the life of the Prophet concerning the connection between patience and jihad is the Treaty of Hudaybiyya. A prominent event in the life of the nascent Muslim community, the treaty was an accord established in the sixth year (628 CE) of the Prophet's emigration from Mecca to Medina (*hijra*) between Muhammad's followers and his enemies in Mecca. The Prophet and his followers had set out to perform their pilgrimage. Given that this took place during the sacred months, no conflict was expected. In the pre-Islamic period, Arabs considered four months of the lunar calendar as sacred. According to their culture, fighting was forbidden during these months. Meccans had respected this practice. The Muslim community was now a major force challenging Mecca. According to this agreement, they would have peace for ten years. The treaty granted Muhammad and his followers the right to perform their pilgrimage the next year, but it also included a challenging condition. As pointed out in chapter 2, according to the deal, if a young man from Mecca converted to Islam and became part of Muhammad's community, he would be returned to Mecca. However, if anyone decided to leave the Muslim community in Medina and go back to the Meccans, this person would not be returned back to Medina. The companions of the Prophet were devastated by this agreement. They found it unfair and unjust. The treaty, however, would work to the benefit of the Muslims, allowing them to enter Mecca on pilgrimage and conquer their enemy's heart without bloodshed. Their patience had won out.

The hadith collections usually include a section on the virtue of jihad. In one, the Prophet remarks that a person who does jihad (*mujahid*) is dealing with his lower self, or ego. When the Prophet's wife Aisha asked his permission to participate in jihad, the Prophet said, "For you, the best form of jihad is to perform your hajj or pilgrimage."[8] In another hadith, the Prophet said, "The best jihad is to speak the

---

7. Qur'an 39:10.
8. Al-Bukhari, *Sahih al-Bukhari*, book 56, hadith 91.

truth to a tyrannical ruler." On one occasion, as the Prophet and his companions were returning from battle, he told them, "You have returned from the lesser struggle (jihad) to the greater struggle." Muslims have interpreted the Prophet's statement as a return from physical fighting to spiritual struggle. The Prophet also said, "Shall I tell you of your best deed, the most pleasing to your King, the loftiest in your ranks, better than the giving of gold and silver, and better than meeting your enemy in battle, beheading him whilst he beheads you? The remembrance of God."[9]

The Question of Violence

Muslim scholars speak of multiple categories of jihad. In his book *Zad al-Maʿad*, Ibn Qayyim al-Jawziyya (d. 1350) mentions fourteen categories—among them, jihad with heart, tongue, and wealth. Only one of these categories refers to outward jihad. Similarly, in his *Muqaddimah*, Ibn Rushd (d. 1198), known in the West as Averroes, talks about four types of jihad: jihad fought through the heart, the tongue, the hand, and the sword. The concept of jihad thus has never had to do with outward violence alone.

Nevertheless, one cannot dismiss the violent aspects of jihad. Muslim scholars acknowledge that the struggle might also take an outward form against threats to Muslims or Islam. This type of jihad might be violent and could involve war. During the Prophet Muhammad's thirteen years in Mecca, God forbade the Prophet and his companions to use violence, despite the fact that they were severely persecuted. As a result, some of his followers immigrated to Abyssinia as refugees. The major principle during this period of dealing with the enemy was to "turn the other cheek." However, this approach changed when they immigrated to Medina. In one chapter of the Qur'an, God permits Muslim believers to fight: "To those against whom war is made, permission is given to fight, because they are wronged; and verily, God is most powerful for their aid. Those who have been driven from their homes unjustly only because they said: Our Lord is God. Did not God check one set of people by means of another, there would surely have been pulled down monasteries, churches, synagogues, and mosques, in which the name of God is commemorated in abundant measure. God will certainly aid those who aid his cause; for verily God is full of strength, exalted in might."[10]

9. Quoted in Caner Dagli, "Conquest and Conversion," in Nasr et al., *Study Quran*, 1806.
10. Qur'an 22:39–41.

The Qur'an also includes verses that are frequently incorporated into the rhetoric of Muslim extremists and critics of Islam. One of them is Qur'an 9:5: "When the sacred months have passed, wherever you find the idolaters, kill them, capture them, besiege them, and lie in wait for them at every place of ambush."[11] Although the Qur'an does not employ the word *sword*, many refer to this passage as the "sword verse." Critics often refer to this passage when arguing that Islam is an inherently violent religion.

Unfortunately, some Muslim extremists pick up the same verse. By twisting the overall message of the Qur'an, they attempt to "develop a theology of hate and intolerance and to justify unconditional warfare against unbelievers."[12] Both camps distort the implications of these divine words, as the reference is actually to the Meccan unbelievers and their allies, who were breaking their treaty with Muslims and continuously waging war on them.[13] They also completely disregard the second part of the verse, in which the Qur'an instructs believers to do the following: "But if they repent, perform the prayer, and pay the alms, then release them. Indeed God is Forgiving and Merciful."[14] Even in this case, which has a particular context, the Qur'an favors peace and reconciliation over war and conflict.

In truth, as with most religious communities, war and violence have been part of Muslim societies from the beginning. The Prophet said, "O people! Do not long to encounter the enemy, and ask God to grant you safety and security. However, if you face them, be patient and know that the heaven lies under the shadow of the swords."[15] The Prophet Muhammad himself participated in many wars, and after his death, Muslims were involved in many battles. As did adherents to countless other religions during the time Islam emerged, Muslims also embarked on journeys of conquest and military expeditions. In this environment, two major empires, the Byzantine and the Sasanian, were in a war of "territorial expansion" in the name of religion.[16] It is worth remembering that religion was about not only individual spirituality but also identity in that context:

11. Qur'an 9:5.
12. John Esposito, *What Everyone Needs to Know about Islam* (Oxford: Oxford University Press, 2013), 138.
13. Esposito, 138. See also Nasr et al., *Study Quran*, 506–7.
14. Qur'an 9:5.
15. Al-Naysaburi, *Sahih Muslim*, book 32, hadith 23.
16. Reza Aslan, *No God but God: Origins, Evolution, and Future of Islam* (New York: Random House, 2006), 80.

Your religion was your ethnicity, your culture, and your social identity; it defined your politics, your economics, and your ethics. More than anything else, your religion was your citizenship. Thus, the Holy Roman Empire had its officially sanctioned and legally enforced version of Christianity, just as the Sasanian Empire had its officially sanctioned and legally enforced version of Zoroastrianism. In the Indian subcontinent, Vaisnava kingdoms (devotees of Vishnu and his incarnations) vied with Saiva kingdoms (devotees of Shiva) for territorial control, while in China, Buddhist rulers fought Taoist rulers for political ascendancy. Throughout every one of these regions, but especially in the Near East, where religion explicitly sanctioned the state, territorial expansion was identical to religious proselytization. Thus, every religion was a "religion of the sword."[17]

There were occasions in Islamic history when the discourse about jihad provided an ideological basis for territorial expansion. For example, according to historian Reza Aslan, "[The Umayyad] caliphate constituted the jihad state par excellence. Its main reason for existence, aside from maintaining God's law, was to protect Islam and to expand the territory under its control, and its reputation was strongly bound to its military success."[18] With territorial expansion and conquests, Muslims were faced with the ethics of conducting war. Within this framework, Muslim scholars began to propound a theory of jihad. Before the development of this theory, "Muslim scholars and judges had tried to make judgments not only with pragmatism and common sense but also, above all, in a true spirit of piety and with a sincere desire to follow Qur'anic principles and the model conduct of the Prophet."[19]

During the Abbasid dynasty (750–1258 CE), Muslim scholars wrote extensively on jihad and developed a classical Islamic legal theory in the process. Muslim jurists of this era divided the world into two abodes: the abode of Islam (dar al-Islam) and the abode of war (dar al-harb).[20] On the one hand, the abode of Islam referred to lands that Muslims ruled but that, according to Islamic law, could also include

---

17. Aslan, 80.
18. Khalid Yahya Blankinship, The End of the Jihad State: The Reign of Hishām ibn 'Abd al-Malik and the Collapse of the Umayyads (Albany: State University of New York Press, 1994), 232.
19. Carole Hillenbrand, Introduction to Islam: Beliefs and Practices in Historical Perspective (London: Thames and Hudson, 2015), 223.
20. Hillenbrand, 224.

non-Muslims, including Jews and Christians who are called *dhimmis*, which literally means "protected people." Muslim governments would protect these groups, ensuring the security of their life and property, upholding their freedom of religious practice, and exempting them from military service. In return, they paid a tax (*jizya*). However, their status would be inferior to that of Muslims, and they would also face certain restrictions such as prohibitions against bearing arms, wearing religious symbols, and performing religious rituals in public. In other regions and times, different religious groups (e.g., Zoroastrians, Hindus, and Buddhists) enjoyed similar protections and restrictions under Muslim rule.[21]

The abode of war referred to lands that were ruled by non-Muslims or places where Muslims lived as a minority, and thus Islamic law was not the law of the land. Occasionally, a Muslim caliph would call for a jihad against the abode of war. In accordance with Islamic law, people of that region would first be invited to accept Islam. If they agreed, the war would end. The other option for them was "to submit to Muslim rule and pay the poll tax." Some Muslim scholars later introduced another category known as the abode of truce (*dar al-ahd*) or the abode of peace (*dar al-sulh*). Based on this territorial classification, a Muslim state could be in peaceful relations with other non-Muslim states regardless of their religious status.[22]

The traditional legal theory of jihad introduced regulations for peace treaties as well as guidelines for the proper ethics of war. According to the new guidelines, combatants and noncombatants should receive different treatment—children, women, clergy of any religious tradition, and the elderly would be considered noncombatants and thus should not be harmed. The law was later expanded to "outlaw the torture of prisoners of war; the mutilation of the dead; rape, molestation, or any kind of sexual violence during combat; the killing of diplomats; the wanton destruction of property; and the demolition of religious or medical institutions."[23] Today, modern international law has similar principles.

As Islamic thought and jurisprudence continued to develop, scholars of Islamic law took a range of positions on jihad, with context playing a significant role in their interpretations.[24] For example, during the era of Islamic theorist Ibn Taymiyya (d. 1328),

21. Hillenbrand, 224.
22. Hillenbrand, 225.
23. Aslan, *No God but God*, 80.
24. Asma Afsaruddin, *Striving in the Path of God: Jihad and Martyrdom in Islamic Thought* (Oxford: Oxford University Press, 2013), 94.

Muslims had been dealing with a dual threat: crusaders from the west and Mongols from the east. By the end of the thirteenth century, Muslims had expelled the crusaders from their kingdom in Syria, but the Mongols' destructive influence continued. In 1258, they had destroyed Baghdad, the center of the Abbasid Caliphate and Islamic civilization at the time. And although the Mongols eventually converted to Islam, this created a further dilemma, as the Mongols did not relinquish all their cultural practices, particularly their own legal code (*yasas*). Ibn Taymiyya (and others) felt that Christian and Mongol superstitions and practices had become embedded in Muslim society. He also criticized the Shiites of his time for collaborating with the Mongols. Thus Ibn Taymiyya "condemned many practices and concepts—visiting graves, the veneration of saints, sharing religious festivals with other faiths, theology, philosophy, ostentatious dress, backgammon, chess, and music."[25] He eventually concluded that jihad against the Mongols was a religious obligation. Ibn Taymiyya's interpretation of jihad has had a significant impact on some of the modern Islamic movements, especially among Wahhabis and Salafis.[26] Both Muhammad Abd al-Salam Faraj and Usama bin Laden drew significantly on Ibn Taymiyya's legal thoughts in justifying contemporary violence against civilians in the name of religion.[27]

In the context of colonialism in Muslim countries in the early eighteenth century, jihad took a different turn. The notion of jihad would come to mean tackling the challenges of Muslim societies. In some situations, this meant resisting colonialism; in other contexts, it was a means to promote the interests of independent nation-states.[28] A more distinctive interpretation of jihad emerged as a response to undemocratic secular governments of Muslim countries in the early twentieth century. During that era, jihad became "a means of effecting sociopolitical reform in Muslim-majority societies by the removal (through violence and by other means) of indigenous authoritarian, secular governments"[29]—a model of jihad that had not been employed in the premodern period.

This model of struggle against a Muslim government was unusual because traditionally in Islamic law, anyone who resisted lawful Islamic authority had been

25. Hillenbrand, *Introduction to Islam*, 236.
26. Afsaruddin, *Striving*, 200.
27. Afsaruddin, 216, 220.
28. Hillenbrand, *Introduction to Islam*, 223.
29. Afsaruddin, *Striving*, 205.

regarded as a rebel (*baghy*). Such resistance was seen as a major crime, which Muslims of the time called *hiraba*—a word that carried a connotation similar to the word *terrorism* today. According to Asma Afsaruddin, "Armed uprising against a well-entrenched government, however tyrannical it might be perceived to be, was usually not justified under the rubric of *jihad* in the pre-modern period. This development alone marks a radical departure from pre-modern juridical and political thought."[30]

Another term deserving attention is *shahid* (martyr), which derives from the Arabic verb *shahida*, meaning "to witness" or "to testify." Like jihad, *shahid* has various connotations in Islamic literature. In the Qur'an, it appears as one of God's beautiful names (*asma al-husna*). In some qur'anic contexts, *shahid* refers to someone who is a model or an example of living according to God's will. For example, the Qur'an says, "We have made you [believers] a middle community, that you might be witnesses over the nations, and the Messenger a witness over yourselves."[31]

One hadith of the Prophet explains that *shahid* might have many different implications. According to this tradition, the Prophet visited one of his companions who was ill. When he entered his friend's house and found his companion's mother crying because of her son's illness, the Prophet said, "You think that one can only become a martyr while fighting in the path of God. In that case your martyrs would be few." The Prophet continued, stating that "being killed in the path of God is martyrdom, dying of an abdominal complaint is martyrdom, being burned to death is martyrdom, drowning is martyrdom, being crushed beneath a falling wall is martyrdom, dying of pleurisy is martyrdom, and the woman who dies along with her fetus is a martyr."[32]

In relation to military jihad, the term *shahid* is understood as a witness or martyr who lays down their life for the religion of Islam. The Qur'an also refers to those who barter their life and wealth in exchange for rewards in the hereafter: "God has bought from the believers their lives and wealth in exchange for the Garden being theirs. They fight for the cause of God, they kill and are killed. It is a promise which is binding on Him in the Torah, the Gospel, and the Qur'an. Who is more faithful to his covenant than God? Rejoice then in your bargain that you

30. Afsaruddin, 206.
31. Qur'an 2:143.
32. Al-Nasa'i, *Sunan al-Nasa'i*, book 25, hadith 110.

have made, for that is the great triumph."[33] In another verse, the Qur'an says, "Let those fight in the cause of God Who sell the life of this world for the hereafter. To him who fights in the cause of God, whether he is slain or gets victory, We shall bestow on him a great reward."[34]

While the word *shahid* has broad connotations, over the course of time and under the influence of different social and historical contexts, the interpretation of martyrdom that "privileged the military martyr over all other believers" came to predominate.[35] Along with the concept of jihad, martyrdom makes a frequent appearance in the literature promoting extremism. Even modern secular nation Muslim states call their fallen soldiers martyrs.

*   *   *

As this chapter has shown, jihad and martyrdom have had many different connotations and interpretations in Islamic literature over the centuries. And contrary to what some today might believe, these concepts have never been limited solely to fighting and violence. Rather, they have encompassed many distinct aspects of Islamic spirituality, including worship and charity. In some contexts, however, jihad as an effort to wage war has become the principal interpretation of the word, both in premodern and in modern times. One can observe a similar evolution of the approaches to martyrdom. In this regard, there have been occasions when both jihad and martyrdom have served as a means of achieving political goals. In these situations, there would be scholars who would "lend support to the king—such as the scholar whom the king had appointed to be chief preacher at the royal mosque." But it is also important to note that there have been Islamic scholars who would not sanction a war as jihad simply because the king said so. Instead, many "would only support those who followed the strict application of Islamic teachings. By these standards, it is probably safe to say that there have been few, if any, valid [in other words, in accordance with Islamic teachings] jihads in the past century, and perhaps not for the past several hundred years."[36]

---

33. Qur'an 9:111.
34. Qur'an 4:74.
35. Afsaruddin, *Striving*, 114.
36. Sachiko and Chittick, *Vision of Islam*, 22.

20 The Woman Question

Emna is a US Muslim who was born and raised on Maui, Hawaii.[1] Although her parents, who had emigrated to the United States from Tunisia, were not observant Muslims, Emna's mother still taught her the basics of Islam. While Emna identified as a Muslim, she didn't look or dress much differently than anyone else on the island, which did not have a visibly active Muslim community. Things changed, however, when Emna left Maui to attend college in Washington, DC, where she was exposed to a vibrant Muslim community on her campus and began to notice how little she knew about her Muslim identity. Emna began to seek opportunities to learn more about Islam and engage with her religion by attending events and services offered by the Muslim community. She cherished these new relations and opportunities to rediscover her faith.

Her growing exposure to Islam influenced how Emna practiced Islam, and it began to become a part of her everyday life. She started to pray five times a day for the first time and to dress more modestly. Her change in attire not only served the purpose of fulfilling religious requirements but also facilitated her prayers. Soon, the only thing she needed to don to begin her prayer was the scarf that she typically carried around her neck. But then she decided to wear a hijab so when it came time to pray, she would be fully clothed and ready for prayer. Wearing a hijab and doing her prayers became the best moment of her day, as it filled her with a deep sense of peace and security. Emna often left her hijab on even after prayer and, at the end of her freshmen year, decided to wear it permanently.

For Emna, contrary to many stereotypes, the hijab has symbolized a renewed freedom, a freedom from the constraints of society's expectations about how women should dress in order to look beautiful. She says that it gave her and continues to give her confidence, pride, security, and peace while she wears it. Since the hijab for her is so strongly associated with being ready for ritual prayer, having it on makes her feel like she is in constant prayer. Emna also points out that although she sometimes gets hot and uncomfortable, the inner comfort she feels

---

1. Emna's last name will not be provided for reasons of privacy.

far outweighs any physical discomfort that sometimes accompanies wearing the hijab. For her, the hijab is an outward, visible sign that shows God and the world her dedication to living the beliefs she holds so close to her heart.[2]

Perhaps no area of Islam has been more controversial than the status of Muslim women, particularly as they are represented in Western media. Muslim women are often presented as ignorant, oppressed, uneducated, poor, voiceless, antimodern, and invisible. In this chapter, we begin with women's status in pre-Islamic seventh-century Arabia. We then move to the Qur'an and hadith's approach regarding women. In the last section, we address some key issues concerning women in Islam as well as the situation of Muslim women in the United States.

Women in Pre-Islamic Arabia

Most books written in the few centuries after the life of the Prophet and the birth of Islam include a section on cultural practices in pre-Islamic Arabia, which is often referred to as the era of *jahiliyya* (ignorance). According to these narratives, society was highly patriarchal, and men saw women as objects rather than as individuals in what were predominantly tribal communities. People were valued according to their physical strength, and women were regarded as weaker and therefore inferior to men. Forced marriages were common, polygamy was widespread, female infanticide was common, and women did not have the right to own property or receive an education. However, occasional historical and traditional accounts relate stories of women in pre-Islamic times who enjoyed privilege and power. Among them are Khadija, the Prophet's wife, who was a prominent businesswoman and Muhammad's employer. Another woman, Hind bint Utbah, wife of Abu Sufyan bin Harb, was an influential woman in Meccan society.

Women in the Qur'an

The revelation of the Qur'an transformed women's status in seventh-century Arabia. One of the Qur'an's most important messages was that being superior in the eyes of God was about not strength or power but rather piety and devotion.[3] The Qur'an

---

2. Emna, email interview with the author, February 19, 2020.
3. Qur'an 49:13.

acknowledged women as individuals. According to the Qur'an, "Whoever does righteous deeds, be they male or female, and have faith, they will enter Heaven, and not the least injustice will be done to them."[4] In another verse, the Qur'an states, "Whoever does a good deed, whether male or female, and has faith, to them will We [God] give a new life, a life that is good and pure and We will bestow on such their reward according to the best of their actions."[5]

Considering that the new revelation was accessible to every member of the community through recitation, some women complained that the Qur'an almost always addressed men and did not mention women. In other words, they believed the language of the Qur'an was patriarchal. Not long after women began to voice these complaints, the following verse was revealed in which the scripture addresses both men and women: "For Muslim men and Muslim women, believing men and believing women, devout men and devout women, truthful men and truthful women, patient men and patient women, humble men and humble women, charitable men and charitable women, men who fast and women who fast, men who guard their private parts and women who guard their [private parts], and men and women who engage much in God's praise, for them God has prepared forgiveness and great reward."[6] With this verse, the Qur'an affirmed that God does not differentiate between men and women when it comes to spiritual rewards.

On one occasion, an elderly woman, Khawla bint Thalabah, came to the Prophet and complained about a common social practice of the time known as *zihar* (literally, "back"). Her husband had gotten upset with her and said, "You are to me as my mother's back." According to this practice, if a husband uttered these words, he would be free of all responsibilities toward his wife, but the wife could neither leave the marriage nor enter into another one. Concerned about her situation, Khawla complained to the Prophet as well as to God about the unfair nature of this practice.[7] Not long after, the Prophet received the following revelation: "God has indeed heard the words of the woman who argued with you [Prophet] concerning her husband and complained to God. And God hears your conversation. He is all-hearing, all-seeing."[8] This was major news, as the revelation affirmed that God

4. Qur'an 4:124.
5. Qur'an 16:97.
6. Qur'an 33:35.
7. Lumbard, Commentary on *Surat al-Mujadilah*, Nasr et al., Study Qur'an, 1241.
8. Qur'an 58:1.

was not indifferent to the complaint of an old woman. With the revelation of the verses in the chapter aptly titled "She Who Disputes" ("Al-Mujadilah"), the Qur'an dismantled this pre-Islamic tradition (*jahiliyya*).[9]

The Prophet Muhammad and the Status of Women

A number of hadiths indicate that, at least in the context of his time, the Prophet Muhammad attempted to improve women's status in many ways. One hadith reported that the Prophet said, "The believer with the most complete faith is the one with the best character, and the best of them are those who treat their women the best."[10] In another, Muhammad explained, "Whoever has three (or two or one) girls or sisters and treats them well, [does not prefer male children over them,] and educates them in the best manner; God will make them a shield against hell and will put them in heaven."[11] In light of the prevalence of domestic violence during his time, the Prophet made clear that "the best of you are those who are good to your wives."[12] According to a report attributed to Umar bin al-Khattab—the second caliph after the Prophet Muhammad—women had no value for men before the coming of Islam. "We realized," Umar said, that "God was addressing them in the Qur'an, which made us think that we had responsibility for our women; but we still thought we did not need to involve them in our affairs." However, one day Umar was arguing with his wife and told her that she needed to know her limit. She responded, "You are admonishing me, but don't you know that your daughter, Hafsa—who is married to the Prophet—argues with him freely, to the extent that she makes him sad?"[13]

Khadija, the Prophet's first wife, played a key role in the early years of Islam. As mentioned previously, when the Prophet received his first revelation, he went to Khadija, who comforted and supported him. Khadija would become the first woman to convert to Islam. Additionally, the Prophet's youngest wife, Aisha, transmitted many hadiths and often corrected important companions of the Prophet concerning their narratives about women.[14]

---

9. Qur'an 58:2–4.
10. Al-Tirmidhi, *Jami' al-Tirmidhi*, book 12, hadith 17.
11. Al-Sijistani, *Sunan Abu Dawud*, book 43, hadith 376; al-Tirmidhi, *Jami' al-Tirmidhi*, book 27, hadith 22; Ibn Majah, *Sunan Ibn Majah*, book 33, hadith 13.
12. Al-Tirmidhi, *Jami' al-Tirmidhi*, book 49, hadith 4269.
13. Al-Bukhari, *Sahih al-Bukhari*, book 77, hadith 60.
14. Brown, *Hadith*, 71.

Women in Islamic Law

Issues related to women became a key area of Islamic law. Muslim scholars derived laws concerning women from verses in the Qur'an and hadith narratives. According to Islamic law, marriage is defined as a contract that requires the groom's family to give the bride a dowry. Women have the right to choose their partner as well as the right to divorce. The law also requires the husband to financially support his divorced wife. Women have the right of inheritance and could control their own property and money. By comparison, English women did not enjoy full property rights until the Married Women's Property Acts of 1870 and 1882. When Lady Mary Wortley Montagu, an English aristocrat and poet, traveled to Istanbul in 1716 with her husband, she was astonished by the freedom that Muslim women enjoyed under the Ottomans. They not only owned large estates but also managed their own property independently of their spouses.[15] Additionally, Islamic law limited polygamy and made education compulsory for both men and women. Indeed, female scholarship has played a key role in Islamic education. However, the following areas of Islamic law have become especially controversial in modern times.

Marital Issues

One issue that has arisen is the question of interfaith marriages. The consensus of Muslim scholars has been that while a Muslim man can marry a Jewish or Christian woman, a Muslim woman cannot marry a Jewish or Christian man. At the heart of this discussion is the issue of how to raise children. It is important to note that since men had more power than women in the early centuries of Islam, scholars concluded that with this law, it was possible for men to raise children as Muslims. However, this rule has brought unique challenges to Muslim women living in the West, where Muslims are a minority. Given that love recognizes no boundaries and that Muslims have often lived in religiously pluralistic societies, Muslim scholars have had to address this question in new ways. As noted in chapter 12, scholars have concluded that once a non-Muslim husband makes the *shahada*, thereby professing

---

15. Ernst, *Following Muhammad*, 27.

the faith of Islam in public, they can get married. Whether or not the person sincerely believes in Islam is irrelevant.[16]

A second issue revolves around polygamy. While qur'anic law limits polygamy, men are still allowed to marry up to four wives, with the condition that justice be maintained in the marriage.[17] Many Qur'an scholars understand this condition to be treating wives "equitably with regard to financial support, love, companionship, and conjugal relations."[18]

The third issue is about the roles of men and women in marriage. Several verses in the Qur'an point to the husband as the head of the household. The Qur'an also implies that the husband is in charge of the family and that his wife should be obedient to him: "Men are the protectors and maintainers of women, because God has given the one more (strength) than the other, and because they support them from their means. Therefore the righteous women are devoutly obedient, and guard in (the husband's) absence what God would have them guard. As for those from whom you fear rebellion, admonish them and banish them to beds apart, and scourge them. Then if they obey you, seek not a way against them. God is most high and great."[19]

This has been one of the most contentious verses in the Qur'an concerning marriage. According to Al-Zamakhshari (d. 1144), a prominent Muslim exegete, this verse was revealed following the story of a man who had slapped his wife. The wife's father went to the Prophet arguing that she was from a noble family and did not deserve such treatment. The Prophet suggested that there should be a form of retaliation (qisas) against the husband. Then this verse was revealed. In reaction to this story, the Prophet remarked, "I wanted one thing and God wanted another."[20]

Traditional Muslim scholars have interpreted this verse as an indication that the husband was the protector and maintainer of the family and that his wife should be obedient to him. If she were not, then there was a process to control her—and that included hitting her. Scholars maintained that the verse showed the improving status of women in the Arabian context and that "beating" should be taken as more symbolic than literal. Al-Shafi'i (d. 820), for example, indicated that beating one's wife is hardly permissible and that men should avoid doing so. Scholars

16. Sachiko and Chittick, Vision of Islam, 39.
17. Qur'an 4:3.
18. Maria Massi Dakake, Commentary on Surat al-Nisa', Nasr et al, Study Qur'an, 190.
19. Qur'an 4:34.
20. Nasr et al., Study Quran, 208.

justified their interpretations based on some of the hadiths of the Prophet in which he strongly discouraged domestic violence among his followers. Modern scholars have also interpreted this verse through other verses in the Qur'an. Verse 128 of the same chapter, for example, refers to a husband's mistreatment of his wife. In this situation, either party could seek a settlement.[21] In one of the hadiths, Muhammad said, "Could any of you beat his wife as he would beat a slave, and then lie with her in the evening?"[22]

Inheritance

The Qur'an allocates one-third of an inheritance from the woman's family to female descendants and two-thirds to male descendants.[23] According to Islamic law, a husband is responsible for taking care of his family financially. The wife does not have this responsibility, but she does receive her share. Many Muslim scholars have produced new interpretations of this approach. However, dealing with inheritance remains a question today in Muslim societies.

The Veil

Another major issue for many Western people regarding Islam is the covering of women. Veiled women are one of the most visible aspects of Muslim societies. The question of the veil is discussed as not only a religious matter but also a political issue in both Muslim-majority countries and the West. Many qur'anic verses and hadiths address ways of dressing for both Muslim women and men. It is important to note, however, that covering oneself has never been considered a matter of faith; rather, it is a matter of practice, piety, devotion, and modesty. While Islam puts forward some principles concerning dress, it also takes into consideration cultural contexts, which is why there are diverse ways of meeting the Islamic dress code in Muslim societies. Muslim scholars have disagreed and still disagree about attire; the headscarf, especially, has become an important political issue in many Muslim countries. Some Muslims have argued that it should be banned in the public sphere.

21. Qur'an 4:128.
22. Al-Bukhari, *Sahih al-Bukhari*, book 78, hadith 72.
23. Qur'an 4:11.

For them, the headscarf is a visible religious symbol and inconsistent with secular values. In Turkey, for example, it was banned for a time. Those who advocated for the headscarf discussed it in the context of religious freedom and practice. The overwhelming majority of Muslims, however, believe that wearing the headscarf is a personal choice and that each woman should make her own decision about whether to wear it.[24]

Questions remain today about the status of women in some Muslim-majority countries, especially surrounding patriarchal power structures, domestic violence, female mutilation, lack of education, and forced or child marriages. Many of these issues are related to the cultural context of particular Muslim societies. While the message of Islam has elevated women's status, in various cultural contexts, it has been unable to transform deep-rooted patriarchal beliefs about women's "proper," subservient role in society. In other words, the culture of the society has dominated the religious message. According to one study, in such societies, the education of Muslim women is often limited not because of Islam, as is commonly perceived in the West, but because of economic conditions—a woman's access to education depends more on a society's wealth than its culture or laws.[25] According to a Pew survey from 2010, the average years of education in Qatar is 10.2 for females and 11 for males. In the United States, there is no gender gap; the average years of education for American Muslim women and men is 13.6. The average years of education for US women and men is 12.6. However, in Yemen, Muslim females only average 0.5 years of education, while men average 2.5 years. In Somalia, Muslim women average 2 years of education, while men average 5.1 years.[26]

Muslim Women in the United States

In 2009, a US Muslim woman wearing a headscarf was working for the clothing retailer Abercrombie & Fitch. Four months later, she was fired. The company argued that the headscarf violated the company's "look policy" and would negatively affect

---

24. See "Chapter 4: Women in Society," Pew Research Center, April 30, 2013, https://www.pewforum .org/2013/04/30/the-worlds-muslims-religion-politics-society-women-in-society/.
25. See Conrad Hackett and Dalia Fahmy, "Education of Muslim Women Is Limited by Economic Conditions, Not Religion," Pew Research Center, June 12, 2018, https://tinyurl.com/4y5x73xe.
26. "Educational Attainment of Religious Groups by Country," Pew Research Center, December 13, 2016, https://www.pewforum.org/interactives/educational-attainment/.

their sales. The woman sued, and in 2013, a judge ruled against the company. The judge concluded that the company failed to provide any evidence of a decline in their sales because of the woman's way of dressing.[27]

Muslim women in the United States enjoy great freedom as well as many opportunities compared to women in Muslim-majority countries. Nearly one-third of US Muslim women always wear head coverings or hijabs in public. While 24 percent of US Muslim women say they wear the headscarf most or some of the time, around 40 percent report that they never wear the hijab.[28]

Being visibly Muslim because of their attire creates challenges for US Muslim women. According to a survey conducted in 2017, nearly half of US Muslims reported experiencing some form of discrimination in the past year. However, the percentage reporting this, among those who could be identified as Muslim because of their appearance, was 64 percent. Among Muslims who did not have a distinctively Muslim appearance, around 39 percent reported that they had experienced discrimination in the past year.[29]

Despite many challenges, Muslim women have been at the forefront of change and progress within the US Muslim community. For example, in 2006, Ingrid Mattson became the first female president of the Islamic Society of North America (ISNA), the largest Muslim organization in the United States. The scholarship of such US Muslim women as Riffat Hassan, Azizah al-Hibri, Amina Wadud, and Asma Barlas has had a significant impact on Muslims around the world. Amina Wadud's *Qur'an and Woman: Rereading the Sacred Text from a Woman's Perspective* and *Inside the Gender Jihad* have become classics in the field of women in Islam.

Muslim women in the United States have also addressed challenges within their own community. A key issue has been the role of women in religious leadership. As in the internal controversies of other religious traditions in the United States, the question has been whether a Muslim woman can lead congregational prayer. But in 2005, Amina Wadud led a gender-mixed congregation during Friday prayer. Another

27. For the story, see Reena Ninan, "Muslim Fired by Abercrombie for Head Scarf Says Policy 'Very Unfair,'" ABC News, September 10, 2013, https://abcnews.go.com/Business/muslim-fired -abercrombie-head-scarf-policy-unfair/story?id=20208124.
28. For the study, see "Section 2: Religious Beliefs and Practices," Pew Research Center, August 30, 2011, https://www.people-press.org/2011/08/30/section-2-religious-beliefs-and-practices/.
29. See "U.S. Muslims Concerned about Their Place in Society, but Continue to Believe in the American Dream," Pew Research Center, July 26, 2017, https://www.pewforum.org/2017/07/26/findings -from-pew-research-centers-2017-survey-of-us-muslims/.

issue Muslim women have confronted is the space mosques provide for women. In keeping with tradition, women pray behind the men's section, often in a designated space at the rear of the mosque. In many cases, these spaces are inadequate, if not discriminatory, often even removed from the main sanctuary. In addition, women often need to use a side entrance into the mosque instead of the main entrance. In addressing the need for better space for women in mosques, Hind Mekki, a US Muslim woman, established a blog called *Side Entrance*.[30] Perhaps as a reaction to the realities of the spaces for women in mosques, a number of US Muslim women established the first female-only mosque in the United States in 2015.[31]

30. For more information, see Side Entrance, accessed April 18, 2020, https://sideentrance .tumblr.com.
31. For more information, see Women's Mosque of America, accessed April 18, 2020, https:// womensmosque.com.

Conclusion

Rev. Bruce McPherson, the interim rector of St. John's Episcopal Church, Lafayette Square, in Washington, DC, invited me to speak about Islam and Christian-Muslim relations in America at his church's adult forum on March 17, 2019. The church is a block away from the White House. It is known as the church of presidents because many US presidents have frequented the church for worship. When I arrived at St. John's, I was surprised by the presence of an unusual number of security guards. Reverend McPherson informed me that President Donald Trump and First Lady Melania Trump would attend the worship service after the forum. It was just two days after the Christchurch mosque shooting in Australia, in which a white supremacist killed more than fifty worshippers during the Friday prayer service.

St. John's was offering an adult series on world religions. For that week, the focus was Islam. It was not just me who would talk about Islam; Reverend McPherson would also engage with the tradition in the context of interfaith understanding. Given that the president and the first lady were among his audience, I decided to observe the sermon after my presentation. I wanted to know how Reverend McPherson would talk about Islam. Would he criticize some of the policies of the Trump administration concerning Muslims? Would he dedicate part of his sermon to the sectarian divisions and conflicts in the Muslim world? Would he address Islamophobia?

To my surprise, Reverend McPherson focused on the five daily prayers of Islam. He emphasized that we can learn from the egalitarian nature of the five daily prayers as people stand shoulder to shoulder to worship God regardless of their status. He noted that the daily ritual of Islam could prompt a "holy envy," an approach developed by Krister Stendahl (d. 2008), a Lutheran bishop who served as the dean of Harvard Divinity School from 1968 to 1979. Bishop Stendahl offered three rules for interfaith understanding: "First, let people of other religions define themselves. Don't allow their enemies to do it for them. Second, compare like with like. Don't compare the positive qualities of our religion with the negative qualities in other religions. Finally, develop 'holy envy.'"[1] Bishop Stendahl's holy envy is often interpreted as the courage

---

1. Todd Green, *Presumed Guilty: Why We Shouldn't Ask Muslims to Condemn Terrorism* (Minneapolis, MN: Fortress, 2018), 166.

to find what is "beautiful and moving within the religion of the other."[2] I was moved by Reverend McPherson's approach as he talked about Islamic spirituality with great appreciation during his sermon. He was given the opportunity to choose among many aspects, but instead, he highlighted a side that is connected to the heart of Islamic spirituality and relatable to his Christian congregation.

I tried to employ a similar approach in this work on Islam and its practice in America. In the end, one can take many different directions in an introductory book. I could have focused on the history of Islam, divisions, Islam and politics, gender issues, Islamic institutions and movements, or simply Islamophobia. However, this would not do justice to how Muslims experience and relate to their religion on a daily basis. The essence of religion would be lost in information. This would not help us understand the tradition, as is wisely put by T. S. Eliot: "Where is the knowledge that is lost in information? Where is the wisdom that is lost in knowledge?"[3] On the journey, I aimed to take this perspective as my departure point. That is why I spotlighted Islamic theology and its spiritual practice in the United States along with providing living examples from the lives of American Muslims. On the journey, we had five stations.

The first station was the historical background in which Islam emerged and the life of the Prophet Muhammad. We have demonstrated that Muhammad and some of the aspects of his life can be understood in his own context. Holding Muhammad to our time's standard concerning politics, war, pluralism, and marriage would not help us understand him. Muhammad's spirituality; piety; generosity; courage; work for peace, justice, and equality; and sufferings as a human being are often lost in the controversies about him. Our second station was the foundations of Islam: the Qur'an, the legacy of Muhammad, and sharia, or Islamic law. We have shown that these foundations are interconnected and complete each other. Muslims turn to these sources in their responsibilities to God, to themselves, and to society. At the third station, we turned to Islamic theology. We have learned that like adherents of other traditions, Muslims had questions and struggles about God and his nature, prophets, scriptures, the status of other religions, ontological beings such as jinn and angels, resurrection and the hereafter, predestination, good and evil, and the relationship between faith and works. Based on the sacred sources

2. Green, 166.
3. T. S. Eliot, quoted in Huston Smith, *The World's Religions* (New York: HarperOne, 2009), 5.

of Islam, Muslim scholars eventually developed a creed that is known as the six articles of faith: faith in God, angels, the prophets, scriptures, resurrection, and the hereafter, as well as belief in predestination.

At our fourth station, we examined the spiritual practices of Islam in the United States. While Muslims enjoy great freedom in practicing their religion in the United States, based on the case studies from the lives of American Muslims, we have learned that they also face challenges. In addition, the spiritual practices of Islam bring a different dynamic to our understanding of religion in public. Examples of Islam becoming more visible include fasting during the month of Ramadan; building mosques, worship spaces in workplaces, and proper washing rooms for ablution on college campuses or at airports; holding communal worship on Fridays; sounding the call to prayer; and making sacrificial rituals during Eid al-Adha. While some Americans may see this increasing visibility as the Islamization of America, it should be interpreted as part of the nature of the spiritual practices of Islam. At the fifth station, we tried to engage with some common questions about Islam: Who are Muslims? What is Sufism? What is jihad? How does Islam view women? We have learned that we need to be more nuanced and thoughtful in our approaches to some contemporary questions about Islam.

There is no doubt that this book has its limitations. But I hope that in this work, Muslims can see their own stories, and the readers of other religions or no religion can find something that prompts a "holy envy."

Bibliography

Abdel Haleem, M. A. S. *The Qur'an: English Translation and Parallel Arabic Text*. Oxford: Oxford University Press, 2010.

Afsaruddin, Asma. *Striving in the Path of God: Jihad and Martyrdom in Islamic Thought*. Oxford: Oxford University Press, 2013.

Ágoston, Gábor, and Bruce Masters, eds. *Encyclopedia of the Ottoman Empire*. New York: Facts on File, 2009.

Allison, Christine. "The Yazidis." *Oxford Research Encyclopedia of Religion*, January 25, 2017. https://tinyurl.com/ndtt5u78.

Alryyes, Ala. *A Muslim American Slave: The Life of Omar Ibn Said*. Madison: University of Wisconsin Press, 2011.

Aminrazavi, Mehdi. *Sufism and American Literary Masters*. Albany: State University of New York Press, 2014.

Anas, Malik bin. *Muwatta*. Sunnah.com. Accessed April 28, 2021. https://sunnah.com/malik.

Armstrong, Karen. *Twelve Steps to a Compassionate Life*. New York: Anchor, 2011.

Aruçi, Muhammad. "Ülü'l-'Azm." In *İslam Ansiklopedisi*, vol. 42, 294–295. Istanbul: TDV, 2012.

Asad, Muhammad. *The Message of the Qur'an*. Islamic Bulletin. Accessed April 18, 2020. http://muhammad-asad.com/Message-of-Quran.pdf.

Austin, Allan D. *African Muslims in Antebellum America: Transatlantic Stories and Spiritual Struggles*. New York: Routledge, 1997.

Baquaqua, Mahommah Gardo, and Samuel Moore. *Biography of Mahommah G. Baquaqua, a Native of Zoogoo, in the Interior of Africa [. . .]*. Detroit: Geo. E. Pomeroy, 1854. https://docsouth.unc.edu/neh/baquaqua/summary.html.

Baysa, Hüseyin. "Ömer Müftü Kilisinin sigaranın hükmü hakkındaki görüşünün değerlendirilmesi." *Kilis 7 Aralık Universitesi Dergisi* 1 (2015): 37–57.

Bazzy, Najah. "Personal Reflections of a Hajjah and Others." In *Pilgrimage and Faith: Buddhism, Christianity, and Islam*, edited by Virginia C. Raguin and Dina Bangdel with Francis E. Peters, 332–342. Chicago: Serindia, 2010.

Becker, Ernest. *The Denial of Death*. New York: Free Press, 1997.

——. *Escape from Evil*. New York: Free Press, 1985.

Berkey, Jonathan P. *The Formation of Islam: Religion and Society in the Near East, 600–1800*. Cambridge: Cambridge University Press, 2003.

bin Said, Omar. *"Oh Ye Americans": The Autobiography of Omar ibn Said, an Enslaved Muslim in the United States, 1831*. National Humanities Center Resource Toolbox, The Making of African American Identity, vol. 1, 1500–1865, 2007. http://nationalhumanitiescenter.org/pds/maai/community/text3/religionomaribnsaid.pdf.

Birışık, Abdulhamit. "Kur'an." In *İslam Ansiklopedisi*, vol. 26, 383–388. Istanbul: TDV, 2002.

Blankinship, Khalid Yahya. *The End of the Jihad State: The Reign of Hishām ibn 'Abd al-Malik and the Collapse of the Umayyads*. Albany: State University of New York Press, 1994.

Bonner, Michael David. *Jihad in Islamic History: Doctrines and Practice*. Princeton, NJ: Princeton University Press, 2006.

Brown, Jonathan A. C. *Hadith: Muhammad's Legacy in the Medieval and Modern World*. London: Oneworld, 2009.

——. *Misquoting Muhammad: The Challenge and Choices of Interpreting the Prophet's Legacy*. London: Oneworld, 2014.

——. *Muhammad: A Very Short Introduction*. Oxford: Oxford University Press, 2011.

——. "Stoning and Hand Cutting: Understanding the Hudud and the Shariah in Islam." Yaqeen Institute, January 12, 2017. https://tinyurl.com/fmkcdj8.

Broyde, Michael. "Sharia in America." *Washington Post*, June 30, 2017. https://www.washingtonpost.com/news/volokh-conspiracy/wp/2017/06/30/sharia-in-america/.

Bukhari, Muhammad bin Ismail al-. *Sahih al-Bukhari*. Sunnah.com. Accessed February 8, 2021. https://sunnah.com/bukhari.

Bullis, Douglas, and Norman MacDonald. "From Pilgrim to World Traveler: Tangier to Makkah." *Aramco World* 51, no. 4 (July/August 2000). https://tinyurl.com/mdshd9sd.

Burge, Stephen. *Angels in Islam*. New York: Routledge, 2012.

Burke, Daniel. "Imam Delivers Message to Trump at Inaugural Service." CNN, January 21, 2017. https://www.cnn.com/2017/01/20/politics/trump-imam-magid/index.html.

Çağrıcı, Mustafa. "Taziye." In *İslam Ansiklopedisi*, vol. 40, 202–203. Ankara: TDK, 2011.

Chappel, Bill. "World's Muslim Population Will Surpass Christians, Pew Says." NPR, April 2, 2015. https://tinyurl.com/5u9db65t.

Chidester, David. *Christianity: A Global History.* New York: HarperOne, 2000.

Chittick, William C. *The Sufi Path of Love: The Spiritual Teachings of Rumi.* Albany: State University of New York Press, 1984.

———. *Sufism: A Beginner's Guide.* Oxford: Oneworld, 2007.

Clarke, J. H. *Malcolm X: The Man and His Times.* New York: Macmillan, 1969.

Curtis, Edward E. *Muslims in America: A Short History.* Oxford: Oxford University Press, 2009.

Daftary, Farhad, and Azim Nanji. "What Is Shi'a Islam?" In *Voices of Islam*, vol. 1, edited by Vincent J. Cornell, 217–244. Westport, CT: Praeger, 2007. https://iis.ac.uk/what -shia-islam.

Dagli, Caner. "Conquest and Conversion." In Nasr et al., *Study Quran*, 1805–1817. New York: HarperOne, 2015.

Deak, Mike. "N.J. Officials to Pay $3.5M to Settle Mosque Lawsuit." *USA Today*, May 31, 2017. https://www.usatoday.com/story/news/politics/2017/05/31/mosque-lawsuit -settlement/357349001/.

Diyanet İşleri Başkanlığı. *Hadislerle İslam.* Vols. 1–7. Istanbul: Diyanet Yayınları, 2011–2014.

Doğan, Ali Fahri. "Tasavvuf Ehlinin Namaz Hakkındaki Görüşleri ve İki Örnek." *Bingöl Üniversitesi İlahiyat Fakültesi Dergisi* 1 (2013): 69–95.

Donner, Fred. *Muhammad and the Believers: At the Origins of Islam.* Cambridge, MA: Harvard University Press, 2012.

Doyle, Dennis M. *What Is Christianity?* New York: Paulist, 2016.

Dursunoğlu, Halit. "Klasik Türk Edebiyatında Ramazan Konulu Şiirler." *A.U. Türkiyat Araştırmaları Enstitüsü Dergisi*, no. 22 (2003): 9–29.

Dutton, Yasin. *The Origins of Islamic Law: The Qur'an, the Muwatta' and Madinan 'Amal.* New York: Routledge, 2002.

Elgot, Jessica. "Mecca Crane Collapse." *Guardian*, September 11, 2015. https://tinyurl .com/59htkuyy.

Ergin, Nevit O., and Will Johnson. *The Forbidden Rumi.* Rochester, VT: Inner Traditions, 2006.

Ernst, Carl W. *Following Muhammad: Rethinking Islam in the Contemporary.* Chapel Hill: University of North Carolina Press, 2003.

———. *Sufism: An Introduction to the Mystical Tradition of Islam.* Boston, MA: Shambhala, 2011.

Erul, Bünyamin. "Veda Hutbesi." In *İslam Ansiklopedisi*, vol. 42, 591–593. Ankara: TDV, 2012.

Esposito, John. *What Everyone Needs to Know about Islam.* Oxford: Oxford University Press, 2013.

Fakhry, Majid. *An Interpretation of the Qur'an: English Translation of the Meanings.* Albany: New York University Press, 2004.

Friedersdorf, Conor. "Singling Out Islam: Newt Gingrich's Pandering Attacks." *Atlantic,* January 31, 2012. https://tinyurl.com/yjdjrbe5.

Furber, Musa. UNHCR *Zakat Collection and Distribution.* Tabah Report no. 1, May 2017. https://unhcrzakatfatwa.com/.

Gandhi, Mahatma. "My Fasts." Mkgandhi.org. Accessed May 17, 2020. https://www.mkgandhi.org/momgandhi/chap06.htm.

GhaneaBassiri, Kambiz. *A History of Islam in America.* Cambridge: Cambridge University Press, 2010.

Ghazali, Abu Hamid al-. *Ihyā' 'Ulūm al-Dīn.* 5 vols. Cairo: al-Quds, 2012.

——. *Inner Dimensions of Islamic Worship.* Translated by Muhtar Holland. Leicestershire: Islamic Foundation, 2006.

——. *Ninety-Nine Names of God in Islam.* Translated by Robert Charles Stade. Ibadan: Daystar, 1970.

——. *On the Boundaries of Theological Tolerance.* Translated by Sherman A. Jackson. Oxford: Oxford University Press, 2002.

Green, Todd. *Presumed Guilty: Why We Shouldn't Ask Muslims to Condemn Terrorism.* Minneapolis, MN: Fortress, 2018.

Hackett, Conrad, and Dalia Fahmy. "Education of Muslim Women Is Limited by Economic Conditions, Not Religion." Pew Research Center, June 12, 2018. https://tinyurl.com/4y5x73xe.

Haley, Alex. *The Autobiography of Malcolm X.* New York: Grove Press, 1965.

Hallaq, Wael. *An Introduction to Islamic Law.* Cambridge: Cambridge University Press, 2009.

——. *Shari'a: Theory, Practice, Transformations.* Cambridge: Cambridge University Press, 2009.

Hanson, Hamza Yusuf. "The Sunna: The Way of the Prophet Muhammad." In *Voices of Islam,* vol. 1, edited by Vincent J. Cornell, 125–145. Westport, CT: Praeger, 2007.

Hart, Michael H. *The 100: A Ranking of the Most Influential Persons in History.* New York: Citadel, 1978.

Hermansen, Marcia. "Hybrid Identity Formations in Muslim America: The Case of American Sufi Movements." *Muslim World* 90, nos. 1–2 (Spring 2000): 158–197.

———. "What Is American about American Sufi Movements?" In *Sufism in Europe and North America*, edited by David Westerlund, 36–64. London: Routledge, 2004.

Hillenbrand, Carole. *Introduction to Islam: Beliefs and Practices in Historical Perspective*. London: Thames and Hudson, 2015.

Hodgson, Marshall G. S. *The Venture of Islam: Conscience and History in a World Civilization*. Vol. 1, *The Classical Age of Islam*. Chicago: University of Chicago Press, 1977.

Horwitz, Sari, Susan Svrluga, and Pamela Constable. "Muslim Call to Prayer Sounds at Duke University, but Not from Chapel Tower." *Washington Post*, January 16, 2015. https://tinyurl.com/4ap87bmk.

Ibn Ishaq. *The Life of Muhammad*. Translated by A. Guillaume. Oxford: Oxford University Press, 1967.

Ibn Majah, Muhammmad bin Yazid. *Sunan Ibn Majah*. Sunnah.com. Accessed February 2021. https://sunnah.com/ibnmajah.

Ingalls, Matthew B. "Aqiqah." Oxford Islamic Studies Online. Accessed January 20, 2020. http://oxfordislamicstudies.com/article/opr/t349/e0002#.

Irmscher, Silke. "10 Facts about Ramadan in Indonesia." CulturEnergy, June 9, 2016. https://www.culturenergy.com/11-facts-about-ramadan-indonesia/.

İşcen, Ayhan. "'Türkiye'deki hafız sayısı 150 bini geçti.'" AA.com, May 10, 2019. https://www.aa.com.tr/tr/turkiye/turkiyedeki-hafiz-sayisi-150-bini-gecti/1603171.

Junod, Tom. "The Greatest, at Rest." ESPN. Accessed April 18, 2020. http://www.espn.com/espn/feature/story/_/id/19409912/the-planning-muhammad-ali-funeral.

Kandemir, M. Yaşar. "Muhammed." In *İslam Ansiklopedisi*, vol. 30, 423–428. Istanbul: TDV, 2005.

Karimi, Nassim, and Amir Vahdet. "Iran to Call Dead Medical Staff 'Martyrs' as Virus Kills 291." AP News, March 10, 2020. https://apnews.com/12c49ab6a3f3dbc19fc1fc99dc9daa58.

Kaur, Harmeet. "Muhammad Makes List of Top 10 Baby Names." CNN, December 6, 2019. https://www.cnn.com/2019/12/06/us/muhammad-top-10-baby-names-trnd/index.html.

Khan, Adil Hussain. *From Sufism to Ahmadiyya*. Bloomington: Indiana University Press, 2015.

Kisakürek, Necip Fazıl. *Çile*. Istanbul: Büyük Doğu Yayınları, 2014.

Kramer, M. "Syria's Alawis and Shiism." In *Shiism, Resistance and Revolution*, edited by M. Kramer, 237–254. Boulder, CO: Westview, 1987.

Lawrence, Miles. "My Fasting Experiment: Ramadan in Saudi Arabi." Al Arabiya News, July 1, 2016. http://english.alarabiya.net/en/blog/2016/07/02/My-fasting -experiment-Ramadan-in-Saudi-Arabia.html.

Lewin, Tamar. "Some U.S. Universities Install Foot Baths for Muslim Students." New York Times, August 7, 2007. https://www.nytimes.com/2007/08/07/world/americas/ 07iht-muslims.4.7022566.html.

Lings, Martin. Muhammad: His Life Based on the Earliest Sources. Rochester, VT: Inner Traditions, 2006.

Lipka, Michael. "Muslims and Islam: Key Findings in the US around the World." Pew Research Center, August 9, 2017. https://tinyurl.com/2kzm9y39.

Manseau, Peter. One Nation, under Gods: A New American History. New York: Little, Brown, 2015.

Mattson, Ingrid. The Story of the Qur'an: Its History and Place in Muslim Life. Oxford: Wiley-Blackwell, 2013.

Mitchell, Abdullah. "Go Green This Ramadan." Council of Islamic Organizations of Greater Chicago, March 31, 2017. https://www.ciogc.org/5-31-17-go-green-this -ramadan-2/.

Mitchell, Travis. "Americans Express Increasingly Warm Feelings toward Religious Groups." Pew Research Center, February 15, 2017. https://tinyurl.com/4asr3dbh.

Mohamed, Besheer. "New Estimates Show U.S. Muslim Population Continues to Grow." Pew Research Center, January 3, 2018. https://tinyurl.com/56v97n87.

Mohamed, Besheer, and Jeff Diamant. "Black Muslims Account for a Fifth of All U.S. Muslims, and about Half Are Converts to Islam." Pew Research Center, January 17, 2019. https://tinyurl.com/25kferb4.

Mohamed, Besheer, and Elizabeth Podrebarac Sciupac. "The Share of Americans Who Leave Islam Is Offset by Those Who Become Muslim." Pew Research Center, January 26, 2018. https://tinyurl.com/z6934cy3.

Muslim Advocates. Fulfilling the Promise of Free Exercise for All: Muslim Prisoner Accommodation in State Prisons. Free Exercise Report, July 2019. https://tinyurl .com/vazukx3v.

Nasa'i, Ahmad bin Shu'ayb al-. Sunan al-Nasa'i. Sunnah.com. Accessed February 2021. https://sunnah.com/nasai.

Nasr, Seyyed Hossein. The Heart of Islam. New York: HarperOne, 2002.

Nasr, Seyyed Hossein, Caner K. Dagli, Maria Massi Dakake, Joseph E. B. Lumbard, and Mohammed Rustom, eds. *The Study Quran: A New Translation and Commentary.* New York: HarperOne, 2015.

Nawawi, Imam al-. "Forty Hadith of an-Nawawi." Sunnah.com. Accessed February 8, 2021. https://sunnah.com/nawawi40.

Naysaburi, Muslim ibn al-Hajjaj, al-. *Sahih Muslim.* Sunnah.com. Accessed February 8, 2021. https://sunnah.com/muslim.

Nettler, Ronald L. "People of the Book." Oxford Islamic Studies Online. Accessed April 18, 2020. http://www.oxfordislamicstudies.com/article/opr/t236/e0628.

Ninan, Reena. "Muslim Fired by Abercrombie for Head Scarf Says Policy 'Very Unfair.'" ABC News, September 10, 2013. https://abcnews.go.com/Business/muslim-fired -abercrombie-head-scarf-policy-unfair/story?id=20208124.

Nursi, Bediuzzaman Said. *The Flashes.* Translated by Şükran Vahide. Istanbul: Sözler, 2004.

———. *İşaratül İ'caz.* Istanbul: Söz, 2009.

———. *Işaratu'l I'jaz.* Istanbul: Söz, 2009.

———. *Lem'alar.* Istanbul: Söz, 2009.

———. *The Letters.* Translated by Şükran Vahide. Istanbul: Sözler, 2001.

———. *Mesnev-i Nuriye.* Istanbul: Söz, 2009.

———. *Mektubat.* Istanbul: Söz, 2009.

———. *Signs of Miraculousness.* Translated by Şükran Vahide. Istanbul: Sözler, 2004.

———. *Sözler.* Istanbul: Söz, 2009.

———. *Şualar.* Istanbul: Söz, 2009.

———. *The Words.* Translated by Şükran Vahide. Istanbul: Sözler, 2008.

Ormbsy, Eric. "Islamic Theology." In *The Oxford Handbook of World Philosophy*, edited by William Edelglass and Jay L. Garfield, 432–446. Oxford: Oxford University Press, 2011. https://tinyurl.com/2h7jzxhr.

Özer, Sükrü. "Tütün." In *İslam Ansiklopedisi*, vol. 42, 5–9. Istanbul: TDV, 2012.

Özervarli, M. Sait. "Selefiyye." In *İslam Ansiklopedisi*, vol. 36, 399–402. Istanbul: TDV, 2009.

Pashman, Manya Brachear, and Marwa Eltagouri. "Wheaton College Says View of Islam, Not Hijab, Got Christian Teacher Suspended." *Chicago Tribune*, December 16, 2015. https://tinyurl.com/zwyc9ja9.

Paul VI. "Declaration on the Relation of the Church to Non-Christian Religions: *Nostra Aetate*." October 28, 1965. Vatican archives. Accessed March 3, 2020. https://tinyurl.com/44hehnhn.

Pengelly, Martin. "Ben Carson Says No Muslim Should Ever Become U.S. President." *Guardian*, September 20, 2015. https://www.theguardian.com/us-news/2015/sep/20/ben-carson-no-muslim-us-president-trump-obama.

Peters, F. E. *The Hajj: The Muslim Pilgrimage to Mecca and the Holy Places*. Princeton, NJ: Princeton University Press, 1994.

Peters, Rudolph. *Crime and Punishment in Islamic Law*. Cambridge: Cambridge University Press, 2016.

Pickthall, Marmaduke. *The Meaning of the Glorious Qur'an*. New York: Everyman's Library, 1992.

Porter, Venetia, and Liana Saif. *The Hajj: Collected Essays*. London: British Museum Research Publication, 2013.

Qaradawi, Yusuf al-. *The Lawful and Prohibited in Islam*. Plainfield, IN: American Trust, 1999.

Qurtubi, Muhammad bin Ahmad al-. *Jami' Ahkam al-Qur'an*. Altafsir.com. Accessed April 18, 2020. https://www.altafsir.com.

Rabb, Intisar A. "'Reasonable Doubt' in Islamic Law." *Yale Journal of International Law* 40, no. 1 (2015): 41–94.

Ramshaw, Gail. *What Is Christianity? An Introduction to the Christian Religion*. Minneapolis, MN: Fortress, 2013.

Reza, Aslan. *No God but God: Origins, Evolution, and Future of Islam*. New York: Random House, 2006.

Rong, Rosa. *Ramadan Report: A Survey of Mobile Internet User Behavior in Indonesia, Malaysia, and Singapore*. Cheetah Global Lab, IAB Southeast Asia and India. Accessed April 18, 2020. http://iabseaindia.com/wp-content/uploads/2017/03/CheetahMobile_Ramadan_Report.pdf.

Rumi, Jalaluddin. "On the Day of My Death." In *Diwan-e Kabir*, translated by Ibrahim Gamard. Accessed May 17, 2020. http://www.dar-al-masnavi.org/gh-0911.html.

Russell, Gerard. *Heirs to Forgotten Kingdoms*. New York: Basic Books, 2015.

Sachiko, Murata, and William C. Chittick. *The Vision of Islam*. Saint Paul, MN: Paragon House, 1994.

Saeed, Abdullah. *The Qur'an: An Introduction*. New York: Routledge, 2008.

Sanders, Sam, and Arnie Seipel. "Cruz: 'Empower Law Enforcement to Patrol and Secure Muslim Neighborhoods.'" NPR, March 22, 2016. https://www.npr.org/2016/03/22/471405546/u-s-officials-and-politicians-react-to-brussels-attacks.

Sawyer, Wendy, and Peter Wagner. *Mass Incarceration: The Whole Pie 2019*. Prison Policy Initiative, March 19, 2019. https://www.prisonpolicy.org/reports/pie2019.html.

Schleifer, Theodore. "Donald Trump: I Think Islam Hates Us." CNN, March 10, 2016. https://www.cnn.com/2016/03/09/politics/donald-trump-islam-hates-us/index.html.

Selcuk, Mervan, and Sakir Gormus. *Zekâtın Kurumsallaşmasının Seçilmiş İslam Ülkeleri Tecrübeleri Çerçevesinde Analizi*. Istanbul: ICPESS, 2016. https://www.pesa.org.tr/single-post/2016/12/23/icpess-2016-proceedings-bildiriler-kitab%C4%B1.

Serrano, Delfina. "Mālikīs." Oxford Bibliographies. Last modified July 30, 2014. https://tinyurl.com/pzaafb6b.

Shafi'i, Muhammad bin Idris al-. *Islamic Jurisprudence: Shafi'i's Risala*. Translated by Majid Khadduri. Baltimore, MD: Johns Hopkins University Press, 1961.

Shariati, Ali. *Hajj*. Costa Mesa, CA: Evecina Cultural and Education Foundation, 1993.

Siddiqi, Muhammad Zubayr. *Hadith Literature: Its Origin, Development, and Special Features*. Cambridge: Islamic Text Society, 1993.

Slight, John. *The British Empire and the Hajj: 1865–1956*. Cambridge, MA: Harvard University Press, 2015.

Smith, Huston. *The World's Religions*. New York: HarperOne, 2009.

Smith, Jane I. *Islam in America*. New York: Columbia University Press, 2010.

Soloman, Job Ben. "*A Slave about Two Years in Maryland*": *Some Memoirs of the Life of Job, the Son of Solomon, the High Priest of Boonda in Africa . . . Compiled by Thomas Bluett, 1734, Excerpts*. National Humanities Center Resource Toolbox, Becoming American: The British Atlantic Colonies, 1690–1763, 2009. http://nationalhumanitiescenter.org/pds/becomingamer/growth/text5/diallo.pdf.

Stockton, Ronald R. "Muslim Gravestones in Detroit: A Study in Diversity." *Journal of the Association of Gravestone Studies* 24 (2018): 52–85.

Sijistani, Abu Dawud al-. *Sunan Abu Dawud*. Sunnah.com. Accessed February 8, 2021. https://sunnah.com/abudawud.

Tarakçı, Muhammet. "Tahrif." In *İslam Ansiklopedisi*, vol. 39, 422–424. Ankara: TDK, 2010.

Tirmidhi, Muhammad bin Isa, al-. *Jami' al-Tirmidhi*. Sunnah.com. Accessed February 8, 2021. https://sunnah.com/tirmidhi.

——. *Shama'il Muhammadiyya*. Sunnah.com. Accessed February 10, 2021. https://sunnah.com/shamail.

Turner, Colin. *The Qur'an Revealed: A Critical Analysis of Said Nursi's Epistles of Light*. Berlin: Gerlach, 2013.

van Ess, Josef. *The Flowering of Muslim Theology*. Translated by Jane Marie Todd. Cambridge, MA: Harvard University Press, 2006.

Wadud, Amina. *Inside the Gender Jihad*. London: Oneworld, 2007.

Warren, Christie S. "The Hanafi School." Oxford Bibliographies. Last modified May 28, 2013. http://www.oxfordbibliographies.com/view/document/obo-9780195390155/obo-9780195390155-0082.xml.

Watt, Montgomery W. *Muhammad: Prophet and Statesman*. Oxford: Oxford University Press, 1978.

Wilson, Gaye. "Tunisian Envoy." Jefferson Monticello, 2003. https://www.monticello.org/site/research-and-collections/tunisian-envoy.

Winter, Tim, ed. *Classical Islamic Theology*. Cambridge: Cambridge University Press, 2008.

Wright, Robin. "Humayun Khan Isn't the Only American Hero." *New Yorker*, August 15, 2016. https://www.newyorker.com/news/news-desk/humayun-khan-isnt-the-only-muslim-american-hero.

Yavuz, M. Hakan. "Nur Study Circles (Dershanes) and the Formation of New Religious Consciousness in Turkey." In *Islam at the Crossroads: On the Life and Thought of Bediuzzaman Said Nursi*, edited by Ibrahim M. Abu-Rabi', 297–317. Albany: State University of New York Press, 2003.

Yavuz, Yusuf Şevki. "Peygamber." In *İslam Ansiklopedisi*, vol. 34, 257–262. Ankara: TDK, 2007.

Yediyıldız, Bahaeddin. "Vakıf." In *İslam Ansiklopedisi*, vol. 42, 479–486. Ankara: TDK, 2012.

Yilmaz, H. Kamil. *Ana Hatlariyla Tasavvuf ve Tarikatlar*. Istanbul: Ensar, 2017.

Yusuf Ali, Abdullah. *The Meaning of the Holy Qur'an*. Beltsville, MD: Amana, 2003.

Index